DISTORTING DEMOCRACY

*The Forgotten History of the Electoral College—
and Why It Matters Today*

CAROLYN RENÉE DUPONT

Prometheus Books

Essex, Connecticut

Prometheus Books

An imprint of The Globe Pequot Publishing Group, Inc.
64 South Main Street
Essex, CT 06426
www.globepequot.com

Distributed by NATIONAL BOOK NETWORK

British Library Cataloguing in Publication Information Available

Library of Congress Cataloging-in-Publication Data

Names: Dupont, Carolyn Renée, author.
Title: Distorting democracy : the forgotten history of the Electoral College—and why it matters today / Carolyn Renée Dupont.
Description: Lanham, MD : Prometheus, 2024. | Includes bibliographical references. | Summary: "Distorting Democracy will awaken Americans to the perils of our system by unveiling the Electoral College's origins, history, and present operations. This book demonstrates that the system has no principled foundation, that it has changed dramatically in its 230-year history, and that it threatens the legitimacy of our political system in the present"—Provided by publisher.
Identifiers: LCCN 2024005828 | ISBN 9781493085989 (paperback)
Subjects: LCSH: Electoral college—United States—History. | Presidents—United States— Election—History. | Representative government and representation—United States. | Democracy—United States.
Classification: LCC JK529 .D87 2024 | DDC 324.6/3—dc23/eng/20240625
LC record available at https://lccn.loc.gov/2024005828

Contents

Introduction: Electile Dysfunction 1

Part I: The Origins of the Electoral College **9**
CHAPTER 1: Philadelphia, 1787: Fumbling Their Way 11

CHAPTER 2: The Best Attainable Solution 33

CHAPTER 3: Electoral College Origins Myths 53

**Part II: The Electoral College since the Founding: Party
Politics and Change** **71**
CHAPTER 4: The Electoral College and the Election of 1800 73

CHAPTER 5: "Hideous the Deformity of the Practice": The
Tortured Path to Winner-Take-All 99

CHAPTER 6: "The Everlasting Principle of Equal and Exact
Justice": Reconstruction's Radical Vision, the Electoral College,
and the Election of 1876 125

CHAPTER 7: "Samson with His Locks yet Unshorn": The White
South, the Electoral College, and the Civil Rights Movement . . . 149

Part III: The Electoral College Today **175**
CHAPTER 8: Deceptions, Distortions, Dangers, and
Dysfunction: The Electoral College Today 177

CHAPTER 9: An Indefensible System 197

Contents

Conclusion: "The Earth Belongs Always to the Living Generation". 215

Acknowledgments 223

Notes. 225

Introduction

Electile Dysfunction

Danger lurks in American presidential elections. This peril manifested spectacularly on January 6, 2021, when thousands of rioters overran police barricades at the United States Capitol, leading to nine deaths, 138 injuries, more than 1,000 indictments, hundreds of prison sentences, and tens of millions of dollars in damage. Every day since, analysts and pundits have rehearsed the social, political, and cultural factors that precipitated this melee.[1]

But what if our very method of selecting the president creates unique vulnerabilities and increases the motivations for such frightening unrest? Joe Biden's decisive popular-vote margin of more than 7 million mattered little that day, because his Electoral College win hung precariously on fewer than 50,000 votes in three key states. In that razor-thin finish, Donald Trump's supporters found ample incentive to embrace swirling allegations of voter fraud. Just as troubling, if those strategic 50,000 votes had gone the other way, a completely different group of Americans would rightly have felt aggrieved.

In recent decades our strange presidential election mechanism has produced these kinds of quirky results with increasing frequency. Who can forget the Bush-Gore contest of 2000, when the results hinged on "hanging chads" and less than 1,000 votes in Florida? After weeks of a messy single-state recount, the Supreme Court halted the process, and George W. Bush won by a single Electoral College vote, even though a half-million more Americans chose Al Gore.

Most notoriously among these recent anomalies, in 2016, Donald Trump stunned the world with an Electoral College victory of 302–227, while losing the popular vote by 3 million.

This system increasingly returns results that threaten to undo the expressed wishes of a majority of voters, and these "misfires" profoundly damage the body politic. Election outcomes of doubtful legitimacy weaken governing mandates and deepen partisan suspicion. As of this writing, well more than half of Republican voters believe that Democrats "stole" the 2020 election, and members of both parties express grave fears about integrity and fairness. At the center lies a method for choosing the president that few Americans understand, and many do not trust.[2]

More Electoral College agitation may await in our immediate future, and many Americans rightly wonder if the country's deteriorating social fabric will hold against such stress.

Compounding these troubling developments, misconceptions and gross misinformation about the Electoral College proliferate. Partisans who see advantages in this design have furthered a cascading series of myths to bolster its legitimacy. They depict the Electoral College as an elegant and pristine device that emerged from the framers' principled wisdom. They mistakenly suggest that today's Electoral College functions in accord with its original design, and they argue that this plan produces positive effects on American political processes.

None of the above is true. But the seeming high stakes of the present moment drive fabulists and spin doctors to spout these myths, and large numbers of Americans embrace them. One video promoting such ideas garnered more than 60 million hits in the aftermath of Donald Trump's 2016 Electoral College win. No wonder public opinion showed a dramatic uptick in public support for the Electoral College at that precise moment.[3]

The looming crisis of the American presidency will not yield to easy solutions. But one thing is certain: Americans need accurate information about the way we select the president. We can open a meaningful dialogue about our future only by understanding why the framers chose an Electoral College, how it evolved into our current system, and how it impacts today's political landscape.

Otherwise, contested elections and political violence may well sabotage our domestic peace and even the very existence of our democratic republic.

About This Book

Distorting Democracy grounds its approach in history, a contrast with many excellent treatments of the Electoral College written by journalists, political scientists, or legal scholars. History guides us in understanding ourselves and the world we have inherited, and it matters enormously for grasping important truths about today's Electoral College.[4]

Credible history plays by certain rules—it requires more than simply mining the record for quotes that support a predetermined viewpoint. It demands attention to context—that is, to the larger world that produced a specific set of ideas. Credible history asks for consideration of forces beyond the choices of a few individuals, as well as awareness of the play of events that led to one path rather than another. It rejects notions of inevitability and compels us to bury our most cherished notions about the superior virtue or vice of figures from the past. Above all, credible history means we must ask why we tell stories about the past that prioritize one set of historical facts rather than another.

Good history also requires an examination of the historian's assumptions, so let me come clean about mine. I'm a moderate Democrat who has twice run (unsuccessfully!) for a seat in my very Red state's legislature. Like many Americans these days, I fear that our political silos and extreme polarization are sending us to dark places. From the late 2010s onward, I've purposefully formed relationships with fellow citizens who don't necessarily share my political ideology. In fact, this book originated in an email conversation with two such people, as I tried to explain my objections to the Electoral College. In making my case, I recognized holes in my own understanding, and these gaps sent me to the historical record to test what I thought I knew. Soon thereafter, I was researching and writing this book.

Distorting Democracy makes its case in three distinct sections, each featuring a key argument.

Part I examines the origins of the Electoral College system. Buried somewhere in the records of the 1787 Constitutional Convention, Americans assume, lies a compelling speech delivered by one of the framers. Surely, George Washington, James Madison, Alexander Hamilton, or Ben Franklin must have laid out the principled foundations that led clearly, logically, and inexorably to this method for selecting the president. In our minds, this lofty discourse rang with Truth so self-evident and compelling that the delegates rose to cheer in glorious consensus. As resplendent beams of light streamed in and an angel chorus swelled, the framers penned Article II of the Constitution.

Except, that speech does not exist and that moment never happened.

Contrary to our cherished ideals, the framers did not create an Electoral College to satisfy deep political principles or philosophical commitments. And though the absence of an exalted underpinning for an Electoral College hasn't prevented pundits from putting high-minded rationales in the framers' mouths, their arguments often rely on rhetorical sleight of hand and historical malpractice.

Equally surprising to some, however, the Electoral College's un-immaculate conception and messy birth doesn't make its opposite equivalent true. It is not the bastard spawn of nefarious intentions or backroom bargains, where the winking and smirking framers conspired to subvert the popular will or to protect slavery.

In truth, the framers followed a zigzagging, convoluted, and bumpy path to the Electoral College during that summer of 1787 in Philadelphia. During the course of many weeks, they wrestled with the question of how to select the nation's leader. They considered and rejected five different proposals for an Electoral College, while they weighed other methods as well. Frustrated and irritable, out of options and out of time, they settled on a plan of electors only in the Convention's final days, primarily to avoid a dangerous and problematic alternative. They adopted this mechanism over the objections of several prominent framers, including one who accused the others of "cramming" the system down their throats. The complicated reasons for this decision and the forces that pushed the framers toward it only become clear in the context of the entire Constitutional Convention. That story forms part I of this book.

Their reasons for choosing an Electoral College aside, the framers created a form of proxy election, where discerning and knowledgeable individuals would assemble in an atmosphere conducive to good decision-making, free of perverse influences on their judgment. These electors would make the choice of president on behalf of those who selected them for this task.

But this concept—the one laid out in the U.S. Constitution—did not survive. Almost immediately, the system of electors worked differently than anticipated, as political operators manipulated it to their own ends. Part II traces 200 years of alterations—many of them subtle but highly consequential—to the plan described in the Constitution. As the new nation descended rapidly into bitter political conflict, partisan operators, including some of the framers themselves, massaged its operations into a form that differed greatly from their own founding intentions. Subsequent generations continued to tinker with the systems' possibilities, always exploiting its potential for political gain. The protocols of today's presidential elections arose mostly from these partisan efforts, though one constitutional amendment and state statutes have given some features a formal sanction.

As with so much of the American past, the Electoral College has been deeply intertwined with the troubled racial hierarchy in the United States, even though the framers did not choose this plan explicitly to protect slavery. Their design did boost slaveholding states' weight in presidential elections, giving the South a leg up in electing slavery-friendly candidates. But the Electoral College's connection to race did not end with the abolition of legalized human bondage. After Reconstruction's demise and the disenfranchisement of black Americans through Jim Crow, the system of electors boosted the South's power even more significantly. Ironically, then, southern white leaders used their inflated power, derived from the people whom they robbed of their political rights, in their fight to preserve white supremacy.

From its inception, Americans have disliked the Electoral College. In recent decades this dissatisfaction has shown up in polling, but it has manifested over the life of our nation in other ways. In the earliest days of our republic, even the men who helped create the Electoral College recommended key changes. Since then, more than 700 proposals to alter or abolish it have been introduced into Congress—more than on any other topic. On seven occasions an amendment to change it has passed one house of Congress, only to fail in the other.

Today, then, the United States does not select presidents the way the framers described in Article II of the Constitution. Two centuries of partisan massaging have long since disfigured the original concept and distorted its operations. We retain only the shell of the framers' design—a set of hollow rituals that lack merit and fail to offer the substance of a true democratic choice.

But, what if, despite this vast departure from the founding vision, this method of choosing the president works well? What if it confers benefits that make our system superior to all others, including a direct, national popular vote? These questions inform this book's third and final section.

As part III explains, today's Electoral College distorts Americans' votes to an astounding degree. It dramatically magnifies the weight of some votes, while completely discounting others and leaving a large percentage of our citizens voiceless in presidential contests. In ways we would never tolerate in any other election, each vote for president does not count equally. These utterly arbitrary weights are accidents mostly of geography and politics.

Moreover, our ballots deceive us and prevent us from grasping the extent of the Electoral College's distortions. Americans participate in a process that looks and feels like a democratic choice, but in fact voters merely plug one variable into a complicated algorithm that warps the outcome like a fun-house mirror.

The Electoral College system negatively impacts our political processes in other significant ways. It shapes political campaigns, so that most of us receive little attention from the candidates, while election messages inundate a small minority of Americans. At present, this mechanism facilitates a movement to the extremes and stifles needed innovations in our rigid, two-party structure. Most troublingly, it opens the door for a winner to occupy the White House without the support of most Americans and offers ample opportunity for the kind of manipulation and violence we witnessed in 2020.

The United States of America, then, elects its president by a method that rests on no important principle and reflects no cherished or widely shared political values. The plan has grown even more troubled than its decidedly earthly origins might have portended, but we've never been able to discard it. Consequently, we've adapted our election system to look and feel like something other than the distorting and dangerous mechanism that it is. And frustrated by repeated failed efforts to change it, we've adjusted our tolerance and expectations.

* * *

Writing from Paris in September 1789, as the convulsions of the French Revolution shook the foundations of Europe's old order, Thomas Jefferson offered his friend James Madison some thoughts about constitutions. "The earth," he explained, "belongs always to the living generation. They may manage it then, and what proceeds from it, as they please."[5]

Indeed, the framers once pursued a sacred obligation to put the nation on the firmest available foundation. They labored mightily under eighteenth-century conditions—a world remarkably different from our own—and achieved remarkable results. The torch they lit has passed through succeeding generations and now lies in our hands. No less than the framers, we must embrace the responsibility to contemplate and choose the best ways to govern ourselves.

Read on and join that noble endeavor.

PART I

The Origins of the Electoral College

With good reason, Americans regard the Constitution as a repository of timeless and foundational truths. Certainly, important principles guided the men who framed it, and they wrote their values of government by the people, separation of powers, and proper limits on authority into that document.

Yet, as much as we'd prefer to believe otherwise, not every feature of the U.S. Constitution arose directly from vaunted philosophical underpinnings. Some constitutional provisions stemmed from necessary compromises, practical considerations, power struggles, and political brinksmanship. The American system for choosing the president—called the Electoral College today, but not so named by the framers—fits this messy description. It emerged mostly as a workable enough solution that satisfied most delegates at the time. It remains among the Constitution's most controversial and problematic features.

The two chapters that begin part I follow the framers as they struggled to agree on the best method for choosing the president. This story captures the overlapping and contradictory considerations that shaped the framers' deliberations, as well as the more silent forces that pressed them toward a final outcome. The third chapter excavates four myths about the Electoral College's origins, demonstrating how these fables fail as explanations for the framers' decision.

A great deal lies at stake in this story. Understanding the Electoral College's decidedly un-immaculate conception can free us from slavish loyalty to a device that has served us poorly and may even endanger our republic.

CHAPTER 1

Philadelphia, 1787

Fumbling Their Way

A WORRIED JAMES MADISON STRODE THE TWO BLOCKS FROM HIS LODG-ings to the Pennsylvania State House. After the better part of a year in preparation, he had arrived in Philadelphia early and waited for eleven anxious days. Now May 14, the day appointed for the Convention to begin, had arrived. So much lay at stake, and with every step he obsessed over opportunities for disaster.

Turning through the gate into the statehouse's manicured gardens, Madison continued to fret. How many men would show up? Rhode Island's explicit refusal even to participate had not surprised him, given the "folly" that dominated that state's legislature. But Connecticut's delay in choosing a delegation did not auger well, and neither did the fact that Maryland kept electing men who declined to serve.

Madison entered the statehouse, threaded his way through the people waiting for court, and headed toward the Assembly Room. In that exact spot, members of the Continental Congress had signed the Declaration of Independence eleven years earlier, but the preoccupied Madison felt no sense of history. The country's problems seriously threatened its survival, and many feared it might splinter into rival and hostile confederacies. Madison and others selected by their states hoped to put the new United States on a sounder footing. Despite instructions from Congress merely to strengthen the Articles of Confederation, the country's existing frame of government, Madison thought the dire situation warranted an overhaul even more fundamental—a completely new constitution.

In letters and memoranda in the preceding months, Madison had spun out a tapestry of fears about the Union's stability and the prospects for change. Only five and a half years after the war's end, domestic unrest and financial instability roiled the country, while the paralyzed government aggravated its own problems. Under the Articles of Confederation, the United States functioned more as a loose collection of thirteen independent sovereignties than a nation. The Articles created only a single branch of government consisting of a one-house legislature with narrowly limited authority. The hamstrung Congress often sat weeks at a time without sufficient delegates to conduct business. Since amendments required unanimity and each state voted as a unit, one state could smack down the most modest proposals for change. Tiny Rhode Island had done exactly that when it single-handedly rejected a small tax measure that would have eased the country's mushrooming financial difficulties. Madison called such episodes to mind when he bemoaned the government's lack of "energy and dispatch."[1]

The present Confederation's weakness manifested most acutely in the economy. The United States owed significant sums to foreign governments, to its own citizens, and to soldiers who had served in the Continental army. Congress lacked any powers of taxation and relied for revenue solely on contributions from the states but possessed no means to collect its due. The states decisively preferred to address their own economic needs rather than ante up for the Confederation. Problems multiplied when the retaliatory British closed foreign ports to American goods. The nation's bounty rotted on warehouse shelves and the country spiraled into depression, but Congress remained powerless to force a change in British policy. It could pursue no unified foreign trade measures because each state crafted policies in its own interests. Making matters worse, some states even printed paper money, inflicting heavy losses on creditors who got rapidly depreciating currency as payment.

Civil unrest cascaded from these economic troubles. In March 1783, officers in the Continental army had nearly mutinied over their meager provisions and lack of pay. Extraordinary leadership from George

Washington had averted that crisis, but, just a few months later, unpaid and angry soldiers surrounded Independence Hall while Congress sat in session there. Even now, Madison could summon the frightful memory of 400 soldiers heckling the members, brandishing their muskets, and blocking the exits. More recently, turmoil had spread to the civilian population. Months before Madison traveled to Philadelphia, cash-strapped farmers in western Massachusetts took up arms to forcibly shut down the courts and stop foreclosures on their property. With no federal authority to quell this uprising, private citizens in Boston raised an army to stop the insurgents. Washington's friend Henry Knox identified the Articles of Confederation as the problem: "The source of the evil is in the nature of the government."[2]

Madison had witnessed these "embarrassments and mortal diseases" firsthand, both as a member of Congress and during his service in the Virginia House of Delegates. His frustration and fear sent him looking for answers in works of history and political theory. Surrounded by books his friend Thomas Jefferson had sent from Paris, Madison holed up in the second-floor study of his family home in the Virginia piedmont. There, he contemplated the course of other republics and wrestled with how their examples might apply to the United States' unique circumstances.[3]

He almost trembled at his own conclusions, acknowledging privately that the solution would "strike . . . deeply at the old Confederation." Though many others admitted that the government required powers it presently lacked, such as trade regulation and taxation, Madison believed that simply augmenting Congress's powers would not suffice. He thought the government needed complete restructuring into a truly national system that acted directly on the people, without the states as intermediaries. This overhaul would require representation of the people, not just the states, in the national legislature. To achieve this vision, the legislature would have two houses—not one, as in the Confederation— with representation proportional to population in both. To give this legislature stability, the representatives would serve longer than their current one-year terms. Appreciating the far-reaching and fundamental nature of these changes, Madison worried that his colleagues might "think this project, if not extravagant, absolutely unattainable and unworthy of being attempted."[4]

Madison also believed a more effective government needed a separate executive, though he had given this topic less thought. Confiding the embryonic nature of his thinking on this subject to George Washington, Madison explained, "I have scarcely ventured as yet to form my own opinion either of the manner in which it ought to be constituted or of the authorities with which it ought to be clothed."[5]

Taking the final steps through the hall of the Pennsylvania State House, Madison opened the door to the gray-paneled Assembly Room. Only a small group sat waiting. Aside from his fellow Virginian, George Washington, only a few members of the Pennsylvania delegation had arrived, and their appearance indicated little since they all lived in the city. What of the others, the seventy-odd men chosen by their state legislatures? Did their absence indicate apathy, or were they simply delayed by the heavy spring rains and bad roads? If this Convention failed to attain a quorum and had to abandon its task, Madison and the others could only return home to watch as the country hurtled toward inevitable catastrophe—likely splintering into rival confederacies, spiraling into civil war, or possibly succumbing to foreign invasion.[6]

Madison, Washington, and the Philadelphians could only wait and plan. They imagined a variety of ways the Convention could fail. The expected delegates' wide range of experience, interests, and opinions portended inefficiency and chaos. As men from large states, these Pennsylvanians and Virginians worried that the small-state delegates might cling to the Confederation's structure as a collection of independent sovereign states with equal representation, sabotaging the obvious solution of a truly national government. Even if the Convention ultimately concurred in a plan, the new system would require the sanction of Congress and buy-in from the people. Given that the necessary solutions departed so radically from the existing Confederation's structure, ratification itself would present a formidable challenge. The endless obstacles to success tempted Madison to despair.[7]

The Virginians and Pennsylvanians felt irritated by the other delegations' failure to appear on time, but they made good use of the wait.

They met daily to discuss strategies for overcoming opposition. Hoping to seize the momentum once the Convention began, they drafted eleven concrete proposals—soon dubbed the Virginia Plan—to present at the outset.

Though Madison's ideas deeply informed the Virginia Plan, he would not be the right person to present it once the Convention got under way. With a small frame that stood just a few inches over five feet, his physical presence never commanded attention. He sometimes spoke too quietly for others to hear, and his often-self-conscious demeanor did not project "presence." Madison excelled in logic, not public speaking.[8]

Madison's nationalist allies turned instead to thirty-four-year-old Virginia governor Edmund Randolph, who counted great oratorical prowess among his many assets. Randolph descended from one of the country's oldest and most powerful political families. His fine elocution, striking manners, and resonant voice exuded authority. The tall and elegant governor claimed reputations as both statesman and scholar. Best of all, he believed fervently in this project. In fact, it was Randolph's persistent coaxing that had convinced George Washington to leave retirement and join the Virginia delegation in Philadelphia.[9]

Even by May 25, a full eleven days after the scheduled starting date, only seven delegations had trickled into the city. But these seven delegations made a majority, and the Convention could begin. The cohort that came to be known as the nationalists—Pennsylvanians, Virginians, and others sympathetic to Madison's vision—stood well positioned to shape the proceedings. The coming days would require all the unity, patience, and thoughtfulness they could muster.

THE FIRST DEBATE ON CHOOSING THE EXECUTIVE

A week into the proceedings, forty or so men worked their way through the Virginia Plan's proposals. Light from tall windows filled the room where ten delegations sat, grouped by state, around tables covered in dark-green cloth. Vacant chairs peppered the room, and three tables sat entirely empty. Everyone knew that Rhode Island had declined to participate. New Hampshire seemed to be on the way, and as for Georgia, the great distance surely explained the delay.

On a slightly raised platform, flanked by two fireplaces, George Washington's desk faced the room. As presiding officer, Washington preferred to act mostly as a referee, rarely venturing his opinion during the discussions.

Madison could have sat with the Virginia delegation, but he positioned himself instead at a table in front, next to Washington's desk. From this vantage point, he could see the delegates' faces and hear every word, necessities for recording the Convention's proceedings in meticulous detail, as he had determined to do.[10]

He kept an especially wary eye on the desks of New Jersey and Delaware, the likely origins of opposition to the extensive overhaul he sought and, especially, to his plan for representation proportional to population in both houses of the new Congress. Already, a few troubling signs had sprouted from the Delaware delegation, and he wondered about William Paterson's frequent and intense scribbling at the New Jersey table. Of course, notetaking might indicate any number of things. Besides, Madison trusted that logic, reason, and the demands of fairness would win them over if they did raise concerted opposition to the Virginia Plan. Even more important, the few small states could never outvote the greater number of populous northeastern states. The southern states would also help Madison's cause, he thought, because everyone believed that migration patterns portended strong population growth in the South.[11]

The Virginia Plan recommended a separate, strong executive, and Madison listened as the delegates digested this proposal. He knew that Americans remained wary of concentrated executive power, given their recent convulsions under a monarchy. This caution manifested in the design of the Articles of Confederation, which provided for no separate executive. A similar concern informed many of the state constitutions, which created weak chief executives who could exercise little meaningful agency. These feeble governors offered no restraint on legislatures whose capricious and intemperate measures often reflected the whims of a fleeting majority. Madison regarded a strong executive branch as essential, but designing a vigorous executive that could not abuse power demanded a delicate balance.[12]

The delegates' shared experiences and political philosophies did not lead inevitably to a single conception of the executive and his powers, and Madison watched his colleagues wrestle with several options. Roger Sherman of Connecticut struggled even to conceive of the executive as a separate branch—in his mind, the executive remained an instrument of the legislature's will. Several delegates preferred a plural executive to dilute concentrated power and abort the "fetus of monarchy."[13]

Everyone recognized that the method for choosing the president remained intimately tied to questions of executive power. Since only a person of highest character deserved this grant of public trust, a body well acquainted with the qualifications of potential candidates should appoint the chief executive. Furthermore, whoever chose the president would, in a sense, own him.

The Virginia Plan called for Congress to select the president, modeling the most common practice in the states. In eight states, the legislatures selected governors. The other five used a mishmash of methods, but only two states chose their governors through direct popular election. Many delegates thought that legislators, who worked with leading figures, seemed best equipped to assess candidates' qualifications for the executive.

James Wilson of Pennsylvania rose to advocate an alternate method for choosing the president. He already embraced Madison's plan for a new, invigorated national government with a strong and separate executive, and he spoke from a special set of credentials in constitution making. Like Madison, he was a passionate student of history and political theory, repeatedly impressing his colleagues with a sweeping knowledge of world governments. He claimed revolutionary bona fides on par with any member of the Convention. Early in the conflict with Great Britain, he had eloquently critiqued the British Parliament's overreaching taxation. But perhaps his most significant experience came from opposing Pennsylvania's new state constitution for its lack of adequate checks on the legislature. That opposition had set a target on his back, and during a wartime panic, a violent mob surrounded his house while he cowered inside. Yet even this traumatic experience had not diminished Wilson's fierce advocacy for representative government and a vigorous chief executive.[14]

Now Wilson introduced a measure he knew would seem radical: direct popular election of the president. Based on this method's success in New York and Massachusetts, Wilson believed it could work for the national executive as well. Furthermore, Wilson thought the people would choose someone "whose merits have general notoriety," and thus popular election would produce the most qualified person for the job.[15]

But no other delegate seconded Wilson's suggestion. Elbridge Gerry opposed it, probably surprising no one acquainted with his suspicious cast of mind. A thin, odd-looking fellow with a high forehead and strong nose, Gerry was one of the wealthiest men at the Convention. This unpredictable Massachusetts "Grumbletonian" doled out objections like candy, bristling even at popular election of representatives. He tended, thought one colleague, to object "to everything he did not propose."[16]

Yet, Gerry had plenty of company in opposing Wilson's proposal for popular election of the president. The delegates smothered Wilson's idea in alternate proposals.

Nonetheless, Wilson persisted in advocating for a president who represented the people and owed his election to them. The next day, he introduced the Convention's first system of electors. The straightforward proposal provided that the people would choose electors who then would select the president. Wilson thought this system would inspire greater confidence in the executive than selection by Congress. Importantly, in his mind, the move to a system of electors did not render the choice any less "by the people," since the electors served as the people's proxies.[17]

Still, Wilson's proposal gained no traction. When put to a vote, eight delegations rejected his system of electors, and only two approved it.[18]

The delegates turned again to the Virginia Plan's provision for Congress to select the president. True to form, Elbridge Gerry did not like this method either. He feared that "the Legislature and the Candidates would bargain and play into one another's hands, votes would be given by the former under promises or expectations from the latter, of recompensing them by services to members of the Legislature or to their friends." These were no idle fears, and other delegates echoed them. How could the executive serve as a check on the very body to whom he owed his office?[19]

Despite this frank admission that a provision for Congress to select the president invited real trouble, the Convention endorsed it rather overwhelmingly. Nine states voted "yes"; only Pennsylvania said "no."[20]

Now it fell to Gerry to persist. Reiterating his fears, he proposed yet another system of electors, this time with governors serving as the electors. But Gerry's proposal failed to win a single favorable vote. For the second time, the Convention had rejected a system of electors for choosing the president.[21]

Selection of the executive by Congress stood as the Convention's choice, and they would leave it there for now.

JUNE 9 TO JULY 16: A CONVENTION IN CRISIS

From the New Jersey table, William Paterson had observed the proceedings and pondered the developments carefully. He did not want to be in Philadelphia. At home on his 350-acre Raritan River estate, he had to contend with man's sinful nature only in the controlled protocols of a lucrative law practice. Here in the city, he confronted it at every corner. Prostitutes and pickpockets imperiled a man in the great open City Market. Even turning into the lovely gardens of the statehouse required him first to pass the massive city jail, where inmates hooted through the windows for money or attention.[22]

And the stench. The city reeked from the press of people and horses, the dogs that roamed the streets, the offal of cows and pigs butchered in the market, the rotting carcasses of animals in the tanning yards, waste from the breweries, and human excrement that flowed from privies into Dock Creek. The whole place stewed noxious odors, contaminations of the body, and hazards of the soul. Even Philadelphia's fine homes, gardens, and churches lay as islands in this swamp of working-class labor, entertainment, vice, and disease.[23]

A strict man of the law and New Jersey's former attorney general, Paterson had come dutifully to Philadelphia to fulfill a single charge: to revise the Articles of Confederation, as described in the authorization from Congress and from his state legislature. Nothing less and nothing more. The current frame of government had weaknesses, to be sure. Citizens from his beloved New Jersey, lacking any real harbor, suffered a great deal from the taxes New York and Pennsylvania slapped on foreign goods that passed through. And the rage for paper money, with its damaging impact on creditors, had ravaged New Jersey as well as six other states. Paterson had expended a good bit of his professional energy suing on behalf of injured creditors. But he believed the delegates could achieve solutions to these problems under the existing Articles of Confederation, with an expansion of Congress's powers on a narrow set of issues.

Of one thing he was certain: He would protect New Jersey's interests. Paterson knew New Jersey, having spent almost his entire forty-six years there. While Madison possessed a "continental" outlook, zipping constantly up and down the seaboard between Virginia and New York City, and other delegates could boast of their British educations or their time at the Inns of Court in London, Paterson contented himself with New Jersey, where life had planted him. As attorney general, he worked to make the state its most virtuous version of itself.

While the other delegates prattled on about the length of the executive's term and where to lodge treaty powers, Paterson focused on more fundamental concerns. The Virginia Plan seemed to move inexorably forward, but in Paterson's view it represented too radical a departure. Most of all, the plan for proportional representation troubled him greatly. It would deprive his small state of the weight it presently enjoyed in Congress. Outside the Convention meetings, Paterson took his concerns to other small-state delegates. He found ready allies in men from Delaware and some from Connecticut and Maryland.

Two weeks into the proceedings, Paterson took the floor to halt the Virginia Plan's momentum. Though small and not physically imposing, Paterson possessed oratorical skills Madison could only envy. Now he rose to deploy them in defense of the small states' interests. He announced that the small states "had everything to fear" from the plan under consideration. They would sooner "submit to a monarch, to a despot, than to such a fate." The New Jerseyan denounced the very foundations of the Virginia Plan—a bicameral legislature with proportional representation based on population. Paterson aimed to preserve the Articles of

Confederation's loose association of states, its single legislative house, and especially the states' equality of representation. The Convention needed merely to strengthen the Articles, he proclaimed, not discard them.[24]

Madison had anticipated this moment. Months before his arrival in Philadelphia, he predicted the small states' objections. For the nationalists committed to his plan, proportional representation in a bicameral legislature formed the essential basis of a more stable and effective government. The new constitution, they hoped, would rest on the sovereignty of the people and act directly on them, without the intermediary of the states. Paterson now advocated exactly the kind of patch job they feared.

Madison answered Paterson's objections in a careful and methodical discourse: Government of the people required equal representation of those people. Equal representation of the states was "confessedly unjust" and would "infuse mortality into a constitution which we wished to last forever." Moreover, equal representation of the states would allow the representatives of a minority to legislate for the entire country.[25]

The lines of disagreement had been clearly drawn, and Madison's nationalist faction felt safe. Their plan had shaped the discussion thus far, and they had the votes on this one. Only New Jersey and Delaware truly qualified as small states, destined by geography to remain so. New York, oddly, joined the small states because its two antinationalist delegates outvoted the third, Alexander Hamilton. New Hampshire might have helped the small-state coalition, but that delegation remained absent. A test vote of 7–3, with Maryland divided, confirmed the small states' weakness: The Virginia Plan triumphed over Paterson's proposal for preserving the structure of the Articles of Confederation.[26]

But outvoting the opposition really offered no solution. No lasting union could grow from seven states in thirteen. Moreover, the small states signaled their intention to die on this hill. Without equal representation of each state in Congress, they were out. Out of the Convention, and out of the Union.

Still, Madison and his cohort saw no reason to compromise. Equal representation of the states would undermine the efficacy of the entire structure. The Convention sat at an impasse, but he urged the others in his camp to stand firm. They should not "depart from justice in order to conciliate the smaller states." Without proportional representation, he argued, the government could remain "neither lasting nor solid." He had known all along that this issue would create difficulties. Time, patience, and logic would prevail, he counseled.[27]

The small states weren't exactly helping their case. A bizarre, two-day declamation by a nearly incoherent and possibly inebriated Luther Martin of Maryland exasperated and alienated everyone. Known for coarse language, rough manners, and a sloppy appearance, Martin rambled on so long that he exhausted even himself, and Madison wearied of trying to follow his remarks, noting simply that Martin spoke with "much diffuseness and considerable vehemence." The small states would need to find new strategies and rely on their better spokesmen, like Paterson, if they wanted to prevail.[28]

Weeks with no progress proved an effective tactic. Another test vote revealed cracks in the nationalist coalition. Some nationalists appeared eager—perhaps too eager—to break the stalemate. The ever-conciliatory Connecticut delegation signaled a change of heart, and another test vote confirmed: Six states now favored the Virginia Plan for proportional representation in both houses of Congress, four stood against it, and Maryland remained divided.[29]

The nationalists worked hard to prevent more losses. They identified a weakness in the small states' position: the very notion of "states." James Wilson asked if the delegates "forget for whom we are forming a government? Is it for *men*, or for the imaginary beings called *states*?" "Metaphysical distinctions" would not satisfy the people. Rufus King of Massachusetts dismissed the states as "wonderful illusions." Alexander Hamilton asked, "as the states are a collection of individual men, which ought we to respect most: the rights of the people composing them, or of the artificial beings resulting from the composition?" Hamilton homed in on the real motivation for the small states' obstinance: "It is a contest for power."[30]

The attack on the notion of states only confirmed the fears of Paterson's small-state coalition, who thought Madison's cohort had finally revealed their true intent: destruction of the states altogether. In a young country where identities remained local and loyalties attached citizens to their states more than to the country, a national way of thinking warred against provincial sensibilities. The small states clung to their position. They would accept no plan without equal representation of the states, and they vowed to go it alone if the nationalists persisted. Gunning Bedford of Delaware declared his willingness for the country to splinter into two confederacies, rather than forsake the small states' interests. He even hinted that the small states might find protection in a foreign ally if they found themselves alone.[31]

Bedford's threats touched the fear that had driven the delegates to Philadelphia in the first place: The Confederation was doomed. No patch job, no surface tinkering could save it, and failure here would lead to convulsions surpassing the war still so present in memory. Madison urged the small states to "ponder well the consequences of suffering the Confederacy to go to pieces." Hamilton spelled out those consequences: If the Union broke apart, foreign powers would provoke the states to war with one another and then step in to their weakened and vulnerable condition to obliterate all they had sacrificed. Gouverneur Morris of Pennsylvania added chilling predictions: "If persuasion does not unite" the country, "the sword will . . . the gallows and the halter will finish the work of the sword." Too old and weak to read his own speeches, Benjamin Franklin suggested that prayer alone could save the work of the Convention now, but the delegates seemed uninterested in divine intervention.[32]

As June waned, a dispirited Madison and the other nationalists felt the tide turning against them. Massachusetts appeared to be slipping— though Rufus King would hold firm, no one could read Elbridge Gerry. And some North Carolina delegates displayed a troubling impatience. A shift of one state would create a tie; a change in two delegations would spell defeat for the nationalists. Had Madison overestimated the power of persuasion and underappreciated the force of frustration?

Alexander Hamilton quit the proceedings on June 30, calling the whole affair a "waste of time." To George Washington, he confided his concern that the Convention would "let slip the golden opportunity of rescuing the American empire from disunion, anarchy, and misery." As the other delegates prepared to leave for a long Fourth of July weekend, it seemed Hamilton's fears might be prophetic. The Convention teetered on the brink of dissolution. Members appointed a committee, hoping it could devise a compromise that might save them.[33]

But the delegates returned from the holiday to entertain yet another contentious issue that poured brine into their wounds. Laser-focused on representation, the southern states complicated the issue even further. They demanded that any formula for proportional representation include slaves. Delegates of the mid-Atlantic and northern states bristled at this prospect because it implied a racial equality that would "give disgust" to their constituents and bolster the power of the sparsely populated South.[34]

The debate about including slaves in the formula for representation threatened to shatter the fragile Convention. Having measured one another's fears, threats satisfied more than reasoned arguments. William Davie of North Carolina stepped first to the brink: If "some gentlemen [intend] to deprive the Southern states of any representation for their blacks," he announced, "the business [of the Convention] was at an end." An exasperated Gouverneur Morris suggested that perhaps the delegates did not share enough in common for a lasting union: "Let us at once take a friendly leave of each other."[35]

The Convention had made no progress for a month. Hamilton's two colleagues followed him out the door on July 10, leaving the New York table vacant. That same day, George Washington wrote Hamilton, bemoaning "narrow-minded politicians . . . under the influence of local views." He added that matters stood "in a worse train than ever; you will find but little ground on which the hope of a good establishment can be formed. In a word, I almost despair of seeing a favorable [outcome] and do therefore repent having had any agency in the business."[36]

Late July: A Different Debate on Choosing the President

With stooped shoulders and grim faces, Madison and his nationalist allies—Gouverneur Morris, James Wilson, Edmund Randolph, George Mason, and others—trudged into the Assembly Room early on July 17. In the angular morning light, the caucus of defeated men considered their options after the previous day's devastating vote, which had finally settled the question: the states would retain equal representation in the Senate.

The nationalists' dream of proportional representation in both houses of Congress, and with it their entire plan for a national government, lay dead. How much of their original vision could they salvage? Should they even continue, now that the Convention had affirmed, to their minds, a fundamentally unjust principle of representation? The razor-thin margin of the vote—one state—drove the pain of this moment even deeper.[37]

The preceding four days had also settled the fundamental question about representation in the House of Representatives. The Convention agreed that representation in the House would reflect the population of each state, with three-fifths of a state's enslaved persons figuring into the calculation.[38]

The early morning meeting of defeated and despondent nationalists produced nothing more than an airing of collective frustration. No option remained but to press on and formulate the best plan possible in this new reality. The fate of the nation lay entirely with a favorable outcome to this Convention.

The other delegates filled the room at the usual starting time of ten o'clock. As the afterlife of animosity radiated about the floor, the New York, New Hampshire, and Rhode Island desks remained unoccupied, and empty chairs stared from other tables. The ten beleaguered delegations began anew, picking up again with matters left hanging a month before.

The two new decisions about Congress upended every assumption upon which the work of the Convention to that date rested. Every provision required reconsideration—none more than the matter of choosing the president.

The delegates revisited the formula they had taken for granted for more than a month: selection of the president by Congress.

But the context had changed significantly. The two decisions on representation dramatically altered the Congress that would choose the president. That body would no longer directly mirror the population, as assumed in the earlier deliberations. Now, by virtue of the three-fifths provision, the slave states would enjoy inflated numbers in the House of Representatives. With its large slave population, South Carolina would gain an additional three representatives. The bonus would only increase as its population of enslaved individuals grew. Virginia would add a whopping six members to a delegation that would otherwise have included only nine representatives. Among northern states, only New York might add even a single representative on account of its enslaved population.[39]

The small states also gained an enormous advantage by virtue of their equal vote in the newly constituted Senate. A tiny state like Delaware, with only 1.5 percent of the entire U.S. population, matched the voting weight of Virginia, where nearly one in five Americans lived. For delegates from these two classes of states—slaveholding and small—the stakes for keeping presidential selection in Congress rose exponentially. They grasped these new advantages and held them tightly.

Gouverneur Morris of Pennsylvania would reinvigorate this wounded assembly, if anyone could. The Convention's most compelling orator, Morris "charmed and captivated" his listeners as his tall frame paced the hall and his wooden peg leg tapped an accompaniment on the floor. The affable Morris had been absent from the first round of conversations about the executive. Now he made up for lost time.[40]

He summoned the full measure of his gifts to argue for popular election of the president. "If the people should elect, they will never fail to prefer some man of distinguished character or services; some man . . . of continental reputation." Congressional selection, he argued, would lead to corruption: "If the Legislature elect, it will be the work of intrigue, of cabal, and of faction . . . real merit will rarely be the title to the appointment." Indeed, an executive chosen by the legislature "will not be independent of it; and if not independent, usurpation and tyranny on the part of the Legislature will be the consequence."[41]

But as previously in the Convention, and despite Morris's eloquence, the idea of selecting the president by direct popular vote met resistance. Several delegates doubted citizens' ability to make this choice. Their misgivings rested on the public's lack of information about potential candidates. In the words of Roger Sherman of Connecticut, "The [people] will never be sufficiently informed of characters and besides will never give a majority of votes to any one man. They will generally vote for some man in their own state, and the largest state will have the best chance for the appointment." Virginian George Mason thought that "the extent of the country renders it impossible that the people can have the requisite capacity to judge of the respective pretentions of the candidates."[42]

These objections to popular election grew not from fears about the tyranny of the majority or a wish to subvert the popular will. Rather, they reflected three realities: (1) In an America where few men enjoyed a national reputation, where news often spread slowly and only locally, few people knew anything about leaders outside their own state; (2) voters would thus invariably choose someone from their own state, and candidates from larger states would always win; and (3) such a process would return too many candidates and almost never provide a true consensus choice.

Given these concerns, the Convention overwhelmingly rejected Morris's motion on election of the president "by the people."[43]

Still, the idea of Congress selecting the president gnawed at the delegates, and many wanted another option. Now, for the third time, the Convention considered a system of electors. This proposal, brought by Luther Martin, called for the state legislatures to choose electors. But Martin's earlier embarrassing performance and his reputation for drink made him a poor advocate. Moreover, many delegates objected to the state legislatures' involvement in the process. Just as they had dismissed two other systems of electors in June, the delegates rejected this proposal, unanimously reaffirming their original plan for Congress to choose the president.[44]

Yet, two days later, the haunting danger of putting this power in Congress drove the Convention to reconsider this method. Oliver Ellsworth of Connecticut rose with the Convention's fourth proposal for electors. Under this plan, the state legislatures would appoint the electors, with the number allotted to the states on a sliding scale, based on population. No state would receive more than three electors, and all would receive at least one.

Ellsworth's plan seemed workable. By a vote of 6–3, with one state divided, the Convention approved it.[45]

Progress washed over the frustrated delegates. Eight weeks into the Convention, they had finally hit on an agreeable method for choosing the president.

But their relief lay as ephemeral as morning mist.

Four days later, business opened with a significant development: The New Hampshire delegates had finally arrived, a full two months into the Convention. The trouble all along had been the state legislature's refusal to finance their participation, a matter only solved when one member agreed to personally cover the costs. Meanwhile, William Paterson had abandoned his chair at the New Jersey table and headed for home.[46]

That afternoon, the weary delegates voted to take a ten-day recess beginning in four days, on July 27. The break would allow a five-man Committee of Detail to prepare a working draft of the Constitution, drawing from the provisions agreed to thus far. Others could rest or travel.[47]

The prospect of a break brought renewed purpose and energy to the assembly. But their improved mood evaporated when, just before ending the day's business, William Houston of Georgia asked the Convention to reconsider the method for choosing the president. The delegates grasped that continually undoing every provision already decided would keep them in Philadelphia longer than anyone wanted.[48]

Nonetheless, the reconsideration commenced immediately. The next morning, the delegates scrapped the system of electors that had seemed such a breakthrough only days before. A telling argument prompted this about-face. Houston and Hugh Williamson of North Carolina both expressed misgivings about the quality of potential electors. Because electors would make the all-important choice of president, they should come from the wisest persons a state had to offer—men of experience, integrity, knowledge, and sound judgment. Not just anyone would do, because electors would make an all-important choice. Persons of the best character, they argued, would prefer service in the legislature, rather than the time-consuming task of traveling to the nation's capital just to cast a single vote.[49]

Having now rejected yet a fourth system of electors, the delegates reverted to the only plan with sufficient support: selection by Congress. All understood that this method fostered troubling ties between the executive and the legislature, an ecosystem ripe for corruption. Nonetheless, they stuck to this admittedly perilous plan, choosing it over both popular election and any Electoral College plan on offer.

The arguments rang tired. Someone found shortcomings in every alternative. Round and round they went.

Madison followed the developments carefully. The matter was of utmost importance, and he hoped to push the Convention to new ground. Taking the floor with a lengthy speech, he laid out the Convention's three options for choosing the president. Congressional selection presented "insuperable objections," including tendencies to throw the legislature into "intrigue, agitation, and corruption" and even vulnerability to foreign manipulation. A system of electors seemed much better. But the delegates had so recently and overwhelmingly rejected a plan for electors, he thought "it probably would not be proposed anew." Turning to election "by the people," Madison confessed that, "with all its imperfections," he liked it best.[50]

Bringing his oration to a close, he addressed the silent weight that sank popular election and, indeed, every proposal except selection by Congress: Popular election, like all systems of electors presented, did not give Southerners any weight for their large populations of enslaved persons who, of course, could not vote. The Southerners' awareness of this disadvantage wedded them to congressional selection, a method where they retained an advantage. But the continentally minded Madison urged his fellow Southerners not to sacrifice the good of all for petty regional gains: "Local considerations must give way to the general interest." As a Southerner, Madison declared himself "willing to make the sacrifice."[51]

Madison had named the problem. Southerners clung to congressional selection because it preserved their advantages, but they were not the only obstacle. They had eager partners in the small-state delegates, who also rejected both popular election and every system of electors. Hugh Williamson followed Madison's lead in laying this reality on the table: "The principal objection against an election by the people seemed to be the disadvantage under which it would place the smaller states."[52]

Little wonder, then, that the eloquent and principled oratory of Wilson, Morris, and Madison proved to be of no avail, and that repeated warnings against the danger of congressional selection could not budge the Convention from this method. The small and slave states had won a great victory in the previous decisions on representation. They determined to carry those wins into selection of the president.

Now John Dickinson of Delaware added his voice. The seasoned legislator whose labors for his country stretched back to the Continental Congress had spoken little on this issue. He had "long leaned towards an election by the people which he regarded as the best and purest source." Though a small-state delegate himself, Dickinson supported the method he believed in the country's best interest.[53]

Yet no one advanced a motion for popular election. Instead, they chased the familiar choices on their well-worn tracks. Charles Pinckney and George Mason urged selection by Congress. Pierce Butler pushed for a system of electors. Elbridge Gerry cast up his hands: "We are entirely at a loss on this head."[54]

Their hard-earned recess waiting, the exasperated delegates voted once more on a resolution the Committee of Detail would write into a draft constitution.

As so many times before, they affirmed: Congress would select the president.

Most delegates left town the next day. George Washington did some fishing. Dying of tuberculosis, William Churchill Houston went home to New Jersey for good. Elbridge Gerry met his new wife for a rendezvous in New York City. Most of the Georgia delegation also traveled to the city to perform their duties as members of the Confederation Congress, but William Pierce encountered a creditor there and only narrowly escaped a duel. Madison passed the recess in Philadelphia, laboriously copying, clarifying, and editing the exhaustive notes he had taken over the preceding two months.[55]

While the others took their well-earned recess, the five-member Committee of Detail set to work, composing a draft constitution that reflected the provisions thus far approved.

Into the draft it went: a chief executive selected by Congress.[56]

Repeatedly, the Convention had spoken. They knowingly chose a dangerous method for selecting all future presidents. Power and interest, not lofty principles and thoughtful political theory, dictated this choice.

In fact, for many, this method flew in the face of every principle they cherished in a republic.

Yet they had affirmed the provision again and again. Like a person who knowingly marries a philanderer, they did it with eyes wide open.

CHAPTER 2

The Best Attainable Solution

SINCE THE DELEGATES HAD TRUDGED BACK FROM THEIR RECESS THREE weeks earlier, every day brought new anxieties, and the August heat wore on them all. They inched through the draft Constitution, wrangling over every line. Gouverneur Morris feared the Convention would thwart his hopes to create a strong national government.

Morris still agonized about the provision for Congress to choose the executive. But after his efforts the previous month, he doubted the wisdom of pressing again for either popular election or a system of electors. The delegates had exhaustively discussed and repeatedly rejected both options in July. The small and slave states continued to prefer selection by Congress for the advantages it gave them. Still, choosing the president with a method so ripe for corruption troubled Morris deeply. He could not let it rest. Not just yet.

Morris had proven himself a leader in the Convention, speaking more often than any other delegate. He rose naturally to the role, with every requisite to inspire self-confidence: family pedigree and wealth, first-rate education, deep intelligence, height, good looks, and buoyant demeanor. The same qualities made the young bachelor a magnet for women, and he enjoyed uncommitted, serial erotic liaisons with both married and single partners, often to his colleagues' dismay. Even the oak peg replacing his lower left leg, lost in a carriage accident in 1780, did not seem to diminish his sexual appeal. His friend John Jay lamented that the accident had taken a leg and not *"something* else."[1]

As a legislator, Morris possessed real substance, but occasionally someone wondered whether his gifts masked an empty shell. He had helped steer New York's course toward independence and through the war, joining the Continental Congress in 1778 as one of its most hardworking and productive members. Now he served in the Convention as a delegate from Pennsylvania.

Before Morris found opportunity to address his pressing concern about selection of the executive, the Convention weathered yet another ugly and alienating confrontation. Trouble erupted over a draft provision that prevented Congress from interfering in the slave trade. While the Convention never entertained the idea of ending slavery, most delegates drew bright distinctions between slave ownership and the international trade. Even George Mason, who was attended in Philadelphia by two of the approximately 300 human beings he owned, professed a loathing for the trade and a wish to prevent the institution's growth. In Mason's Chesapeake region, a naturally sustaining enslaved population cultivated tobacco, and planters needed no more slaves. The Virginia legislature had already halted slave importation, fearful that an oversupply would drive down the value of those enslaved persons already in the state. Furthermore, the ever-present threat of revolt meant that no white Virginian wanted an enslaved population approaching the dangerous levels of South Carolina's.[2]

But in Deep South states where economies depended on slave importation, settlers who streamed into the western reaches clamored for slaves. Moreover, their victory on the three-fifths clause meant that Deep South states now had a political incentive to boost their slave populations by continuous importation. More than one speaker laid this reality in the open.[3]

Morris had already provoked the Southerners with a fiery denunciation of slavery, the slave trade, and the impacts of the three-fifths clause. Now he watched silently as Deep South delegates cast their trump card on the table. John Rutledge reminded his colleagues that South Carolina and Georgia would settle for nothing less than protection of the slave trade as the price of a new constitution. Without it, they would walk away. To those who pled the inhumanity and immorality of the slave trade, Rutledge answered, "Religion and humanity have nothing to do with the question. Interest alone is the governing principle with nations."[4]

The South Carolinians stoked the delegates' deepest fears to press them through this significant impasse. The provision preventing Congress from stopping the slave trade stood, with only the modification that it would expire in twenty years. After all, opined Madison sardonically, "twenty years will produce all the mischief that can be apprehended from the liberty to import slaves."[5]

This multiday confrontation thickened the Assembly Room's already toxic fog. Morris watched as the delegates' private irritations sabotaged their efforts. He knew some delegates worried about ill family members back home. At the dinner table, he listened to George Washington fret about his drought-parched crops. Morris's friend and fellow Pennsylvanian James Wilson pined for his recently deceased wife and anguished over a pending financial debacle. Then there was the humiliation of William Samuel Johnson, the Connecticut delegate forced to vacate his lodgings for cheaper accommodations.

Vacant chairs peppered the Assembly Room more liberally. William Paterson and James McClurg of Virginia had not returned after the recess. As the days inched on, impatience siphoned off more. William Pierce and William Houston returned to Georgia, Caleb Strong to Massachusetts, and Alexander Martin and William R. Davie to North Carolina. The departure of the slovenly and oft-inebriated Luther Martin of Maryland felt like good riddance.

Morris also smelled trouble in the caucus of "dissidents" who assembled in the evenings to air their displeasures. Everyone found troubling elements in the emerging document, but for some, the "obnoxious ingredients" accumulated to levels they could not accept. Elbridge Gerry thought the Constitution "full of vices." George Mason vowed he would "sooner chop off [his] right hand than put it to the Constitution as it now stands." Neither would commit to supporting it, though each day they flung themselves fully into the fray. Edmund Randolph, so hopeful when he introduced the Virginia Plan back in May, now thought the Constitution contained "features so odious" he might not endorse the outcome. Even if they produced a flawed constitution—as they inevitably would—lack of unanimity on the outcome would create openings that malevolent or demagogic actors could exploit.[6]

As the Convention turned at last to the draft provision on selecting the executive in Article X, Morris knew the brittle atmosphere did not bode well. Another slave-trade worthy moment might erupt if he challenged the plan for Congress to select. He watched appreciatively as Daniel Carroll of Maryland risked the delegates' ire with a motion for popular election of the executive. Popular election had never garnered a majority—the delegates from small states and slave states saw to that. Now it failed overwhelmingly again.[7]

Still the danger weighed heavily on Morris. He knew Madison, Wilson, Gerry, and many others also feared the consequences of congressional selection. But the group had circled these tracks so wearingly a month before. What cost would come with reopening the issue?

The future of the American presidency was worth at least a shot.

Morris ventured a proposal for a system of electors—a method the delegates had already refused four times. Recapitulations of this sort usually provoked complaints.

The Convention voted it down, marking the fifth time they had rejected a system of electors. But now the measure failed by only a single vote, a clue that pervasive dissatisfaction with congressional selection simmered just below the surface. Morris recognized possibilities in that narrow margin.[8]

"By the legislature" stood as the method for choosing the president, and the delegates moved on. There remained many problematic provisions requiring resolution—deep ties between the executive and the Senate, a worrisome provision for a standing army, and a federal judiciary that might impinge on state courts.

Everyone wanted to go home. More and more often, John Rutledge shut down proposals simply "on account of the delay" they would produce. Continued deliberation only brought more wheel-spinning, and another committee seemed the best way to wrap up their business. The delegates selected a "Committee on Unfinished Parts" to find solutions for those remaining thorny issues.[9]

Here—Morris found the opening he sought. It was the last day of August. They had labored in Philadelphia for more than three months. One after another, delegates rose to identify clauses for the committee to resolve.

Morris rose, too. He moved that the Convention refer "this point, of choosing the President," to the committee.[10]

And the delegations of nine states agreed that a committee of eleven men would hash out the method for the United States to choose its president. All the weeks of wrangling, the hours of debate, and the months of tedium had brought the matter down to this. They tossed the entire matter into a small committee's hands.[11]

SEPTEMBER 1 TO SEPTEMBER 3: THE WORK OF ELEVEN MEN

Morris, Madison, and the other nine members of the Committee on Unfinished Parts streamed upstairs to the Library Room on the Pennsylvania State House's second floor.

John Dickinson joined the committee a bit late. The Delaware lawyer and veteran of the Continental Congress walked in to find the other members grappling with the issue of choosing the president. Most of the committee seemed ready simply to endorse the provision for Congress to select. And why not? No other method, no matter how frequently proposed, no matter how finessed, had garnered sufficient support. They seemed incapable of finding a workable alternative.

But Dickinson, a small-state man who had already expressed a preference for popular election, suggested that the success of ratification itself lay at stake in this issue. "The people," he argued, would never agree to the Constitution "unless they themselves would be more immediately concerned in [the President's] election."[12]

Morris welcomed Dickinson's reminder, beckoning him to the table.

Ever the vigilant observer, Madison had carefully noted every objection and every obstacle. He had considered some possibilities. Now he drew out a piece of paper and sketched a potential system of electors. It allotted to each state a number of electors equal to their representation in Congress, thus mimicking the actual Congress. This feature preserved the small and slave states' advantages, thus addressing the primary obstacle that had thwarted all alternative proposals. Yet, because the electors performed only one task—choosing the president—this plan avoided the corrupting potential of the actual Congress.[13]

This arrangement might prove a significant breakthrough.

Madison recognized that the method of choosing electors could send the entire system down to defeat. The five plans already rejected by the Convention had foundered, in part, on precisely this problem. In their heightened state of irritability, the delegates would likely find fault with any arrangement and use their dissatisfaction to revert to the dangerous plan for congressional selection. Madison sidestepped these potential objections by proposing that the states could choose electors in any manner their legislatures might dictate.

Madison's plan also closed the several points of entry for corruption, all identified during the Convention deliberations. Electors would meet in their home states, rather than all together as one body, making it harder to coordinate a plan across several states. To mollify the concern that only candidates from the large states would win and to increase the likelihood that the system would return a majority, each elector would vote for two candidates, one of whom must live outside the elector's own state. The plan also required electors to vote by ballot, thus preserving the secrecy and independence of their vote. Finally, Madison drafted a complex contingency procedure in case an election failed to return a majority. In such cases, the Senate would make the choice.

Madison's plan addressed every objection raised by the delegates thus far. Maybe it would get everyone on board. At this point after all, the committee merely aimed to get agreement on something workable that did not leave the choice of president in Congress's sullying hands. They would see how a contentious and impatient Convention responded.

SEPTEMBER 4 TO SEPTEMBER 17: TO THE FINISH LINE
Back in the Assembly Room, Gouverneur Morris presented the committee's work, including its plan for a system of electors. The change surprised the delegates. Edmund Randolph and Charles Pinckney asked why the committee had made this about-face.

Morris responded with the historical record's most direct explanation for the choice of a system of electors. He offered six reasons for the committee's decision, five of them connected to the problems of congressional selection. Finally, he noted, "many were anxious even for an immediate choice by the people."[14]

Though some delegates admired how effectively the plan solved difficulties that had dogged their deliberations for weeks, it immediately found detractors. Richard Dobbs Spaight of North Carolina accused the committee of "cramming" electors down the delegates' throats. Not a single South Carolina delegate approved of it, and John Rutledge urged a return to congressional selection.[15]

Significantly, many—possibly most—delegates predicted that even this Electoral College would rarely return a majority. They worried that even requiring electors to choose a candidate outside their home state failed to assure a consensus choice. The paucity of men with national reputations in 1787 seemed to guarantee it.

If the Electoral College would seldom return a single winner, the contingent election provisions loomed even more consequential. "Nineteen times in twenty," thought George Mason, the contingent election would become the real election.[16]

The plan to resolve an undecided election in the Senate resuscitated fears about an improper connection between the executive and the legislature. Given that the Convention had endowed the Senate with powers—confirmation of judges, ratification of treaties—connecting it dangerously to the executive, several delegates exploded at this prospect. Randolph noted, "We have in some revolutions of this plan made a bold stroke for monarchy. We are now doing the same for an aristocracy." James Wilson agreed, fearing that members of the Senate might even work behind the scenes to engineer a failed election. They might "hold up to their respective states various and improbable candidates, contrive so to scatter their votes, as to bring the appointment of the President ultimately before themselves." He argued that the plan would not make the president "the man of the people as he ought to be, but the minion of the Senate."[17]

For three days, the delegates worked on the contingent election procedure. They finally put a failed election in the House of Representatives, but with voting by states, a provision that preserved the advantage of the small states.

The issue of selecting the president finally resolved, the delegates moved crisply to finalize other provisions. They made difficult decisions about the processes for amendment and ratification. They rejected George Mason's proposal for a bill of rights. The culmination of their work lay tantalizingly in sight.[18]

A Committee of Style met in the evenings to condense the twenty-three draft provisions into seven succinct and graceful articles. Gouverneur Morris's elegant pen polished the Preamble, "We the people of the United States, in order to form a more perfect Union . . ." Yet, even after the application of Morris's gifts, the paragraph on election of the president—the third paragraph of Article II, Section One—remained cumbersome, the longest and most complicated in the entire document.[19]

The assistant clerk of the Pennsylvania Legislature painstakingly and handsomely engrossed the Constitution's completed text on four pages of parchment and laid the finished product on George Washington's desk at the front of the Assembly Room.

* * *

September 17 in Philadelphia dawned clear, fine, and cool. The delegates streamed a final time into the Assembly Room. Alexander Hamilton occupied the New York table again as the state's only delegate—he had returned in mid-August. William Paterson traveled back from New Jersey just to sign.

Not a single delegate thought the Constitution flawless. Morris and Hamilton believed the Convention had failed to create a government with adequate vigor and strength. George Mason feared the opposite. He concluded that "the dangerous power and structure of the Government . . . would end either in monarchy or a tyrannical aristocracy; which, he was in doubt, but one or other, he was sure." Benjamin Franklin shared their misgivings: "It is likely to be well administered for a course of years, and can only end in despotism, as other forms have done before it."[20]

The dangerous dissent that Morris dreaded burst into full display. Here lay an opening sure to be exploited in a deteriorating political climate. Mason and Randolph wanted to call a second convention after the people had time to respond to the current plan, but no one else liked this idea. True to hints they had dropped for weeks, Mason, Randolph, and Elbridge Gerry refused to sign. William Blount of North Carolina had also planned to withhold his name but changed his mind at the last minute.

The delegates steeled themselves for the looming struggle over ratification. The plan called for the people themselves, not the state legislatures, to ratify. In the country's fragile state, ratification itself might trigger the crisis the Convention hoped to avoid. Gerry worried that "a civil war may result" from the effort. Randolph seemed certain that ratification would fail and then "confusion must ensue." Morris predicted that "a general anarchy will be the alternative" if the Constitution failed.

Given these extraordinarily high stakes, Benjamin Franklin urged his colleagues not to air their concerns publicly, but to support the Constitution unequivocally: "The opinions that I have of [the Constitution's] errors, I sacrifice to the public good." Franklin clearly shared Morris's concern about the impact of open disagreement coming out of the Convention, and others echoed Franklin's advice. Their comments seemed directed squarely at the three nonsigners. Despite his own objections, Morris asserted, "the present plan [w]as the best that was to be attained, [and] he should take it with all its faults."[21]

* * *

Of all the issues the Convention faced over the course of these fifteen contentious weeks, the method for choosing the president had confounded and frustrated them most of all, according to several delegates' own testimony. It occupied their attention for twenty-one days, and the Convention took thirty different votes on it. They thought—they hoped—their plan would produce a wise and experienced president not beholden to Congress, but with strong majority support from the American people.

Practical considerations and necessary concessions, not lofty principles, shaped the winding path to this solution. No one in the entire course of the Convention ever pressed for a system of electors as an essential feature of republican government. No delegate ever defended this plan as superior on principle. In the end, the framers chose an Electoral College mostly to avoid the perils of congressional selection. Their system was no one's first choice, but it worked as an acceptable second choice that could muster a majority.

Perhaps just as telling, Madison later acknowledged the system's provisional nature: "That mode which was judged most expedient was adopted, till experience should point out one more eligible." And, he noted, the system of electors reflected the "hurrying influence" of men ready to complete their work and return to their lives.[22]

But for the moment, as they took their leave of Philadelphia, most of the delegates could neither rest on their laurels nor trouble themselves with the Constitution's shortcomings. The labor of the previous four months would be for nothing if the people of nine states did not give their assent to the new frame of government. Mighty battles were taking shape, even before some of them left town.

HOME TO VIRGINIA

In many ways, the struggle to ratify the Constitution all came down to Virginia, for no union could last if Virginia did not join. With 821,287 inhabitants, Virginia, the most populous state by far, dwarfed the nearest competitor by 60 percent. Its massive bulk lay like a wide sash about the country's hips, stretching west through wild mountainous counties, on across the frontier region of Kentucky, and just gracing the country's western border on the Mississippi. The state had supplied some of the Revolution's ablest statesmen, including George Washington, Thomas Jefferson, and Patrick Henry. Indeed, the call to the Philadelphia Convention had issued from Virginia, and the entire affair had commenced on the strength of its ideas. A rejection of the Constitution in Virginia would signal death to the Union.[23]

The five Virginia delegates who remained in Philadelphia until the end grasped fully the significance of their state. After the signing, four different conveyances carried them away from the city. They traveled divergent routes and, most important, followed unique intellectual trajectories to the ratifying convention. On the way home, three suffered serious mishaps that portended the Constitution's course in Virginia.

George Washington wanted badly to get home. He and John Blair hurried out of Philadelphia the day after they signed the Constitution. Heavy rains fell during their first night at an inn near the Elk River in Maryland, but even after delaying their morning departure, they found the river swollen above the level at which the carriage could safely ford it. Impatience pressed the travelers to look for other options, and they spied one in an old and abandoned bridge towering above the waters. The men alighted from the carriage and sent it ahead without them. They would follow on foot after the horses made it safely over. But the wood cracked loudly above the swollen waters as rotting boards collapsed, and one horse plummeted straight toward the water. The traces jerked the horse's fall up short, while the force of its weight threatened to pull the second horse over the edge. The carriage tipped and rolled, and the second steed stumbled on the still-intact portion of the bridge. Moments passed before the remaining horse and tottering carriage stabilized. The fallen horse dangled in his harness fifteen feet below.[24]

George Mason rattled along in the coach carrying him back to Gunston Hall. His journey to Philadelphia had been the farthest of his sixty-one years. He did not feel much like chatting with James McHenry, who would soon disembark for the final leg to his Maryland home. Suddenly the horses snorted loudly. The coach lurched sharply, veered off the road, and toppled to its side. At the mercy of gravity, Mason and McHenry tumbled in a tangle of arms and torsos, necks torquing, heads banging. Stunned, the two men came to rest in a heap against the side of the carriage, next to the earth. Mason's head throbbed and his neck burned. Voices, a commotion, stirred outside. A hand reached down to extract them.[25]

Washington and Mason might have traveled home together and so avoided these near misses. After all, their Fairfax County plantations lay only five miles apart. But the two left Philadelphia in decidedly different moods and with their friendship damaged. Washington returned immediately to the life he loved and had missed these four and a half months: riding about his lands, inspecting his crops, supervising improvements on the house and outbuildings, and entertaining a constant stream of houseguests. He hoped to bolster the Constitution's chances for ratification in his home state, where he feared it dangled as perilously as his steed from the bridge. He immediately sent copies to former Virginia governors Benjamin Harrison, Patrick Henry, and Thomas Nelson Jr., along with a note explaining his belief that "it is the best that could be obtained at this time," adding a wish that the "Constitution had been made more perfect." For Washington, it all came down to the simple question: Was the Constitution "preferable to the government (if it can be called one) under which we now live?"[26]

Mason, however, returned to Virginia in an "exceeding ill humor," determined to sabotage ratification at every opportunity. The ongoing pain in his head and neck exacerbated his sour spirits, which owed mostly to the Convention's course in its final days. He had found his colleagues' manner "precipitate, intemperate, and indecent." Did John Rutledge, always prioritizing finishing up over the quality of their work, fail to grasp the gravity of this task? Mason's mood further darkened when he relived the most galling moment of all, four days before the end, when his own motion for a bill of rights won not a single delegation's approval.[27]

Mason objected to an identifiable set of features in the Constitution. He had listed and carefully spelled them out before the delegates. At a minimum, he thought Congress should call for a second convention after the people had time to digest the delegates' work. But only Randolph seemed interested in that. And then Franklin and Morris had exerted such pressure to sign on the last day. Even before leaving town, Mason had dispatched a copy of his objections to Richard Henry Lee, a member of Virginia's delegation in Congress.[28]

Like Washington, Mason could wield enormous influence. The author of the Virginia Declaration of Rights claimed a sterling reputation as a defender of individual liberties with long service to his state. Washington and Madison could only hope that Mason might ultimately decide that the danger to the Union outweighed his objections. Perhaps

44

he would come around to support it in the state's ratifying convention after all. At present, that seemed unlikely.

For his part, James Madison could not bask in satisfaction and triumph. He had taken too many defeats on crucial measures, and those losses still stung. The finished Constitution bore little resemblance to the plan he had brought to Philadelphia, and it lacked provisions he thought essential to solving the country's crippling problems. He remained disappointed at the compromise over equal representation of the states in the Senate. The Convention had rejected his plan for an executive council and for a federal veto on state laws. On the whole, he thought, the new Constitution did not "effectually answer its national object." In a seventeen-page private letter, he outlined the Convention's failures for Thomas Jefferson.[29]

But despite his cascading disappointments, Madison regarded this flawed Constitution as the best attainable under the circumstances. Without it, the country would fragment. He would heed Franklin's advice, keep his objections to himself and a few close confidants, and advocate fiercely for the Constitution.

Madison tarried at his Philadelphia lodgings. He refined, edited, and copied his notes and dispatched overdue correspondence in the mails. He needed a few more days. But a message from New York City arrived to warn that the new Constitution was already stalling in Congress, thanks to the exertions of Richard Henry Lee from his own home state. Madison thought Congress need not debate the Constitution's merits. It ought only send it to the states with instructions to hold ratifying conventions. He could not stand by while Congress sabotaged the Convention's work, however imperfect. He packed his bags quickly and departed for New York.

While Madison worried and Mason seethed with righteous indignation, Edmund Randolph anguished. He held so many of his colleagues in high esteem. They had labored together for four months, and the undertaking had tested them all. Though he had tempered his refusal to sign with apologies, he held firm on the choice.

As his carriage bounced along the roads toward the capital city of Richmond, the young governor cast his mind back over the previous months, recalling his high hopes at the Convention's outset. He had worked as hard as anyone for its success, believing passionately in its mission. That May day, he had "opened the business" at General Washington's signal, raising all six feet of his elegant frame with both pride and apprehension. Eloquently, he had urged upon the delegates the catastrophic danger of the moment and the hope of the Virginians' proposed solutions.

But then he had watched as the Convention replaced proportional representation in the Senate with a system of representation he regarded as unjust. Afterward, he thought, the delegates proceeded to load far too much power into the executive branch, and they had failed to clearly delineate areas of state and federal authority. Those problems, perhaps, remained surmountable, but the Convention's final choices about the ratification process sealed his decision. The delegates insisted that the people ratify the Constitution "as is." They offered no chance for adjustments in response to the public's concerns, no second convention, as he and Mason recommended. The Convention put only a binary choice—this Constitution or the Confederation—before the state ratifying conventions.

Randolph felt a tremendous sense of responsibility. His position as governor, his wide public esteem, and his family's cachet meant that he could influence many people. He wanted an even better solution to the country's problems. He wondered whether he should throw his considerable political weight behind a flawed document and a disturbingly precipitous process or join the opposition brewing in Virginia.[30]

The state soon seethed with gossip and intrigue. Washington and Madison tried to glean the attitude of leaders from their friends. Still a member of Congress in New York City, Madison waited anxiously for news, but he admitted to only "very faint hopes of its corresponding with my wishes." Both men knew that Mason was sowing his objections widely, in Washington's view, to "alarm the people." But what about Randolph? Washington and Madison also tried to keep an ear out for how former governor Patrick Henry might weigh in. Exceedingly popular, Henry could wield great influence. But reports about him seemed conflicting and unreliable.[31]

By December, several Virginia newspapers had printed George Mason's list of objections. According to reports, one gentleman traipsed about Fairfax County, his "pockets stuffed" with copies, leaving them everywhere. Pennsylvania and Massachusetts newspapers also printed Mason's objections.[32]

Randolph held back. In December he allowed friends to publish his reasons for withholding his name from the Constitution. But he still refused to tip his hand on whether he would support or oppose ratification in his state.

In March 1788, Virginians elected delegates to a ratifying convention scheduled for June. Madison's friends urged him to hurry home and stand for election as a delegate from his Orange County district. Washington assured him that no one could defend the Constitution "with more precision and accuracy than yourself."[33]

* * *

The Constitution itself demanded ratification by nine states to go into effect. By June 1788, when Virginia's ratifying convention met, eight states had ratified. The journey had not been entirely smooth. In smaller states like New Jersey and Delaware, the Constitution breezed through quickly and unanimously. But it met fierce opposition in larger states like Pennsylvania and came down to nail-biting passage in Massachusetts. Rhode Island held a hurried public referendum that rejected the Constitution two-to-one. And then the New Hampshire ratifying convention adjourned without taking a vote, while a fierce fight with powerful opponents still loomed in New York. In general, voters from the coastal and commercial areas of the country responded far more enthusiastically than those in the developing agricultural reaches, where significant opposition percolated. Meanwhile, Americans talked of little else in taverns, town meetings, shops, and farms. In pamphlets, newspapers, and letters, they produced a torrent of political writing on both sides of the ratification question.

With only 300 wooden houses—and goats and pigs roaming the streets—Richmond hardly felt like the capital of the nation's largest state. The city strained to accommodate the 170 delegates and throng of spectators who flocked to the ratifying convention. When the crowd overflowed the statehouse on the first day, the convention moved to a newly erected theater.[34]

A pantheon of the state's luminaries lent their glow to the Shockoe Hill Theater. As president of the state's High Court of Chancery and Supreme Court of Appeals, Edmund Pendleton presided. George Wythe, who had mentored half of Virginia's lawyers, represented York County. The up-and-comers James Monroe and John Marshall served as delegates and so did shoots from the old Tyler, Harrison, Nicholas, Cary, and Lee families.

The Constitution's opponents in Virginia included charismatic and influential statesmen. Patrick Henry worried Madison the most. Henry's words could make "blood run back upon the aching heart," and Thomas Jefferson called him "the greatest orator who ever lived." He had authored Virginia's rebuke of the Stamp Act twenty-three years before. The fiery orator of the Revolution and two-time governor enjoyed enormous prestige.[35]

Madison tried to count the votes, but this exercise produced only grave doubts. Randolph had come around—quite decisively—and that bode well. But here at this gathering, the greatest exertion of Madison's life could come to a summary end. The better part of eighteen months' effort—exhaustive study preparing for the Philadelphia Convention, fifteen weeks of acrimonious debate in the sweltering Pennsylvania State House, long evenings holed up alone revising and editing his notes, hours composing essays that defended the Convention's work—it could all evaporate in a few short weeks here, in his own bailiwick. He had given his best effort to save his country.

In no other state ratifying convention had the method for choosing the president figured as a significant point of contention. But in Virginia, the Constitution's opponents tore into the proposed system of electors as a dangerous and antidemocratic device. The most withering critique issued from the tall, dark-haired, and dashing James Monroe, a thirty-year-old rising star who argued for more direct participation by the people: "The President [should] be elected by the people, dependent upon them, and responsible for maladministration."[36]

48

Randolph countered that "the people" *would* choose the president under the current system. After all, electors served simply as the people's proxies, deputed by them for the express task of selecting the president. Alexander Hamilton and John Jay had spelled out exactly this conception of the system a few months previously in their essays known as *The Federalist.*[37]

But in fact, as Hamilton and Randolph both well knew, the Constitution did not require that the people choose electors. Under Article II, state legislatures would decide how electors were chosen. Monroe fixed on this ambiguity, rejecting Randolph's description of the system as proxy election "by the people." He countered that the plan rendered the president electable by the states: "He is to be elected . . . in a manner perfectly dissatisfactory to my mind. I believe that he will owe his election, in fact, to the state governments, and not to the people at large."[38]

Monroe continued skillfully dismantling the framers' meticulously crafted system of electors. The plan offered insufficient safeguards against corruption, he declared. Monroe believed that the electors could conspire to throw the election to the man they wanted. He thought the whole thing ripe for the intervention of foreign governments, who could influence the process in just a few states to shape the result to their liking.

George Mason watched with delight as his young ally took down the system for choosing the president. When time came to offer his own objections, he rose and amplified Monroe's claims about corrupting operators, arguing that the design failed to protect the process from manipulation: "The electors, who are to meet in each state to vote for him, may be easily influenced." Mason contended that the whole plan was, in fact, a sham, "a mere deception—thrown out to make [the people] believe they were to choose him."[39]

Randolph and Madison vigorously denied these claims. "There can be no concert between electors. The votes are sent sealed to Congress," they countered. Perhaps with a touch of pique as his months of hard work came under fire, Madison impressed upon the assembly the enormous difficulty with which the Convention had arrived at a method for choosing the president.[40]

But in fact, both Randolph and Madison ignored Article II's purposeful ambiguity about who would choose electors and how they would be chosen. With so much at stake, they offered an overly optimistic and simplistic interpretation of the system's design. As the author of the plan, Madison knew full well that the Constitution afforded the states considerable leeway in the method for appointing electors. Events would later force upon Madison and Randolph the murky truth they presently papered over.

The Virginia debates did not linger here long. Too many other features of the executive troubled Mason and Monroe. And provisions beyond the executive gave ample fodder to Virginia's deep bench of Constitutional critics—no bill of rights, fuzziness between state and federal authority, too much power in the Senate. Topping it all off, Patrick Henry popped up repeatedly to play on Virginians' fears. As Henry raised the specter of despotism, his listeners unconsciously touched their wrists to feel the "shackles" they might endure under the new system.[41]

On June 24, the members made their closing arguments. Henry held forth on the new Constitution's dangers a final time, while a heavy summer rainstorm moved in to drive sheets of water against the windows of the Shockoe Hill Theater. The room darkened. Water droplets beat so hard that the sound smothered even Henry's soaring oratory. A clap of thunder rattled the tall windows in their casings, while Convention onlookers gasped. Henry recognized the moment as a heaven-sent warning against the Constitution. Lifting his eyes and fingers skyward, he urged, "*Beings* of a higher order are anxious concerning our decision."[42]

The next day, the delegates strode solemnly into the theater once again. Madison could not tell where things stood. His guessed that the Constitution would pass narrowly, perhaps by only three votes out of the 170 delegates. Newspapers and other observers issued similar predictions. That afternoon, the chair called the vote. A thousand spectators held their breath as the gentlemen rose one by one to announce their decisions. In the gallery, spectators watched "with fear and trembling." Reporters sat with pens poised.[43]

The Virginia ratifying convention approved the Constitution by a ten-vote margin, 89–79. At first, the victors thought Virginia had been the ninth state to ratify, thus earning distinction as the final necessary state to put the Constitution into effect. But then a special rider arrived with news that New Hampshire had achieved that honor four days earlier.[44]

Despite the victory, Madison continued to worry about Patrick Henry's influence, suspecting he would undertake "every peaceable effort to disgrace and destroy" the new Constitution. Perhaps Henry lay behind the anonymous "Obituary for Constitutional Liberty" published in the *Virginia Gazette* three days later. True to its title, the piece presented Virginia's ratification of the Constitution as the death of American liberty: "The corpse preceded by all the patriots in the city—Public Integrity, Virtue, Friendship, and every domestic smile. Pallbearers: Liberty of the Press, Liberty of Conscience, Taxation with Representation, Trial by Jury. The solemn scene was closed by the Goddess Liberty shedding tears for the loss of her departed hero."[45]

After Virginia, only two states remained to vote. In New York, powerful actors mobilized to reject the Constitution, but ratification squeaked out a three-vote margin of victory. North Carolina's advocates for the Constitution could not save it there. Like Rhode Island, the state would not join the Union until it ratified on a second attempt, a full year later.

* * *

Most Americans assume that the Constitution grew inevitably from a broad, holy, consensus around important principles and values. We prefer to believe that deep philosophical commitments led inexorably to a frame of government with quasi-divine perfection.

But the facts point instead to a constitution that emerged as much from pedestrian processes and earthly impulses. Struggle among fifty-five very human men with competing priorities and interests formed its specific features. The final document brims with provisions passed by only narrow margins and after much dissent.

The Constitution's human origins speak loudly in the Convention's last-minute resort to system of electors for choosing the president. The framers did not choose it from high-minded commitments to this device.

Rather, confronted with the Convention's continued preference for an admittedly dangerous method—congressional selection—Madison designed a practical alternative. His plan preserved the advantages that congressional selection gave to the small and slaveholding states, and thus won their agreement. It was a necessary concession made to avoid a disastrous alternative.

The method by which Americans elect their presidents originated here—in overheated, exhausted, and frustrated delegates who needed a practical solution and made accommodations to achieve it. Only huge misunderstandings and historical inventions can follow from elevating the framers' practical concession to the status of lofty principles.

Most Americans would prefer to choose the president by a method rooted in deep principles and widely shared values. Indeed, we deserve such a system, but the one we have does not fit this description.

* * *

No matter how we interpret the framers' Herculean struggles to find a suitable method for choosing the president, one thing is certain: Their plan did not last long.

They created a plan for proxy election. The people would choose wise and experienced individuals, those who knew something about the character of potential national leaders. In a sealed environment, these sages would meet and render their best judgment in a secret ballot. The framers never envisioned a system that translates the "popular vote" of a state or calculates "electoral votes." Indeed, these terms never appear in the Constitution's Article II.

Political parties rose within a few years of the Constitution's implementation. These intensely oppositional factions engaged in bitter political contests that shaped—even warped—the Constitution's operations, especially bending the Electoral College to their will. Over the next few decades, a series of innovations dramatically altered the framers' design. These changes completely subverted the system the framers created.

Thus, Americans no longer choose the chief executive according to the plan so cumbersomely described in Article II. We forsook the framers' design more than two centuries ago. Part II of this book tells that story.

CHAPTER 3

Electoral College Origins Myths

TARA ROSS WANTS YOU TO BELIEVE THAT THE ELECTORAL COLLEGE springs from high-minded ideals. In her books and widely viewed video, she celebrates it as "inspired," drawn from "principled reasons." She is not alone. Many Americans, most often conservatives, defend our method for choosing the president as an important bedrock of American constitutional government. These voices have grown in number and volume since the 2016 election when, for the second time since 2000, the candidate who lost the popular vote won the Electoral College.[1]

On the other hand, critics have recently reinvigorated a long-standing case against the Electoral College. These detractors—many from the left side of the political spectrum—also often make misinformed arguments. Consider Alexandria Ocasio-Cortez's complaint that the framers established the system "because of slavery," a notion echoed and amplified by other pundits. To these Americans, a mode of election tainted with original sin gave the nation's highest office to a singularly unfit and dangerous man in 2016, proof of the system's flaws.[2]

Americans crave a compelling creation story for the Electoral College, one that leads either to celebration or condemnation. But the Electoral College's actual origins story lacks the heroes, villains, righteous fireworks, and shame many seek. As the previous chapters have shown, this system was simply an attainable solution that avoided the dangerous alternative of Congress electing the president. But an "attainable solution" chosen "to avoid a worse alternative" offers all the rhetorical appeal of leftover dishwater, and thus more colorful origins stories pervade our public discourse.

Rather than offer historical truth, the myths that prevail in the moment speak to our contemporary political dilemmas. After an election that put the minority choice in the oval office, Electoral College defenders promoted the fable that the framers designed the system with exactly this outcome in mind. Meanwhile, as the nation struggles to reckon meaningfully with the legacy of slavery, we inevitably ask how this evil sullied even our method for choosing the president. Facile narratives almost always miss the mark.

This chapter concludes part I by examining the most widespread misconceptions about the Electoral College's origins. These fallacies provide poor foundations for understanding a critical element in our political system. How can we honestly and objectively evaluate the Electoral College if partisan fabulists and spin doctors dominate the conversation with arguments based on false premises? Like a right angle that measures only 88 degrees, inaccuracies at the inception lead to catastrophic distortions in the finished structure.

The Origins Myth: The Framers' Design versus Today's Electoral College

Americans often assume—and some state outright—that we select our presidents according to the plan the framers designed and described in 1787. This assumption inspires an instinct to preserve the system, since Americans generally revere the framers' work. But the Electoral College has, in fact, changed dramatically over the roughly 235 years since Madison sketched it out in a second-floor room of the Pennsylvania State House. Since these alterations have so fundamentally transformed its character and dynamics, a defense of today's Electoral College is, in fact, not a defense of the framers' plan at all.[3]

The framers created a pool of people, equipped with experience and wisdom, to choose the chief executive. John Jay called it a system of "select assemblies for choosing the president." The people, he suggested, gave their proxies to these sages, who selected the chief executive on their behalf. In states that allowed it, the people voted directly for electors—not for a presidential candidate. In other states, the legislatures chose the electors. These electors then *voted* for the president—that is, they made a choice, informed by their experience and knowledge.[4]

Notably, the Convention never discussed—and the Constitution does not describe—"electoral votes" or "popular votes." Nothing in the Constitution directs a state to "assign" votes to the winner of the popular vote, and nothing in the framers' recorded conversations suggests an intention for the system to work that way. Rather, the Constitution dictates that *electors* (actual people) will choose the president. Indeed, in eighteenth-century usage, "elector" simply meant "voter."

The framers took great care to guard the environment for this process, so that these electors could exercise their judgment unconstrained. In introducing their plan at the Convention, Gouverneur Morris described protection of the electors' free and unfettered judgment as a key factor in the plan's design. The system, he explained, sought to avoid "the danger of intrigue and faction." To that end, the framers put four corruption-inhibiting mechanisms in Article II of the Constitution.[5]

As a first corruption-retarding device, the framers disqualified as electors individuals who occupied any other federal office. This prohibition guaranteed that no one choosing the president would have the opportunity to help, hinder, influence, or collude with him.

A second anti-corruption mechanism required electors to meet in each of their home states, rather than together in one central location. Morris described this feature as essential: Since "the electors would vote at the same time throughout the U.S. and at so great a distance from each other, the great evil of cabal was avoided. It would be impossible also to corrupt them." Alexander Hamilton offered a similar rationale in *Federalist* 68: "This detached and divided situation will expose [the electors] much less to heats and ferments." Electors could best render independent and wise decisions when removed from collaborators who might whisper in their ears, demanding loyalty or offering favors.

Third, the framers' system required that electors cast two votes for president (not a separate one for vice president). One of these votes had to name a person outside the elector's own state. This rule aimed to produce a true consensus candidate. It forced electors to look beyond their local loyalties and consider someone with a national reputation. Sixteen years after the Constitution's ratification, the Twelfth Amendment altered this provision by requiring electors to designate separate choices for president and vice president.

Finally, the framers demanded that electors vote "by ballot." This word indicated a private, written vote, in contrast to the public voice votes often used in legislative bodies and local elections. A secret and anonymous written vote freed an elector from fear of reprisals and fostered honest judgment.

Each state would tally the votes of its electors and convey the results under seal to Congress. Under the framers' design, no one would know the outcome until the president of the Senate read the certificates before Congress.

But though any American can read these provisions in Article II of the Constitution, none of these meticulously crafted mechanisms matters one whit in today's presidential contests. The system no longer operates as the framers designed it. We no longer give our proxies to a body of sages who choose the president. The anti-corruption features detailed in the Constitution have grown unnecessary, because the electors no longer exercise judgment that requires protection. The "electoral votes" "awarded" in today's system—described nowhere in the Constitution— require no choices, no discretion, and no wisdom on the part of electors.

Today's Electoral College comes down to simple math. The transfer of an allotted number of "electoral votes" to the winner of each state's "popular vote" requires only plugging numbers into the algorithm. Today's system needs only spreadsheets and calculators, not living, breathing humans as electors.

If the framers had sought a mere mathematical formula to transfer and weight "popular votes," they certainly could have designed such a system.

In today's elections, electors assemble in each state capitol to cast predetermined votes for the candidate of their party. This moment that the framers envisioned as the "real" presidential election has evolved into a quaint but essentially empty ritual. Some call it "ceremonial," but the framers created it with real purposes. Much of the long and cumbersome third paragraph of Article II, so carefully crafted by the framers, remains in the Constitution like the dead shell of formerly relevant provisions.

Yet despite dramatic and far-reaching changes, some commentators simply ignore the great gulf between the 1787 Electoral College and the one that operates today. Tara Ross, a Texas lawyer whose website identifies her as "nationally recognized for her expertise on the electoral college," flatly asserts that "America's method of electing its president remains largely as it was first conceived by the Founders in the summer of 1787." Conflating the framers' system with today's operations, Ross never acknowledges in her entire 150-page book that the country long ago forsook that 1787 plan. She praises the system for its embodiment of superior wisdom. But it makes little sense to defend a system for its high-minded principles (or to critique it for ignoble origins) when, in fact, that system has changed almost beyond recognition. It's a bit like arguing that the framers rode horses because they wanted to save on gas.

Anyone who wants to defend the framers' system should, by all means, take that project on. They could begin by urging Americans to embrace the Constitution's widely accepted public meaning at the time of ratification. They could explain how we must get back to that original intent and dismantle all the extra-constitutional practices around presidential elections that have grown up in the last 235 years. Then, we can reinstate the framers' plan. All Americans would relinquish their vote for president, just as citizens did in early presidential contests. Instead, in those states that allow it, people can choose someone they trust to select the president on their behalf. In others, state legislatures will likely relish the opportunity to pick their preferred electors.

Likely, that project will find few takers.

But we can't defend today's Electoral College and pretend we are promoting the framers' plan.

"THE FRAMERS INTENDED" MYTH

"The framers established the Electoral College because they wanted . . ."

"In creating the Electoral College, the framers intended . . ."

"The framers created the Electoral College because they thought . . ."

These sentences are destined for falsehood, for they all begin with the flawed premise that the fifty-five framers shared a sort of Vulcan mindmeld, all drinking from the same cup of high-minded revolutionary principles. Such statements further assume that a straight and inevitable line runs from their beliefs to only one set of possible provisions: the Constitution's seven articles.

This book's first two chapters demonstrate quite the opposite truth: The delegates to the Constitutional Convention followed a winding, pockmarked path to a system of electors. Bumps and ruts troubled their way because these men agreed about precious little. They showed up in Philadelphia with competing ideas and interests. They embraced a variety of beliefs about the features of a well-structured republic, and they demonstrated a range of attitudes about ordinary people, the frailties of human nature, and the corruptibility of legislative bodies. Madison explained to Thomas Jefferson that "the natural diversity of human opinions on all new and complicated subjects" added a layer of complexity to the delegates' work. All that diversity of thought—even within the context of widely embraced eighteenth-century republican ideals—produced fifteen weeks of frustrating stalemates, tense and heated arguments, and painfully slow progress.

When it came to selecting the president, their disagreements blossomed like yeast in a summer kitchen. James Wilson showed up in Philadelphia with deep commitments to popular election. During the course of the summer, Madison grew convinced of the dangers of congressional selection and the benefits of popular election. Alexander Hamilton, John Rutledge, and the other South Carolinians generally preferred a "high-toned" sort of government and favored limiting popular participation. George Mason worried about ordinary citizens' lack of information, but Gouverneur Morris believed the people would choose wisely. The fact that the framers endowed the executive with significant powers (also highly controversial and hotly contested) raised the stakes. Adding to this multiplicity of ideas, eighteenth-century realities about information availability complicated the issue. Furthermore, the interests of small states and slave states shaped the conversation and limited the delegates' options.

Lack of consensus plagued the Convention on almost every issue, but especially on the method for choosing the president. For this reason, assertions about "the framers' intent" in choosing an Electoral College should immediately raise a field of red flags. One single delegate's comment at the Convention does not indicate the shared assumptions of the whole.

Honest evaluation of the sources leads to only one supportable conclusion about why the framers established the system of electors: They chose it to avoid the alternative of congressional selection, and they designed a very specific plan that answered enough objections to secure agreement.

THE TYRANNY OF THE MAJORITY MYTH

The craving for a more principled foundation for the Electoral College drives some commentators to invent lofty rationales and put them in the framers' mouths. The oft-made case about the "tyranny of the majority" falls into that category—these words feel good tripping off the tongue, and any mention of "tyranny" sets Americans' blood boiling with a reminder of their righteous rebellion against King George.

The phrase "tyranny of the majority" refers to the problem of elected majorities violating the rights of their defeated opponents. Tara Ross has emerged recently as the most popular proponent of the argument that the framers created the Electoral College to address this problem. She claims that the framers possessed a "distrust of emotional mobs." According to Ross, the framers "knew that people are imperfect. Emotions can grip a mob and propel voters into unreasonable action. History shows that minority groups tend to be tyrannized in such situations." The framers rejected strict majority rule, she argues, because "bare majorities can easily tyrannize the rest of a country." Opinion writer Donna Carol Voss makes a similar case: "The tyranny of the majority drowns out every last bit of the minority's self-interest. Our framers . . . devised the electoral college to prevent such tyranny from happening here. It works beautifully."[6]

This framing presents the Electoral College as a cool-tempered and reasonable process for choosing the president, protecting minorities from being outvoted by an irrational majority. After all, the majority can be wrong. The Electoral College offers a chance to work around these misguided "emotional" mobs and get the choice of the rational minority in the executive office. In such a light, it seems only wise and fair.

But a plethora of problems attend this argument, despite its commonsense facade. For our purposes, we can identify three serious flaws. In the first place, the framers themselves never offered "the tyranny of the majority" rationale that Ross and others advance. No delegate at the Philadelphia Convention ever argued for an Electoral College on these grounds. This justification appears nowhere in the flood of political writing generated by the ratification debates, including in the essays later collected and published as *The Federalist*. And no framer ever made this case in later years as he looked back on the Convention deliberations. Since the system of electors lacks a strong philosophical underpinning, Ross and Voss have fabricated one. And because no evidence connects the Electoral College to the problem of majority tyranny, they put words in the framers' mouths.

Second, this argument relies on rhetorical sleight of hand. Ross and Voss glibly misrepresent "the tyranny of the majority" as the framers understood it. For the framers, "the tyranny of the majority" had nothing to do with electoral mechanisms. Voters suffer disappointment when their candidate loses, but election losses hardly equate to "tyranny." If losing elections equals "tyranny," then a hefty percentage of American voters are routinely tyrannized in every election. Moreover, don't these "irrational mobs" that Ross describes also vote for other officials, for which the framers made no special electoral provision? No, indeed. Madison, Jefferson, and other founding-era thinkers affirmed the basic rule again and again: Majorities win elections. No framer ever proposed addressing "the tyranny of the majority" by tinkering with this formula.

So, what then did the framers mean by "the tyranny of the majority"? In their descriptions, "tyranny" results when elected leaders, *once in office*, behave despotically. "Tyranny" ensues when legislation violates individual rights or benefits the few while wreaking havoc on large swaths of society. This kind of "tyranny" ran rampant in the years after the American Revolution, such as in 1784 when the Virginia General Assembly tried to tax citizens for the support of religion, a measure that Madison viewed as violating Virginians' rights to choose, follow, and support their own faith. Early American state legislatures often enacted these kinds of measures, since they lacked sufficient checks on their powers.

No early American political thinker wrestled with this problem more exhaustively than James Madison. Indeed, Madison's entire plan going into the Philadelphia Convention aimed to diminish the "tyranny of the majority," but he never once suggested quirky electoral devices to address this problem. In fact, Madison defended the principle of majority rule vigorously and repeatedly, even as he offered prescriptions for preventing elective majorities from trampling rights, acting capriciously, or otherwise menacing the public good. His solutions included specific governmental structures—a bicameral legislature, separation of powers, and checks on the respective branches. He also supported explicit guarantees of certain fundamental rights. Furthermore, Madison believed that, in a large republic like the United States, the multiplicity of competing interests would undermine permanent majorities and thus create a "republican remedy for the diseases most incident to republican government."[7]

In a third serious logical flaw, the "tyranny of the majority" argument relies on another fallacy identified earlier in this chapter: treating today's Electoral College as if it were the one designed in 1787. This elision permits Ross, Voss, and others to depict the mathematical mechanism in today's Electoral College operations (whereby the candidate who loses the popular vote can still win in the Electoral College) as a brilliant and deeply principled calculation on the part of the framers. But the framers' system included no such mechanism. It's saving on gas by riding horses again.

Even in its current form, the Electoral College has only rarely made a winner of the candidate who loses the popular vote. But the dishonest argument that the framers actually sought to enable such an outcome grows attractive when a party repeatedly struggles to win majority support. Rather than craft policies that appeal to most Americans, some would rather pin their hopes for electoral success on a mechanism not designed by the framers and on an electoral map that increases the chances for a minority victory. All the while, they justify this approach by reinventing the framers in their own image—as champions of minority rule.

BECAUSE OF SLAVERY

In his 2018 book, *The Constitution Today,* Professor Akhil Reed Amar of Yale University argues for a relationship between the Electoral College and slavery. Historians have also elucidated this link. Certainly, the Electoral College preserved an advantage to slaveholding states in presidential selection, but we should carefully understand and not simplistically misconstrue this argument.[8]

Slavery indeed exerted a constant influence on Convention deliberations. Madison's Convention notes reveal how conflict connected to slavery sometimes erupted openly and rancorously. At other moments, slavery wielded a silent force, like the earth holding the moon in orbit.

It could scarcely have been otherwise. Twenty-five of the fifty-five framers—not all of them Southerners—were slaveholders. Many of the Convention's most important leaders owed their social, economic, and political existence to the human beings they enslaved and who labored for their benefit. George Washington, George Mason, and all four signers from South Carolina each enslaved hundreds of people. At the time of the Convention, Madison enslaved only a small number of people, but throughout his lifetime, he enslaved hundreds of human beings. Moreover, *every* delegate at the Convention represented a slaveholding state, except those from Massachusetts. Enslaved labor provided the fundamental market activity in more than half the participating states and contributed important economic fuel in the others. At least three delegates—George Washington, George Mason, and Charles Cotesworth Pinckney—brought enslaved people to attend to their needs in Philadelphia while they crafted the Constitution.[9]

Little wonder, then, that Convention conversations related to slavery rarely turned on questions of morality. Equally unsurprising, the framers left Philadelphia with a Constitution marked by this institution in multiple ways. In ensuing decades, representatives of slaveholding states skillfully used their Constitutionally endowed advantages to strengthen and perpetuate this institution. At the very least, such knowledge should undermine our misty-eyed notions of the framers' high-minded idealism and the Constitution's unspoiled design.

So, yes indeed. Slavery played a role in the creation of the Electoral College. Importantly, however, while slaveholding shaped the deliberations about choosing the president, and the final Electoral College design did benefit the slaveholding states and secure their approval of the plan, identifying slavery as *the* driving force behind this choice overstates the case. The driving force was avoiding selection of the president by Congress.

To clarify: Slavery did not cause the framers to choose an Electoral College. But slavery did prompt the Convention repeatedly to reject popular election in preference for Congress selecting the president. The slaveholding states wanted to preserve the advantage congressional selection conferred in the three-fifths clause. These delegates aimed to bolster their political power, not to find the most principled method. Madison laid this reality on the table, noting that popular election put the southern states at a disadvantage "on account of their Negroes." Though Madison declared himself in favor of popular election, he found little support from other Southerners.[10]

Notably, congressional selection of the president also benefited small states, by preserving their two-vote bonus in the Senate. They joined the slaveholding states, blocking popular election in preference for congressional selection. As with the slaveholding states, political power, not principle, guided this choice.

Thus, the small and slaveholding states profoundly shaped the deliberations, quashing every alternative except for Congress choosing the president. Importantly, these states gained nothing in the Electoral College that they did not already possess in congressional selection. They accepted the switch to the Electoral College in the eleventh hour only because Madison's plan mimicked the composition of Congress.[11]

Slavery moved the delegates to reject more principled options for choosing the president, shaping the circuitous path to the system of electors and dictating that only a certain Electoral College design would win acceptance. Understanding slavery's impact in this light differs slightly from "the framers chose an Electoral College because of slavery."

The subtle distinction matters for two reasons. The first speaks to the reasons the framers rejected popular election. They did so largely at the insistence of slaveholding states and small states, not for principled reasons pointing away from a choice by the people.

Second, preserving the three-fifths clause's advantages determined the structure of today's Electoral College, with each state's number of electors matching its representation in Congress. The three-fifths boost has, of course, disappeared, but the system it shaped remains, like a skeleton whose flesh has long since rotted away.

Of course, if the goal is to present the Electoral College as a noble, principled constitutional feature, downplaying this less admirable factor makes sense. Perhaps the simple truth will serve us better.

THE MYTH OF A ROLE FOR THE STATES

A popular argument today maintains that the framers established the Electoral College to preserve a role for the states in presidential selection. This argument presents with two slightly different emphases. On the one hand, some political scientists like the late Judith Best, a university professor who wrote extensively on the framing of the Constitution, defend the Electoral College as fundamental to federalism. Federalism is the uniquely American system of concurrent sovereignties of the states and of the people. Our government acts upon and represents both at the same time. Thus, some argue, the Electoral College expresses the federalist framework in the executive branch by combining votes of the states with votes of the people.[12]

Another variation on the "role for the states" argument maintains that the framers established the Electoral College to prevent the most populous states from dominating the process. Trent England, founder and director of Save Our States, an organization devoted to "defending the Electoral College from the dangerous National Popular Vote campaign," explains: The "Electoral College prevents one region, or a handful of major metropolitan areas, from controlling the White House. Support must be geographically distributed around the country in order to win enough states to capture an electoral vote majority." England emphasizes how the Electoral College makes it necessary to win the votes of states, rather than just people. Others who build on this argument remind us that the final Electoral College design put the manner of appointing electors in the hands of the state legislatures. The framers, they say, wanted the states to control elections.[13]

But as in the argument about the role of slavery, we should not interpret the Philadelphia Convention's necessary concessions as principled commitments. Just as the slave states aimed to preserve maximum political power, so the small states at the Convention also sought to bolster their political power. The small and slave states together formed a bloc that prevented the Convention from approving a general popular vote. Delegates from these two categories of states voted repeatedly to keep the choice of president in the hands of Congress, despite its admitted dangers. To overcome their objections, the final design of the Electoral College mimicked the composition of Congress.

Arguments positing the framers' lofty commitment to a role for the states invent clarity and consensus out of muddy and contradictory Convention conversations about this issue. The Convention delegates disagreed vehemently about the extent to which the states required representation. Moreover, nowhere do the Convention debates describe the delegates searching for a method of presidential selection that would preserve a role for the states. To the contrary, the delegates overwhelmingly rejected one Electoral College proposal that involved state governments.[14]

During ratification, the Constitution's defenders mostly ignored or downplayed any role for the states in presidential selection, describing the Electoral College as mediated election "by the people." Both Alexander Hamilton and John Jay made this case in essays later published in *The Federalist*; James Madison, James Wilson, Edmund Randolph, and Charles Cotesworth Pinckney all defended the system of electors this way at various times during the ratification debates.

The Constitution's opponents, however, seized on the states' role in choosing electors and added this provision to their catalog of complaints. Among them, George Mason and James Monroe described the system of electors as a deceptive device "thrown out to make the people believe they were to choose [the president]," when in fact, they thought the states would do the choosing.[15]

In other words, few conversations at the time, from either supporters or critics of the Electoral College, identified a role for the states as a positive, desirable, or significant feature.

One important source from the time did describe a role for the states as important—James Madison's *Federalist* essays, 39 and 45. The essays of *The Federalist*, all originally published in New York newspapers, aimed to defend the Constitution against powerful opposition from antinationalists in that state. *Federalist* 39 addressed this faction's persistent critique of the Constitution: that it would destroy the state governments. Madison pushed back vigorously against the charge, arguing that nearly every aspect of the Constitution—the methods for ratification, for adopting amendments, and for choosing each branch—combined national and federal features (the people and the states). With respect to the president, he explained, "the executive power will be derived from a very compound source. The immediate election of the President is to be made by the States in their political characters." Reiterating the point in another essay, Madison explained that "without the intervention of the State Legislatures, the President of the United States cannot be elected at all." Yet in the Virginia ratifying convention just a few months later, the same James Madison downplayed a role for the states in presidential selection. While the two aspects of Madison's argument do not necessarily contradict one another, it seems he carefully calibrated his case to respond to the demands of the setting.[16]

Federalism *is* an important part of our system. But a close study of federalism finds its significance mostly in the division of duties and authority between the states and the federal government, not in the mechanism for electing the president. Certainly, the federal nature of our republic matters, but the Electoral College plays little meaningful role in this structure. Federalism will thrive in the United States—with or without an Electoral College.

As to the framers establishing a system of electors to prevent large states or certain regions from dominating, this argument does not appear in any rationale for the system of electors at the time. Morris did not make this argument when he presented the Electoral College plan at the Convention. The argument appears nowhere in the eighty-five essays of *The Federalist*, including number 68, where Hamilton described and defended the Electoral College. No one made this case during the ratification debates. Like the case for the tyranny of the majority, this argument invents a rationale and puts it in the framers' mouths.

Only in a few Convention conversations did a related argument appear when some delegates worried that the larger states "would invariably have the man" in a general popular vote. The possibility that the president would always come from a large state seemed especially likely during an era when so few people enjoyed a national reputation. Importantly, however, delegates made these comments in arguing against a general popular vote, not in advocating for a system of electors.[17]

In any case, the Electoral College failed miserably when it came to preventing dominance of the highest office by a few large states. Eight of the first ten presidential contests returned a winner from the country's most populous state, Virginia. In other words, for thirty-one of the first thirty-five years under the Constitution, chief executives all came from one state. Not until 1828 did the United States elect a president from a state other than Virginia or Massachusetts.

Notably, this argument about preventing the dominance of a few states or a region has surged only in recent years, as our polarized political landscape has increasingly taken on geographic dimensions. In this increasingly hyper-partisan and geographically siloed reality, the argument, once again, reads the past through the lens of our present dilemma. It puts in the framers' mouths both a problem and a solution born, not in their day, but in ours.

THE FRAMERS' ANTIDEMOCRATIC INTENT

Left-leaning Americans often condemn the Electoral College as an antidemocratic device, instituted by elitist framers who aimed to buffer the popular will. Conservative Americans sometimes interpret the Electoral College in essentially the same way—as a mechanism meant to limit the destructive influence of an "excess of democracy." Critics find a problem in the antidemocratic elements of the Electoral College, while proponents sometimes regard this tendency as a positive and refining influence on the process and the outcome.

Indeed, the Constitution brims with democracy-constraining features, especially by comparison to other American constitutions of the time—the state governments and the Articles of Confederation. It created a system far *less* responsive to the popular will than these other constitutions. The Constitution diminished the authority of governments closest to the people (the states), while granting significant powers to a strong national government more distant and removed. It gave powers typically reserved to legislatures—appointment of public officers, for example—to a new and powerful executive branch. In appointing federal judges for life, it completely shielded the judiciary from the popular will. In the legislature, it created a small upper house accountable only to the state legislatures, with lengthy six-year terms. At the time, some Americans complained that House members represented constituencies far too large to foster sympathy and acquaintance with "the people." The framers also put term limits on none of these offices, in stark contrast to the frequent rotation in office required by the Articles of Confederation and the states. Americans at the time noticed these democracy-curbing features, and the Constitution's opponents cited them as powerful arguments against ratification. To the framers, most of these features seemed necessary to prevent the damage of capricious legislation in the states, to bring a new level of energy and authority to the national government, and to keep that new power firmly within its limits.

Many Americans today who understand the 1787 Electoral College find it undemocratic. Putting presidential selection in the hands of a select body of citizens removed this choice from direct popular input. But the framers' plan may not have appeared as undemocratic to eighteenth-century Americans, most of whom did not even elect their governors. While the Electoral College did provoke some criticism on these grounds during the ratification process, the Constitution's other democracy-blunting features invited far more complaints.

As to an antidemocratic intent in the choice of an Electoral College, the Convention delegates displayed a wide range of sentiments on direct election of the president by the people. On the one hand, some of the most influential delegates—James Madison, Gouverneur Morris, James Wilson, and John Dickinson—argued vigorously for direct popular election. At the other end of the spectrum, Elbridge Gerry worried that "the people are uninformed and would be misled by a few designing men," a statement that helps explain why Gerry opposed direct elections for *any* national office, including congressional representatives. And in between, other delegates expressed a range of sentiments, including admiration for the principle of direct popular election but doubts about its practicality at the time. As we so often find, no single framer's words represented a Convention consensus on the best mode of presidential selection.[18]

In fact, for at least some of the framers, their system of electors seemed the most democratic solution attainable at the time. When Gouverneur Morris justified the plan at the Convention, he explained that "many were anxious for an immediate choice by the people."

Today's Electoral College does indeed create serious problems in our political landscape. Perhaps most significantly, it profoundly warps our election processes and props up a badly broken party system, as part III of this book will show. But these ill effects do not necessarily reflect the intentions of the framers, who designed a system utterly different from the one we have today. They thought, under the circumstances, that their plan was the best attainable at the time. It avoided the dangers of Congress selecting the president and gave the people some role.

* * *

Now that we've dismantled some of the most prevalent myths about the Electoral College, let's return once more to Madison's exhaustive and detailed notes on the Convention, a vital source for understanding the framers' motivations. Instead of putting words in the framers' mouths, picking quotes out of their context, offering abstruse explanations, or imposing our present political wishes and sensibilities on them, let's let *them* remind *us* why they created a system of electors for choosing the president.

Only one Convention incident offers the "this is why we did it" explanation that Americans crave. This moment came when Gouverneur Morris presented the Electoral College plan to the Convention on September 4, 1787. Two delegates asked why the committee had switched to a system of electors from the previous plan for Congress to choose. Morris gave six reasons. Five of these rationales identified problems with Congress selecting the president. The sixth explained that many delegates "were anxious for an immediate choice by the people."[19]

Of course, Morris's words only reveal their full significance and meaning in the context of the extended Convention conversations about choosing the president and the delegates' larger goals for this new government. Additionally, Morris's comments require consideration in light of all the other commentary about these matters left by Americans of the time. This exercise reveals neither high-minded principles nor nefarious aims in the framers' pragmatic eleventh-hour decision to put presidential selection in the hands of carefully chosen electors. It seems they created this system as an obtainable solution for one of the most intractable problems they faced. Most delegates to the Constitution accepted it as the best they could achieve under the circumstances, despite expressed preferences for other methods. Most of them also followed Benjamin Franklin's advice, sacrificing their private disappointments about the Constitution to the public good. With a few exceptions, the delegates defended the Electoral College and its benefits as part of their total advocacy of the new system of government.

Ultimately, the most important appraisal of the Electoral College should rest, not on its origins, but on its impact in the present. If it serves the country well, by all means let's keep it. If it acts negatively on our electoral processes and our politics, we should seriously consider making some changes. We take up that evaluation in part III.

This book's next section, part II, details how today's Electoral College came to be. For if the framers' plan lacked deeply principled foundations, today's Electoral College arose from decidedly ignoble forces. Today's system grew from the very political manipulation the framers sought so strenuously to avoid. Perhaps even more troubling, some of the men who helped create the system in 1787 participated in this crass adulteration.

Part II

The Electoral College since the Founding

Party Politics and Change

The framers' plan for an Electoral College did not last long. Deeply antagonistic political parties developed a few short years into George Washington's first term, and these bitterly warring factions utterly transformed the system's operations. Today's method of choosing the president originates more from the manipulations of early political operators than in the framers' careful design.

The four chapters in this section explore Electoral College history *since* the Constitution's ratification. These chapters trace the rise of two features not in the framers' plan: (1) electors pledging in advance to a specific candidate; and (2) the winner-take-all system for allocating a state's electors. These practices have fundamentally converted the Electoral College from the framers' system of proxy election by wise and discerning people into the mathematical algorithm we use today.

This section also tells the story of widespread, ongoing, and deep dissatisfaction with the Electoral College. From early in the life of the nation, Americans have striven to make presidential elections more reflective of the people's wishes and less susceptible to fraud, chaos, and partisan manipulation. More than 700 constitutional amendments to this system have been introduced in Congress. Many early leaders and key framers—Thomas Jefferson, James Madison, Alexander Hamilton,

Gouverneur Morris, and Rufus King—recommended or endorsed these changes.

This story dispels the assumption that the Electoral College has served the nation well. To the contrary, this system has repeatedly produced problematic—even dangerous—outcomes, ranging from inconclusive results to contests riddled with fraud. Moreover, the Electoral College has proven extraordinarily malleable to small groups who openly manipulated it for their aims.

Tellingly, many Electoral College defenders ignore this history of change, frustration, and turbulence. Instead, they sail right over 235 years of the American past, drawing a straight line from the Constitution as written to today's system. By artfully omitting this history, they encourage the misperception that we elect our presidents exactly as the framers intended and that the plan has always worked with clean and principled precision.

Nothing could be further from the truth.

CHAPTER 4

The Electoral College and the Election of 1800

THE EERIE LIGHT OF A SNOWY FEBRUARY NOON GLOWED IN THE NEW Senate Chamber as Vice President Thomas Jefferson raised his tall frame to face the congressmen. Extending nearly thirty-five feet above him, the room's vast empty height contrasted awkwardly with the packed floor below, where men crowded in a tight semicircle. Others crammed under the low arches at the rear, and onlookers filled the gallery above. The room smelled faintly of new construction, damp clothes, and men after a tramp through the snow.

Jefferson's countenance betrayed nothing of his inner agitation. He could not discern whether partisan hatred or hopefulness dominated the room. His gaze passed quickly over the hostile New England faces to linger on the warmer expressions of southern friends. As usual of late, he wore his anti-aristocratic commitments in a simple suit of subdued tones, though once he had enjoyed sporting rich colors and high fashion. Neither did he powder his hair, letting its natural streaks of silver soften the fading ginger.

Only ten weeks before—on December 3, 1800—electors had cast their ballots in the state capitals in this, the country's fourth presidential election. Intrigue had bloomed as the country waited for the official count, but now Jefferson would end the speculation. As sitting vice president, he would take each state's electoral certificate and read the totals aloud. Like everyone present, he expected to announce a tie—seventy-three votes each for himself and his Republican running mate, Aaron Burr. If reports were accurate, incumbent president John Adams would trail with sixty-five votes.

Turbulence simmered beneath this seemingly simple ritual. If the two Republican candidates tied as expected, the election would go to the House of Representatives, where Jefferson's Federalist enemies could wreak havoc. Those Federalist partisans retained many options—all unethical and of borderline legality—to seize the presidency. Republicans would regard such efforts as a coup and violence might erupt, whether from governors summoning their militias or ordinary citizens asserting themselves against a defrauding political elite.

One by one, the three tellers broke the seals on the envelopes, extracted the certificates, and handed them to Jefferson. In his soft voice, Jefferson announced each state's totals. Every announcement moved toward the anticipated result. New England's five densely populated states gave their electors unanimously to John Adams. All twelve New York electors chose Jefferson and Burr. Then Virginia, all twenty-one electors for Jefferson and Burr. So, too, South Carolina, Georgia, Tennessee, and Kentucky—all for Jefferson and Burr.

When Jefferson concluded, the result sat at the predicted seventy-three votes each for himself and Burr. Decisively defeated, President John Adams captured only sixty-five votes.

Jefferson's expression remained inscrutable as the peril of the moment descended on the silent assembly. Eleven years after the Constitution's ratification, the carefully wrought system for choosing the president had produced no clear winner.

But the cloud quickly lifted. Eager to flex their muscle in the next phase of the business, the members did not linger. Low murmurs filled the chamber and then swelled as they filed from the room into the halls of the unfinished Capitol and the gaping hole of unknown and dangerous outcomes.

At the core of a looming catastrophe lay the Electoral College. In just four election cycles and a dozen years, it had produced a crisis with frightening implications.

* * *

Thirteen years earlier, as debates about the Constitution raged in the states, Alexander Hamilton had offered an elegant, idealized explanation of the Electoral College. In *Federalist* 68, he painted it as a pristine and brilliant device that would unfailingly register the "sense of the people." Though he acknowledged that the system fell short of "perfect," he found it at least "excellent."

Hamilton explained how it would work. The "most capable" men, chosen for their "discernment," would serve as electors. They would exercise their wisdom in a protected environment. The "detached and divided" electors could not coordinate with one another, nor could anyone outside "tamper with [them] beforehand." The system's firm barriers "to cabal, intrigue, and corruption" meant the electors would choose without any "sinister bias."[1]

But almost nothing about Hamilton's description fit Electoral College operations in practice. The "sinister bias" of hyper-partisanship gripped the nation in the early years of the Washington administration, and it soon bent the system to its will. As early as 1796—the first truly competitive election—electors pledged themselves to candidates in advance and were chosen exclusively for their political leanings rather than any abstract wisdom and discernment. Party operators routinely "tampered" with electors and carefully coordinated votes. Moreover, in exploiting the tiniest openings to create an advantage for their candidates, state leaders tinkered with elector section methods to extract maximum partisan benefit, suppressing the votes of significant minorities.

No one participated more enthusiastically in these developments than Alexander Hamilton.

Indeed, Hamilton may not actually have believed what he was selling in *Federalist* 68. Less than a year after publishing it, he privately described the Electoral College quite differently. A "defect in the Constitution," he observed, made it possible for the man intended for vice president to win the top spot. Here, Hamilton referenced a potential problem in the double-vote rule: each elector voted for two candidates, and the vice presidency went to the second-highest vote-getter. But if every elector chose the two favorites, they would tie, throwing the election to the House of Representatives, where a very different process would take over. More than a decade before the disastrous election of 1800, Hamilton identified the precise flaw that produced this catastrophe.[2]

But the Electoral College vulnerabilities that spawned the calamity of 1800 went well beyond the one flaw Hamilton pointed out. This debacle owed as much to the many significant departures from the framers' vision, as shaped by the bitter partisan rivalry between Hamilton and John Adams's Federalists and Jefferson and James Madison's Democrat-Republicans.[3]

And many of the Constitution's own authors participated in converting the Electoral College into something they had not originally envisioned or devised.

CONNECTICUT, 1796: THE ELECTORAL COLLEGE IN THE FIRST COMPETITIVE ELECTION

On a crisp December day in 1796, Connecticut governor Oliver Wolcott Sr. strode through the white wooden gate of the brand-new statehouse. A finely dressed man of seventy years with a straight, firm mouth, high forehead, and erect bearing, Wolcott moved comfortably in elite political circles. His father had also served as Connecticut's governor, and recently his son, Oliver Jr., had succeeded Alexander Hamilton as secretary of the treasury. The elegant senior Wolcott looked perplexed as he joined the eight others who had arrived to cast Connecticut's votes for president of the United States.[4]

The nine Connecticut electors gathered with the casual chatter of intimates bound together by ties of family, marriage, and wealth across several generations. As in many other states, these electors reflected little "sense of the people" as Hamilton had promised. Indeed, the people had not chosen them at all. Rather, the Connecticut state legislature appointed them, bypassing "the people" altogether. Fully half the states used this perfectly legal option in 1796, and more would use it in the next cycle.

Connecticut's political traditions removed the electors from the people by still several more degrees. The legislature that chose them came from the same set of wealthy, deeply intermarried families tied to the state's religious and political establishment. With pedigrees extending back into the colonial period, these families monopolized the state's offices through a set of election rules that kept incumbents in power and discouraged competition. These Connecticut families cemented their grip on state power so firmly that sometimes fewer than 3 percent of eligible voters bothered to participate in elections.[5]

Connecticut's intensely partisan Federalist electors exuded the very sinister bias Hamilton had so decried. Their shared disdain for Republican Thomas Jefferson bubbled immediately to the surface. Governor Wolcott regarded Jefferson as a "hypocrite," possessing little "practical ability," a man whose "Machiavellian policy has already done his country great injury and dishonor." Fearing Jefferson's election as "fatal to our independence," the electors perceived dangerous vulnerabilities in his affinity for French thinkers, French wine, and French morals. Indeed, they thought a Jefferson presidency might produce a bloodbath like the ongoing revolution in France. Wolcott had heard that Jefferson's supporters in Philadelphia "went to the polls with French cockades in their hats," though he could not vouch for the story's truth.[6]

These men did not regard themselves as partisans but, rather, as sensible men with "prudence and firmness," possessors of the unvarnished truth. In their view, the country's deep and debilitating partisanship flowed from the "ignorant and fickle" mob, with its "folly and depravity." Highly partisan and "pestiferous" newspapers only published lies against their side. Foreign influence exacerbated it all, especially from the French, who "practiced every species of seduction to divide the country." In the minds of Connecticut's Federalist electors, Jefferson embodied these ills, serving both as French puppet and the people's puppeteer.[7]

Connecticut's electors hoped to shut Jefferson out entirely. To a man, they planned to cast equal votes for Federalist standard-bearer John Adams and his South Carolina running mate, Thomas Pinckney.

Since the very first presidential election, operators like Alexander Hamilton had coordinated with electors in every possible state. Usually, Hamilton urged a calculated "throwing away" of votes from the intended vice presidential choice, to avoid an Electoral College tie. In both 1789 and 1792, Hamilton had arranged with electors in several states to withhold votes from John Adams, so that Adams would not edge Washington out of the top spot. In this way, the very man who so loudly praised the Electoral College's barriers to tampering became the country's chief election meddler.

Now, in 1796, choreographing electors seemed even more crucial. The two parties' apparently equal strength portended an extraordinarily close outcome. Hamilton barraged every available contact with his carefully designed plan. But this time, he urged equal votes for Adams and Pinckney, expecting that undisciplined electors in the South would solve the problem of the tie. Some operatives thought he actually hoped to slip Pinckney past Adams into the top spot.

Others "tampered beforehand" with the electors as well. The chief justice of the United States, Oliver Ellsworth, advised Governor Wolcott exactly how the electors should vote. To be clear, Ellsworth had no official role in this process. In fact, Article II of the Constitution expressly prohibited federal officeholders like Ellsworth from serving as an elector. As a key delegate to the Constitutional Convention who had been deeply involved in the question of presidential selection methods, Ellsworth well understood that provision and the spirit behind it.

There in Connecticut's new statehouse, Governor Wolcott called the electors to their business. The Constitution required them to vote "by ballot"—making a private choice—so that each elector might exercise independent and unfettered judgment. Wolcott, however, thought they should vote strategically and required coordination.

Wolcott and the other electors questioned the wisdom of giving Pinckney their second votes as Hamilton and Chief Justice Ellsworth had advised. Their indecision flowed from two pending nightmare scenarios, and they could not decide which prospect troubled them more. On the one hand, Connecticut men could muster no enthusiasm for the slaveholding Pinckney. If they followed Hamilton's plan and voted equally for the two Federalists, Pinckney might slip ahead of Adams to win the presidency. But on the other hand, if they withheld votes from Pinckney, Jefferson might finish in the vice presidential slot and considerably damage the country.

This dilemma pained Connecticut's electors all the more as they contemplated how the three-fifths clause gave southern states—and thus supporters of Pinckney and Jefferson—an added electoral "bump." Governor Wolcott knew that the electors "would not be satisfied to have a president contrary to our wishes by a Negro representation only."[8]

Wolcott queried the other electors for information that might help the group settle on a voting strategy. Had he wished to adhere to original intent, he might have remembered that the Constitution required electors to assemble in their own states—not all together in the nation's capital—so as to prevent exactly this sort of coordination. But Wolcott proceeded, unaware or unconcerned that his actions conflicted with the spirit of Article II.

Someone suggested that the afternoon mail might bring up-to-date information. No harm in adjourning a few hours and delaying a decision until after the mail arrived.

As the nine men streamed back into the governor's office that afternoon, Wolcott announced that nothing helpful had come in the mail. They would have to coordinate from their own limited information.[9]

Connecticut's electors decided to withhold five votes from Thomas Pinckney. They put their results—nine votes for Adams, five for John Jay, and four for Thomas Pinckney—in a sealed envelope and sent it to Congress. As sitting vice president, Adams himself would read out the official tallies in February. Until then, the mail and the papers would predict the results.

When Congress assembled to count the votes that February, Adams won with seventy-one votes, but Thomas Pinckney finished at only fifty-three. Federalist electors in other states had made the same fatal calculation as their Connecticut colleagues, "throwing away" a combined total of eighteen votes from the South Carolinian. The withheld votes allowed Thomas Jefferson to edge Pinckney out of the vice presidency, just as the Connecticut men had feared. For the next four years, a president of one party served with a vice president of another. Every alert Federalist could only conclude that better party discipline—more careful coordination—would have avoided this result.

Even in this third election, the first true test of the system, Electoral College operations departed vastly from Hamilton's description of electors acting as the people's proxies, making individual decisions from deep wisdom, and casting their independent votes in a hermetically sealed environment. As in Connecticut, the practice in many states ran contrary to Hamilton's description. Small groups of deeply sectarian elites—often chosen by another small group of sectarian elites—coordinated strategy or conferred with party operators to place their men in office.

In the aftermath of this outcome, Americans reflected on their strange method for choosing a president. Connecticut congressman Chauncey Goodrich described its operations as "preposterous." A writer for the *New York Diary* noted, "Mr. Adams' election is not owing to a fair, decided expression of the public voice. . . . Accident alone gave Adams the Presidency."[10]

Four years later, in the election of 1800, those preposterous and accidental elements flourished, as manipulation and tampering of the Hamiltonian style produced the country's first serious electoral crisis.

* * *

John Adams's administration did not retard the nation's zealous factionalism. During his presidency, animosity between Federalists and Republicans fed on the two parties' clashing approaches to foreign affairs, taxation, military expansion, and civil liberties. As the election of 1800 approached, Federalists and Republicans each believed that the other aimed to destroy the country. Each nourished the conviction that the nation's survival hung on getting the right man—their man—in office.

In this high-stakes atmosphere, partisans looked for the best places to gain an advantage. Methods of elector selection—a matter the Constitution left to the states—promised effective control of election outcomes. Focusing on small adjustments in the states, operators charted the path to the disastrous election of 1800.

James Madison—the very man who fought so hard in the 1787 Constitutional Convention for a presidential election method that would avoid "intrigue, cabal, and corruption"—proved extraordinarily adept at these subtle changes.

VIRGINIA: "FOLLY OR WORSE NOT TO FOLLOW"

Virginia's state capitol rose like a Greek temple on the James River's banks. Its glistening whiteness, clean lines, and massive columns embodied an architectural ideal that contrasted sharply with the small town's dark, low-slung dwellings and stores. As James Madison strode into the grand building on a mid-January morning in 1800, he wrestled internally with a similar contradiction.[11]

Madison had recently retired from Congress, returning to his old seat in the Virginia House of Delegates with a single purpose: to thwart Federalists at every turn. Thus far in the session, he and his fellow Virginia Republicans had succeeded stupendously. They purged the opposition from every state office, installing their own partisans. When the popular Federalist Patrick Henry died, Virginia House Republicans refused even to sanction a simple resolution honoring Henry's memory as a Revolutionary hero and multi-term governor. They presented these measures as necessary to halt the "anglo-monarchic-aristocratic-military government" of John Adams. Madison intended to crown these achievements by facilitating Thomas Jefferson's path to the presidency. Republicans outside the state had urged on him the "absolute necessity" of the step he was about to take.[12]

Like other Virginia Republicans, Madison despised the policies of the preceding four years. In their view, President Adams had pursued misguided and dangerous measures. He had stacked the courts, trampled civil liberties, and raised taxes to pay for a wholly unnecessary army. Only a change of administration would halt the Federalist march toward destruction of the country.

Republicans believed that Adams's own writings betrayed his love of monarchy and aristocracy, as did his penchant for titles, pomp, and ceremony. They would not forget the ridiculous sight of "His Rotundity" taking the presidential oath, decked in finery, a wig on his head and a sword at his side. Jefferson, they believed, would initiate a mighty second revolution, returning the country to its authentic, humble republican principles.

Now, inside the Virginia Capitol, Madison rose to address the House of Delegates. Though only forty-eight years old, to some he appeared a "little dried-up creature." His shrunken frame, wrinkled visage, and wispy, unruly hair displayed the physical toll of the last dozen years. Outfitted as plainly as ever, he delivered ineloquent remarks too softly to fill the chamber.[13]

Nonetheless, as Madison introduced his bill, its implications jolted the Virginia House. Everyone immediately perceived it as a bald partisan measure, calculated to give Thomas Jefferson an advantage in the upcoming presidential contest.

Madison's bill would alter the method for choosing electors that Virginians had used since the first presidential election. In contrast to states where aristocratic legislatures monopolized the choice of electors, Virginia had always respected and sought the people's voice. Virginia voters selected their electors in districts. In each of twenty-one districts, voters chose a single elector—usually a "local notable" whose reputation they knew well. They valued this method as a reflection of their republican principles.

Madison did not seek a change so draconian as putting elector selection in the legislature's hands. He advocated only a simple switch to the "general ticket" used by some states. Voters would still select electors, but they would choose state-wide rather than in districts. Thus, each Virginia voter would vote for all twenty-one electors, rather than just one.

In a deeply partisan climate, the choice of district or general tickets carried enormous implications. The general ticket, sometimes known as winner-take-all, helped a state's dominant party capture every single elector, depriving the minority party of any electors at all. The district system, by contrast, allowed the minority party to win at least a few electors in their local pockets of strength. The district system reflected a state's actual political diversity and registered it in the Electoral College.

Virginians had often praised the district system as the fairest and most representative of the people's wishes, and the state's loudest Republican spokesmen had just recently condemned the general-ticket system.

Yet the state's Republicans contemplated with pain how this system had sabotaged Jefferson's presidential hopes four years earlier, costing him the election of 1796. One of the votes against him had come from a single Federalist stronghold in northern Virginia. Madison's bill aimed to neutralize such Federalist pockets and sweep all twenty-one electors for Jefferson.[14]

In the House of Delegates, Virginia's drastically outnumbered Federalists decried Madison's measure for what it was: a blatantly partisan attempt to silence the voice of the minority. The bill would "exclude one-third at least of the citizens of Virginia from a vote for President of the United States."[15]

Even some Republicans pushed back against Madison's measure as a betrayal of their oft-cited values, predicting an outcry from their constituents. The public would recognize and resist the overtly partisan maneuver, they warned. Though they could clearly see how the bill would facilitate a critical presidential victory later that year, it simply felt dirty.

Thus far this session, Virginia Republicans had rammed their anti-Federalist agenda through by huge margins that reflected their two-to-one majority. But Madison's general-ticket bill could not escape the shame of its naked partisanship, and it squeaked by with only five votes to spare.[16]

Having secured this new method for choosing electors, the state's Republican leaders got to work. To maximize its effectiveness, the general ticket demanded extensive voter education. The old district system used "voice voting"—a voter spoke his choice to the clerk, who wrote it down and asked the voter to sign. Madison's measure eliminated voice voting, instead requiring voters to write twenty-one elector candidates on a "ticket" that they signed on the back. Given that election officials offered no preprinted ballots, the new system asked much of voters' advance knowledge and working memory.

Virginia Republicans created and deployed a party machinery to help voters select twenty-one Republican electors. Just three days after passing the new law, they strategically selected twenty-one men who enjoyed far-reaching reputations. Virginians would recognize, remember, and respect names like James Madison, Edmund Pendleton, and George Wythe.[17]

To assure the sweep they wanted, the newly formed Virginia Republican Party apparatus guided voters to all twenty-one electors. Working through a central committee in Richmond and networking with county committees, they handwrote and distributed "tickets" identifying the twenty-one Republican electors. Voters needn't struggle any longer to remember names. They could simply sign the prewritten, party-provided elector ticket and drop it in the ballot box.[18]

The party also molded public opinion. Since Republicans had so long and loudly praised the district system, voters needed a rationale for the shift to the general ticket. Soon a pamphlet "vindicating" the general-ticket system circulated throughout Virginia—possibly financed by Jefferson himself. The twenty-three-page manifesto justified the measure as necessary for preserving majority rule and only needed until a constitutional amendment could prescribe a "uniform mode of election." The author flailed, denying that the law aimed "to promote the election of Mr. Jefferson," while in the next breath admitting he hoped it would have that effect.[19]

Virginia Federalist John Marshall, then a member of the state's congressional delegation, understood clearly that this new law aimed to eliminate his party's influence in presidential selection and to render his own Federalist vote meaningless. He determined never again to vote in a presidential election while Virginia's general-ticket law remained intact. Twenty-eight years later, as the chief justice, he still adhered to that vow.[20]

In private, Jefferson expressed ambivalence about Madison's efforts on his behalf. Everyone agreed, he observed, "that an election by districts would be best," if all states chose their electors this way, but "while ten states choose either by their legislatures or by a general ticket, it is folly or worse for the other six not to follow." If all the other states used a method that conferred a partisan advantage, Virginia could ill afford to remain a purist holdout.[21]

These innovations—the use of the general ticket and party control of electors—utterly transformed Electoral College operations. First, the general ticket altered Electoral College math, weighting the state's vote entirely for a single candidate rather than distributing it proportionally. Second, electors no longer exercised judgment or discernment. Instead, they pledged themselves in advance to a candidate, and voters selected them for their known party affiliations. They assembled to select the president with their "discernment" already promised.

As the election year of 1800 unfolded, other states mimicked Virginia's fine-grade Electoral College tinkering. Shifts in Electoral College outcomes depended on which party controlled the state legislatures. And operators like Alexander Hamilton would stoop to significant lows to game the system.

NEW YORK: "IT WILL NOT DO TO BE OVERSCRUPULOUS"

Alexander Hamilton panicked as New York's state legislative election returns rolled in during early May that year. His Federalists lost their majority in Albany. Their Republican enemies captured a twenty-seat lead, including all thirteen seats from Hamilton's own turf—New York City. Though only a state legislative race, the election's implications extended widely, and Hamilton knew that Aaron Burr lay behind this outcome.[22]

Burr had spared no effort, outorganizing, outsmarting, and outworking his Federalist opponents. Carefully dividing each of New York City's seven wards into districts, Burr and other Republicans launched the country's first urban party machine. They put subcommittees in each district and dispatched house-to-house canvassers. Burr opened his own magnificent home to serve as headquarters. He filled the living room floor with mattresses and piled the tables with food for campaign workers. The party dispatched German-speaking canvassers and organized transportation networks to bring out the vote in poorer and immigrant-heavy wards at the city's north end. During the three days of voting, Burr and his lieutenants stationed themselves outside polling stations to encourage and intimidate voters.

Hamilton immediately calculated the cost of this defeat for the fall presidential race. As in most states, the New York legislature chose electors themselves, rather than relinquish this power to the voters. Before this surprise result, Hamilton had considered the state's twelve electors safely in the Federalist column. But the new Republican-dominated legislature would choose a slate of solidly Republican electors. Hamilton mentally shifted twelve votes to the Republican side and confronted a horrifying prospect: the Electoral College would surely send Thomas Jefferson to the White House.

On a single state election, on the efforts of one savvy political operative, hung the outcome of the presidential election, still six months in the future.

Hamilton sprang into action and dispatched a letter to New York governor John Jay. A committed Federalist, Jay shared Hamilton's partisan convictions, and he, too, feared Republican treachery. Jay would surely see the urgent need to act. In his letter, Hamilton pressed the governor to call the outgoing Federalist-dominated legislature back into a special session expressly to authorize a proposal that would salvage at least some Federalist votes. For this purpose, Hamilton now recommended popular voting for electors in districts, even though New York had never used this method and Federalists themselves had rejected exactly this plan only weeks before.

Knowing that this move would rankle the conscientious Jay, Hamilton urged the governor to weigh his principles against the public good: "In times like these in which we live, it will not do to be overscrupulous." Reminding Jay that this recommendation was technically legal and constitutional, Hamilton dressed the political trick as a virtuous act of saving the republic. He and Jay possessed the "solemn obligation to employ the means in our power . . . for *public safety*." He went on, "The particular nature of the crisis and the great cause of social order" made such steps necessary.[23]

Jay ignored Hamilton's request. He simply filed the letter with a note: "Proposing a measure for party purposes, which I think it would not become me to adopt."[24]

In every state, legislators understood the same truth that drove Hamilton and Madison: the method of elector selection could dramatically alter Electoral College outcomes. As the election calendar raced toward the fall, these legislatures tinkered with elector selection, pursuing the option most favorable to the dominant state party. From state to state, each party displayed a remarkable inconsistency.

In Massachusetts and New Hampshire, for example, Federalist legislatures took elector selection away from voters entirely and appointed them without the people's input. In so doing, they protected themselves from voters' growing Republican affinities and retaliated against Madison's efforts in Virginia.

Partisan competition around Pennsylvania's fifteen electors created a stubborn deadlock that threatened to cost the state its vote entirely. The Federalist-dominated upper chamber wanted voters to select electors in districts, thus preserving some weight for their party. But Republicans, who controlled the lower house, hoped to sweep all the electors with a general ticket. Unable to settle on a provision, Pennsylvania legislators finally selected electors themselves only days before the election.

In December, electors streamed to their state capitols to vote for the president of the United States. In ten of the sixteen states, legislatures had chosen these individuals themselves. A high-stakes election was certainly no time to consult "the sense of the people."

Neither was it a good time for electors to exercise independent discernment. Degrees of party discipline and coordination remained the only potential variables.

Madison left ample time for the seventy-five-mile trip from his Orange County home to the Virginia capital. He would not risk bad weather or impassable roads delaying his arrival in Richmond, where he would cast his vote with other Virginia electors. Contemplating his work of the previous year, he surveyed the political landscape with cautious optimism. The seismic shift in New York had hugely boosted Jefferson's chances, and Madison's efforts in his home state practically guaranteed all of Virginia's twenty-one votes for his friend.

His party stood poised to take a government—to save the Constitution and save the country, he thought.

But the overabundance of coordination produced a problematic outcome.

A SPECTACULAR FAILURE

During the dark days of December 1800, Thomas Jefferson received election reports in his suite at Conrad and McMunn's boardinghouse in Washington. He could consider nothing official, even though the sources—friends in key state positions—claimed inside knowledge. Jefferson would learn the official outcome with everyone else on February 11 when, as sitting vice president, he would open the sealed ballots and read them before Congress. Until then, he could only wait, brood, and prognosticate.

About him lay the awkward and unfinished federal city, an architectural dream awaiting realization. Large swampy areas interrupted a landscape with few finished buildings, and muddy streets oozed through seemingly random clusters of houses, lime kilns, and brickyards. The federal government had resided there only a month, and the city offered few artistic pleasures or entertainments. Congressmen and other functionaries who crammed into partisan boardinghouses spent their evenings playing cards with others of their tribe, warming their sinister bias with drink and talk.

Early information indicated that Jefferson had a clear victory with seventy-three votes. Aaron Burr would trail by three votes to win the vice presidency. Repeatedly performing the calculations, Jefferson assumed someone had arranged to withhold a few votes from Burr—probably one each in Tennessee, Georgia, and South Carolina. Otherwise, the Republican sweep appeared so decisive that the two might tie.[25]

As December's darkness deepened, more complete information arrived, and a troubling reality dawned. Jefferson could learn of no withheld vote in any state. Any arrangement to throw away votes from Burr had "been left to hazard." Tight party discipline prevailed, and every single Republican elector had cast their votes for Jefferson and Burr. The two men tied with seventy-three votes each, beating John Adams's sixty-five votes.[26]

Jefferson contemplated the paths to disaster that might flow from this outcome. He thought it opened "an abyss at which every sincere patriot must shudder." According to the framers' carefully wrought rules, the House of Representatives would now decide the contest. But in contrast to the regular order, they would vote by states—one vote per state. States with evenly split delegations would lose their vote. Jefferson needed nine states to claim a majority. Sizing up each state delegation, he could count on only eight.[27]

Most disturbing, no one could predict what course Federalists might pursue. They had clearly lost the election, but they retained numbers in Congress sufficient to make serious mischief. Jefferson feared they might resort to drastic machinations. They could simply keep the ballots tied up until March 3, when all outgoing officers' terms expired. Then they might declare the election failed and maneuver to place their own men in these offices. Such measures would, of course, amount to a coup and could plunge the country into violence.

Jefferson knew that plenty of Federalists would not consent to such treachery. But what if enough approved of it? Extreme partisan commitments helped bad actors view these machinations as virtuous acts of saving the republic. Even short of such measures, the untried and untested situation gave Federalists ample maneuvering room. Out of partisan animosity and a base desire for control, Federalists would cast their votes for Burr. Burr's malleability and widely acknowledged self-serving nature rendered him a ripe and dangerous target for manipulation.

At the other end of Pennsylvania Avenue, John Adams rambled around a cold and unfinished White House, where he had lived only a few weeks. By now, the outgoing president wore betrayal like well-used slippers. His fractured party had failed him repeatedly, and even men in his own administration had undermined him.

Deep personal grief overwhelmed Adams's election disappointment. The very day electors voted in the state capitals, the president learned that his thirty-year-old son Charles had died. The dark turn of Charles's life—alcoholism, bankruptcy, marital infidelity—only compounded Adams's grief over his second son. Peering into a desolate future, Adams wished that he could have "died for him, if that would have relieved him from his faults as well as his disease."[28]

The cheerless and bereft president plunged himself into final policy achievements and lived for March 4, when he could flee the inhospitable city. His frame of mind suited him perfectly for playing spectator to an unfolding election debacle.

* * *

At his New York City home, Alexander Hamilton writhed. He despised Thomas Jefferson's politics. Indeed, for nearly a decade, the country's partisan animosity had fed at the trough of their mutual disdain. Possibly more frequently and intensely than anyone, Hamilton had cautioned against Jefferson's "fangs" and contrived to keep him out of the White House.

But Hamilton nuanced his hatreds. Sinister bias had not entirely destroyed his ability to distinguish fine points of character. If he detested Jefferson's politics, he feared Burr's character more. Hamilton thought Burr devoid of any principle other than ambition. Now that it seemed the choice of president would go the House, his pen worked steadily, urging Federalists not to "fall into the snare" of elevating Burr to the highest office. Burr was "restrained by no moral scruples . . . too coldblooded and too determined a conspirator ever to change." Burr would "disgrace our country abroad." He loved "nothing but himself; thinks of nothing but his own aggrandizement, and will be content with nothing, short of permanent power in his own hands." Hamilton believed Burr would "use the *worst* part of the community as a ladder to climb to permanent power and an instrument to crush the better part." He called Burr "a profligate, a bankrupt, a man who laugh[ed] at democracy . . . one of the most unprincipled men in the United States."[29]

But Hamilton's fellow Federalists showed little inclination to heed his warnings. Most relished the chance to play kingmaker, licking their lips at the prospect of denying the presidency to Thomas Jefferson.

* * *

As December evaporated into January, intrigue rose like vapors from Washington's frigid swamps. Jefferson would need Federalist votes to win, but did he appreciate that Federalist support would come at a price? What promises would he give? Burr stood similarly well positioned to dispense favors to Republican congressmen who would choose him over

Jefferson. He remained enormously influential in his home state of New York, and that delegation's fractious nature ripened its vulnerability to manipulation.

Jefferson and Burr both played the situation cautiously. They had long since learned not to commit anything to writing. Both had suffered when their words fell into the hands of operators who deployed them for their own aims. Indeed, each had skillfully weaponized the words of others.

Both candidates maintained that they were not for sale. Burr initially claimed to support Jefferson, but he then appeared to back away from that position. No one could say exactly what transpired in private meetings.

Republicans regarded the New York delegation as secure for Jefferson, but they worried when Burr associate David Ogden appeared in Washington in mid-January. Ogden reportedly hounded New York's congressmen, paying particular attention to one outgoing member who had his sights on the New York City mayor's seat. Ogden also met behind closed doors with a member of New Jersey's divided delegation.[30]

Gouverneur Morris hobbled around Capitol Hill on his peg leg, communicating Hamilton's concerns about Burr. The very "cabal, intrigue, and corruption" Morris had so vigorously denounced during the Constitutional Convention now bloomed in front of him. As the senior senator from New York and an ardent Federalist, Morris remained one of few in his party hoping for a Jefferson win. Since a tied vote would go to the House and not the Senate, Morris would have no vote, but he worked on his House counterparts. Watching Burr's agents in the capital, Morris wondered whether Jefferson deployed similar lieutenants, though strict partisan silos kept such information out of his reach.[31]

A mere thirteen years after the framers labored so persistently to protect presidential selection from the basest elements of human nature, those exact forces flourished. They had failed to protect the process from themselves.

* * *

Heavy snow blanketed Washington City on the morning of February 11, 1801. It piled up on construction sites and turned the streets messy and treacherous. Most members of Congress needed only to tramp a block or two from their boardinghouses to the unfinished Capitol, but those coming from outside the city met difficulty. In the high-stakes atmosphere, every vote mattered, and a single missing member could flip an entire state delegation. One Maryland representative who suffered from pneumonia even insisted on coming to the Hill. Others carried him through the snow on a litter.[32]

Only the north wing of the Capitol sat complete, and at noon the members filled the new chamber. Jefferson read out the results and confirmed the tie.

Now a different election would ensue in the House, and the nation would see which party could best marshal their loyalists. The Constitution required the House to vote immediately between the tied candidates, conducting no other business until the nation had a president-elect. The House Chamber remained without a roof, so members crammed into an alternate space to cast their ballots, one vote per state. Jefferson remained confident that he would win eight states, one short of the nine needed for a majority. Everyone anticipated that the six Federalist-dominated delegations would go to Burr, and two states with divided delegations would lose their votes.

The House voted. Exactly as predicted, Jefferson won eight states and Burr six, with two states divided. Neither candidate had won the required majority.

Rumors flew that New York, New Jersey, and Vermont might switch on a second vote. But when the House balloted again, the outcome remained the same. They tried again, with no change. Twenty-two hours later, at eight the next morning, the Capitol disgorged its sleep-deprived occupants after twenty-seven ballots. Each ballot returned eight votes for Jefferson, six for Burr, and two states divided. The nation remained without a president-elect.

Over the next four days, House members streamed back and forth from their boardinghouses into their cramped space at the Capitol. They napped when they could. Mostly, they gossiped, caucused, and schemed.

They sought assurances from the candidates—the high stakes pushed up the value of each vote. Federalists stiffened their resolve. At Conrad and McMunn's one block south of the Capitol, Jefferson's door opened and shut as emissaries churned in and out. On passing through the lobby, some may have relieved their stress by paying fifty cents to view the "Learned Pig," who reputedly could spell and read. By Saturday, the House had voted thirty-three times, with no change.

Violence threatened. Republicans in Congress claimed they would meet with force any attempt to slip a Federalist into the presidency. Jefferson maintained "that no such usurpation even for a single day should be submitted to." Indeed, the governors of Pennsylvania and Virginia put their militias at the ready. Jefferson personally delivered the threat of armed resistance to John Adams.[33]

James Bayard's position as the lone House member from Delaware gave him great power. A strict Federalist partisan, Bayard obligingly cast thirty-three ballots for Aaron Burr over the first four days of House voting. Yet he claimed no love for Burr, and the stalemate wore on him. His cooperation, he thought, ought to warrant something in return. Through an intermediary, he sent Jefferson a message about two friends with federal jobs in Delaware.

Bayard announced in a caucus meeting that he planned to switch his vote to Jefferson, and other Federalists heaped invectives upon his head. The caucus disintegrated in "confusion and discord."

Sunday came, and the House took no vote. Jefferson wrote Virginia governor James Monroe that most on the Hill seemed to believe he would have the necessary votes the next day, though he knew "of no foundation for that belief." He went on to observe that "many attempts have been made to obtain terms and promises from me. I have declared to them unequivocally, that I would not receive the government on capitulation, that I would not go into it with my hands tied."[34]

On Monday, they voted again, with the same deadlocked result. The next day would make a full week of the House's deadlock and the country's precarious uncertainty. The simultaneous boredom and tension exacted a toll.

At noon on February 17, House members dragged themselves back for another vote. The mood seemed different, though Federalists vowed not to support Jefferson. They opted instead for strategic passivity. Not a single Federalist switched his vote from Burr to Jefferson. Bayard simply abstained, leaving Delaware without a vote. Federalist members from Maryland and Vermont did the same, releasing those formerly divided delegations to Jefferson.

Now, on the thirty-sixth ballot, Jefferson won ten states and Burr four.

That very day, Bayard penned a letter to his friend who worked as a federal port collector. "I have taken good care of you," he noted. "You are safe."[35]

The country had survived this serious electoral malfunction. But the process had smacked of all the intrigue, backroom dealmaking, and corruption the constitutional framers had sought so strenuously to avoid. Moreover, it had almost placed a dangerous man at the helm of the nation.

In a little more than a decade, the Electoral College had brought the country to the brink of disaster.

* * *

The entire fiasco rattled Alexander Hamilton, who regarded it as an utter "humiliation." If Hamilton had ever really believed his glowing description of the Electoral College in *Federalist* 68, he thought quite differently now. "The scene of last session," he mused, "ought to teach us the intrinsic demerits" of the system for choosing the president. The catastrophe of 1800 laid bare how a person "by mere intrigue and accident [could] acquire the first place in the Government of our Nation." It also "proved to us how serious a danger of convulsion and disorder is incident to the plan."[36]

Let us review these "intrinsic demerits" in the framers' plan that led to "convulsion and disorder," a mere four presidential election cycles into the country's life under the Constitution. Most obviously and directly, the double-vote rule—requiring electors to vote for two candidates—produced the tie, sending the election of 1800 to the House of Representatives.

But the situation owed as much to partisan operators' electoral choreography: their "tampering beforehand" to organize electors, secure their pledges, and direct their votes. The system proved far less guarded against manipulation than the framers had anticipated. Moreover, partisanship overwhelmed and directed electors' judgment. The vision articulated by Hamilton in *Federalist* 68—that the people's proxies would make independent choices in conditions free from outside influences—had proved a pipe dream.

The states' ability to decide the means of selecting electors also fostered this electoral dysfunction. State partisans gamed the system by switching methods of elector selection. In the brittle and hyper-partisan contest of 1800, five states switched methods. In ten of the sixteen states, *legislatures* chose electors, more than in any other cycle before or since. When the stakes soared their highest, the country's tiny political class seized the process and managed it to their own ends.

Finally, without slaveholding states' inflated representation in the Electoral College, John Adams would likely have won the election of 1800. Southern states, which voted overwhelmingly for Jefferson, owed a total of twelve electors to the Constitution's three-fifths clause, an advantage that the pro-Adams northern states could not overcome. In fact, the slave-state "bump" surpassed the number of electors belonging to any single New England state, save Massachusetts. New Englanders' resentment of the South's an unfair advantage expressed itself in a Boston newspaper's claim that Jefferson had ridden "into the temple of Liberty on the shoulders of slaves." For the next eight years, Federalists decried the Constitution's slaveholder boost with a new appellation for Jefferson: "Negro president."[37]

REFORMING THE ELECTORAL COLLEGE: THE TWELFTH AMENDMENT

Alexander Hamilton converted his dismay over the election of 1800 into action. He thought the nation ought to "derive instruction" from that debacle. Political leaders, he advised, should work "to establish the fortune of a great empire on foundations much firmer than have yet been devised."[38]

At Hamilton's urging, Federalists and Republicans in the New York legislature asked Congress for an amendment to the Constitution. Gouverneur Morris introduced the New York resolution in the United States Senate in February 1802.[39]

The amendment embraced two reforms. First, it required all states to choose their electors in districts. This alteration would not only prevent states from constantly switching elector selection methods but also would guarantee "a full and fair expression of the public will," as the amendment itself explained. Hamilton supported district elections because this method would "let the Federal Government rest as much as possible on the shoulders of the people, and as little as possible on those of the State Legislatures."[40]

The amendment's second provision, "designation," required that electors identify which candidate they preferred for president and which for vice president, instead of naming two undifferentiated choices. This change aimed to prevent another tie by candidates of the same party.

These changes garnered broad support. In addition to Hamilton and Morris's New York resolution, the state legislatures of Vermont, Maryland, and Massachusetts asked Congress for a constitutional amendment requiring states to choose their electors in districts. Individual congressmen from South Carolina and Virginia, one Federalist and the other Republican, submitted similar proposals. Jefferson's own treasury secretary, Albert Gallatin, favored such an amendment. The change seemed uniquely poised to succeed.[41]

The amendment, providing both for district elections and for designation, passed the House of Representatives in 1802.

But the rare moment of bipartisan cooperation ceased. The overwhelmingly Republican Senate altered the amendment to suit their aims, eliminating the section on district elections. In the intensely competitive environment, partisans still wanted options for legislative selection or winner-take-all—two ways they could manipulate the system to their advantage.

Late in 1803, both houses of Congress approved the mutilated version of the amendment on a lopsided, party-line vote. Electors would now designate their choices for president and vice president. The new measure also slightly altered the contingent procedure in the case of a tie.

But by the time the last necessary state ratified the amendment—the Twelfth Amendment—on June 15, 1804, Alexander Hamilton had directed his attention elsewhere: toward Aaron Burr, once again.

Burr lay in the midst of a spectacular political implosion. Jefferson had dropped him as his running mate, a humiliation Burr hoped to assuage by becoming governor of New York. But he lost that race in a landslide. Struggling to salvage some sense of his own significance, he found a provocation in words attributed to Hamilton in the Albany *Register*. Throughout the course of six weeks, Hamilton and Burr charted a path that destroyed them both.

At dawn on July 11, 1804, the two met with their seconds on a small field in Weehawken, New Jersey, across the river and a bit north of New York City. Just after sunrise, they discharged their pistols. Hamilton's shot missed Burr by more than six feet, striking a tree limb instead. But Burr fired more carefully, his bullet piercing Hamilton's abdomen just above the hip. The ball fractured a rib, tore through his liver and diaphragm, and lodged in Hamilton's spine.[42]

Alexander Hamilton would say no more about the Electoral College. Thirty-one hours later, he was dead.

CHAPTER 5

"Hideous the Deformity of the Practice"

The Tortured Path to Winner-Take-All

CONGRESSMAN WILLIAM GASTON HAD DESPISED THIS WAR FROM ITS beginnings in 1812. Now two years in, he surveyed Washington City's charcoal rubble and mentally added humiliation to the war's growing costs. Certainly, the British had lit the match, but he thought the dispiriting scene owed much to the United States' misguided policy, poor preparation, and rank incompetence. On the Capitol's exterior walls, dark deposits testified where flames had licked the once-bright sandstone. Peering through blown-out windows, he noted a blackened mass gaping in the space where he had debated with his House colleagues only months before.

Gaston moved as if in a dream through the city's expanse, meeting rubble everywhere government buildings once stood. The Treasury and War and State buildings lay in damp, inky heaps. At the Navy Yard, he viewed the work of American troops who scuttled two American frigates and burned navy stores rather than let them fall into British hands. Everywhere, the debris of hastily jettisoned possessions—clothes, kitchenware, tools, books—littered the city.

Gaston came to rest at the charred shell of the Executive Mansion. Through the broken windows, he saw the ceiling where it rested on the floor of the gutted interior.[1]

The scenes loomed all the grimmer for their utter senselessness. Like other Federalists, Gaston considered the war an unnecessary ploy for empire and dominance. Brash young "war hawks" from western states like Kentucky and Tennessee had pushed President James Madison into it. Though Madison sold the conflict as necessary to protect American seamen from seizure and impressment into the British Navy, Federalists believed that expert diplomacy could have secured that goal without war. Predictably, the war had hurt Gaston's constituents in trade-dependent coastal North Carolina, just as Republican trade policies had damaged the area since 1808.

Gaston knew the cost of Mr. Madison's war more intimately than most. Residents of his home city of New Bern lived in terror that a British fleet might sail up the Neuse River, disgorge its troops, and commence an orgy of destruction. Those fears materialized and ravaged Gaston's personal life when, just three months into his first term in Washington, he learned that his delicately beautiful, dark-eyed wife Hannah and their unborn child had died. Only on arriving home did he learn the details and trace their deaths to the war. British ships had indeed landed on the coast, fulfilling the fear Hannah had confided so frequently. When rumors of an impending invasion reached New Bern, Hannah fell into convulsions and succumbed within a matter of hours. For the second time in a decade, Gaston buried a young wife. But he soon returned to work 350 miles away from home, leaving behind his three young children and the comfort they might give him.[2]

Now he lingered in Washington's desolation, and the city seemed to mirror his soul. Congress would reconvene the following day in temporary quarters at Blodget's Hotel. He hoped this destruction would sear the war's cost onto every Republican heart.

With the rest of his party, Gaston planned to continue his opposition to tax increases and offensive war measures, but he knew the small Federalist minority could not halt the overwhelming Republican majority. His best prospects for legislative success this session hung on one issue with strong bipartisan support: securing a constitutional amendment on the operations of the Electoral College. Maybe he could salvage something good from Mr. Madison's war.

Gaston would not succeed. Neither would any of the others who joined him in a nearly two-decade struggle to make the country's presidential election system more uniform and representative, though several times Congress almost passed a constitutional amendment that would have transformed American presidential elections. The bizarre, complicated, and chaotic election of 1824 would interrupt this effort, further highlighting the dangers and arbitrariness of Electoral College operations and strengthening the case for reform. But rather than producing meaningful change, that election reinvigorated ferocious party competition. The brutal partisanship following determined the operations of future presidential contests far more than any pristine and principled vision of the framers.

Rising Up from the States

The War of 1812 precipitated a mighty movement to reform the Electoral College, and that effort owed much to events in North Carolina and to William Gaston.

North Carolina selected its presidential electors in districts, just as Virginia had once done. Kentucky, Tennessee, and Maryland used similar systems. Under this method, the state was divided into districts equal to its number of electors, and voters in each district chose one elector. Importantly, this system meant that North Carolina's coastal Federalists typically carried several districts, even though Republicans dominated statewide. Gaston's district elected him as a Federalist elector in 1808, and two other coastal districts also chose Federalist electors that year, though Madison's electors won everywhere else in North Carolina.[3]

But the onset of war heightened Republican fears that a "peace candidate" might win more of North Carolina's districts, resulting in the president's defeat in 1812. To secure their state for Madison, the Republican-dominated legislature copied a high-handed maneuver used in other states. The legislature repealed the state's district elections provision and took to themselves the power to choose electors. Predictably, they appointed a solid slate of fourteen Madison electors, suppressing entirely the voice of the three coastal districts.[4]

Serving in North Carolina's state senate at the time, Gaston watched these proceedings with dismay and disbelief. He read the newspapers and took no comfort in learning that legislatures in other states deployed similarly shameful tactics. The antics in Massachusetts no longer surprised him, given that state's well-earned reputation for switching their elector selection procedure every cycle. This time, prognosticators feared that Massachusetts legislators would not settle on a method in time for the election.

Events in New Jersey troubled Gaston more, especially since his own Federalists were the guilty party there. The war helped New Jersey's Federalist antiwar candidates squeak out a tiny majority in the state legislature. That new Federalist majority in Trenton flexed its muscle just days before New Jersey voters were scheduled to choose electors. All lay in readiness for a popular selection on a general ticket, where each voter named an entire slate of electors. But the new Federalist-dominated legislature abruptly repealed the state's electoral law, took the choice of electors to themselves, and named a solid slate for the peace candidate. Angry at the legislature's revocation of a long-standing right, Republicans in several New Jersey counties showed up at the polls to cast protest votes for Madison's electors.[5]

As part of the Federalist minority in Raleigh, Gaston possessed little power to stop the legislature's steamrolling. But voters' anger crossed party lines. Gaston's Republican colleagues in North Carolina worried about their political futures after this "usurpation." Leveraging Republican shame, Gaston helped secure a resolution instructing North Carolina's congressional delegation to work for an amendment to the United States Constitution. The amendment would require all states to select their electors by the district method, widely regarded as the fairest and most reflective of the people's will.[6]

The next spring, antiwar sentiment in Gaston's district catapulted him to Congress. Now he could work for and defend that very amendment on the Electoral College.

AMENDING THE CONSTITUTION

When Gaston surveyed British troops' destructive rampage in the capital in September 1814, he had served fifteen months in Congress. Already, one battle in the fight for a district elections amendment had concluded. A Senate resolution on district amendments had sailed to success, only to fail in the House. But Gaston and a cadre of others felt encouraged by the strong showing and prepared to try again.

For most of the next decade, Gaston and his allies pursued an amendment requiring district elections. The effort percolated up from the states themselves, as the legislatures of seven states instructed their congressional delegations to work for district elections. Though the proposed amendments varied slightly in their provisions, they flew in so fast and furious that, by 1826, Congress had entertained forty-seven district elections amendments.[7]

Though Gaston advocated effectively and persistently, leadership on this amendment passed among congressmen from every part of the Union, from states large and small, from both slave-holding and free states, and from all political persuasions. This effort's most tenacious spokesmen included Senator Mahlon Dickerson, a New Jersey Republican who witnessed his state's 1812 stunt and introduced an amendment in the Senate each year for eight years. The testy, irritable, and grim-looking South Carolina congressman George McDuffie also fought doggedly for district elections. After Missouri achieved statehood in 1821, Senator Thomas Hart Benton introduced a district elections amendment almost every year for twenty years.

These reformers came extraordinarily close to success under the Constitution's supermajority requirement for amendments. Four times— in 1813, 1819, 1820, and 1822—a district elections amendment passed the Senate with the necessary two-thirds majority. Yet each time, it languished in the House. In January 1821, an amendment that had just cleared the Senate failed to pass the House by a meager six votes.[8]

Only twenty-five years after the Constitution's ratification, these reformers maintained that Electoral College operations had departed dramatically from the framers' intentions. When Gaston rose to support the amendment in January 1814, he explained how current operations "perverted and abused" the Constitution and "frustrated" the framers' goals. Quoting liberally from Alexander Hamilton's Electoral College defense in *Federalist* 68, Gaston detailed the framers' plan. But though "beauteous smiled the theory," he exclaimed, "how hideous the deformity of the practice."[9]

No one spoke more convincingly about the gap between the framers' plans and current operations than Senator Rufus King of New York. One of the few framers still alive and active in public life, King stood uniquely qualified to describe their goals. In 1787, he had served as a highly consequential delegate to the Constitutional Convention, a vigorous ally of James Madison's nationalist plan, and a member of the committee that wrote the Constitution's final language.

Now sixty-one, slightly fleshy and mostly bald, King schooled the Senate on the framers' hopes to place the election of the president "with the people" and their belief that their plan would meet this objective. But, he lamented, "we all know the course which this thing has taken. The election of a President of the United States is no longer that process which the Constitution contemplated." According to King, the current "pernicious" operations of the Electoral College frustrated the framers' aims. He vowed to support any effort that would bring the election "closer to the people," including a national popular vote.[10]

States' ability to choose elector selection methods especially troubled these reformers. A New York representative called this power a "rotten, a gangrenous part of our Constitution, which if not removed will infect and poison the body politic." This ability led to chronic switching of methods of elector selection, creating havoc and disruption every election cycle. Speakers detailed the states' chaotic elections history—Massachusetts changed methods almost every cycle, and Pennsylvania once risked losing its votes altogether when partisan bickering stalled selection of electors. This "constant fluctuation" rendered presidential elections a "farce . . . ridiculous and disgusting occurrences," that tended "to degrade our representative Government in the eyes of the world and to lower it in our own estimation."[11]

Indeed, the reformers understood that this repeated shifting served one simple but deeply dishonorable goal: maximizing partisan advantage. A South Carolinian argued that partisans switched "to insure a result . . . favorable to their wishes and views." These maneuvers served "the ambition, the whim, of caprice of party and faction." "The parties were only influenced by a view to their own purposes" as they sought to make the election "subservient" to their aims. No party could "claim to be guiltless" because partisans in one state justified methods of elector selection that "in another they zealously oppose."[12]

To prevent this switching, the reformers proposed an amendment that required all states to choose their electors by the same method: popular election in districts. As Americans had recognized for more than two decades, the more commonly used general ticket, or winner-take-all, "stifled the voice of the minority." Giving all a state's electors to one candidate under the general ticket rendered the political minority "utterly without weight." General tickets conferred on "the dominant party an undue influence by suppressing . . . the voice of the minority."[13]

But the general ticket's evils extended beyond this silencing of the minority's voice in each state. It presented the dangerous possibility that a man without the support and mandate of the people might rise to the presidency. "By legerdemain tricks" the general ticket made "the minority appear the majority," argued Gaston. He trembled to contemplate the consequences if "a man not the choice of the people should be imposed upon us as President of the United States."[14]

District elections, by contrast, divided the electors proportionally, reflecting a party's geographic pockets of strength. When states returned their electoral votes by districts, their total elector slates divided between the candidates, and the result gave "a fair expression of the sentiments of every portion of the people." Indeed, Gaston implored, "Let the voice of every part of the nation be heard in the appointment of the Chief Magistrate, and the minority in each state acquires an importance which assures to them respect and political freedom."[15]

The unfolding debate between 1813 and 1824 unleashed creative thought about presidential elections, and some congressmen followed the notion that "power derived from the people" to its logical conclusions. Many wondered whether electors now served any purpose at all, especially since they had long since stopped even pretending to choose independently, as it seemed the framers had intended. No one offered a sound reason "why these men should be interposed between the people and the candidates." Several representatives proposed direct elections, without electors.[16]

In 1816, Senator Abner Lacock of Pennsylvania went even further, suggesting the widest departure yet from the current system: a direct national popular vote. The Senate refused even to send Lacock's proposal to a committee, but the debate over his proposal revealed why reformers stuck with a more modest district proposal: District elections preserved the current ratio of electors, keeping both small states and slave states happy.[17]

Now in his seventies and comfortably retired at Montpelier in the Virginia piedmont, James Madison observed these reform efforts with satisfaction. The former president responded to queries from two men interested in his opinion on a district elections amendment. Noting that he did not wish his thoughts to be made public, Madison confessed his preference for district elections over the general ticket, adding that "the district mode was mostly, if not exclusively in view when the Constitution was framed and adopted." Writing to the aged Thomas Jefferson, Madison called the suggested measures a "real improvement."[18]

Jefferson agreed with Madison. Only months later, he offered strong support for a constitutional amendment that would place "the choice of President effectually in the hands of the people." At eighty years of age, Jefferson noted that this improvement would help him "live in more confidence and die in more hope" for the future of the nation.[19]

By the time presidential candidates began lining up for the election of 1824, the movement to reform the Electoral College enjoyed the momentum of a full decade. It had come within a whisker of succeeding.

If anyone needed confirmation of the system's perils, the election of 1824 brought the Electoral College's multiple shortcomings crashing together. Suddenly, every reformer appeared to be a prophet.

The Little Magician
Senator Martin Van Buren did not believe a word of his own speech. On this late December day in 1823, he rose beneath the elegantly coffered half-domed ceiling of the new Senate Chamber to embrace a constitutional amendment like so many others over the past decade. With his short frame draped in fashionable clothes, Van Buren's active, beady eyes moved beneath his high forehead and thinning hair. Yet even as he

turned out one eloquent phrase after another praising district elections, he did not want them, especially in his home state of New York.[20]

His nickname, the Little Magician, owed to his success with exactly this kind of maneuver. Sometimes, after all, a man needed to provide political cover for others, and his perceived support for this amendment would boost the faltering image of his Bucktail faction back home. Meanwhile, New York's legislature would continue to choose the state's electors, exactly as it had always done.

Van Buren enjoyed immense benefits from the present arrangement. He directed the Bucktails, and the Bucktail-dominated legislature selected New York's thirty-six electors. In effect, the Little Magician controlled more than 25 percent of the votes needed to win the White House. This king-making capacity rendered him far more influential—indeed, formidable—than an ordinary U.S. senator. Only a fool would relinquish such power.

Today, Van Buren paid lip service to popular selection of electors in districts only because of a new vulnerability at home. A growing People's Party movement was challenging Bucktail dominance in New York, and its spokesmen advocated this change, along with other democratizing measures.

Just weeks earlier, the People's Party had captured a significant number of state legislative seats in a surprising display of strength. Jolted, Van Buren calculated that his party could prevent future losses by publicly embracing those measures that fueled People's Party success, including district selection of electors. But he intended to work behind the scenes against this change, even as he praised it.

Van Buren excelled at these delicate dances. He thought his speech in Congress, echoed by party leaders back home, would stem party losses. Meanwhile, Bucktails in the New York legislature could oppose a state district elections provision on the grounds that a constitutional amendment appeared poised to pass the U.S. Senate, making a state measure unnecessary. Why, at this very moment, their very own Van Buren championed the cause in Washington!

But they knew full well that an amendment had no chance of passing before the presidential election of 1824, and that contest would unfold as usual. Exactly what they wanted.

Smug in their confidence, six weeks after Van Buren's Washington speech, seventeen Bucktail members of the New York Senate rejected a state bill that allowed voters to select electors in districts. But contrary to their expectations, voters saw right through the strategy, and the betrayed public erupted in outrage. The opposition press identified the seventeen senators under the caption "People of New York: Behold your enemies."

For once, Van Buren's sleight of hand failed. His faction would pay a price at the ballot box in the fall. Meanwhile, his shamed Bucktails walked about with targets on their backs.[21]

RACING TOWARD NOVEMBER 1824

Raising his eyes from the stack of letters before him, U.S. House Speaker Henry Clay gazed out the windows of his beloved Ashland estate in Lexington, Kentucky. Late spring's long tranquil light slanted across the lawn while his sheep bleated their evening chorus beyond the trees. After a winter of Washington's dizzying activity, he relished time at Ashland and the space it gave him to think.[22]

Clay turned away from the farm's nourishing beauty to consider his prospects for becoming the sixth president of the United States. The news in the letters before him entirely changed his strategy. Neither he nor any of the other three presidential candidates stood poised to capture the necessary Electoral College majority of 131 votes that fall. In that event, the Twelfth Amendment's contingent procedure would kick in, and the House of Representatives would choose between the top three finishers. As in 1800, the House would vote by states, with one vote per state.

At first, these reports of his competitors' strength troubled Clay. But as he reflected more on the possibility of the election going to the House, his hope rose. This new calculation actually boosted his chance to win the presidency, and finishing among the top three presented an easier task than winning an outright Electoral College majority.

Clay mentally ticked through the significant advantages he would enjoy in a House vote. For one, his House colleagues generally liked him. They enjoyed the late-night card games where he held court and poured out jokes, conversation, and whiskey under curling cigar smoke. He helped relieve the tedium and loneliness of life in the capital.

But Clay offered much more than agreeable friendship and a good time. His great gifts of communication and diplomacy made him an effective legislator. He delivered clear rationales for infrastructure improvements, tariffs to promote American manufacturing, and sound banking policies. House colleagues from the rapidly growing states west of the Appalachian Mountains especially appreciated his advocacy for their region and for initiatives that would expand their commerce and raise their property values.

What's more, Clay wielded great power in the House, having served off and on since 1810. He knew how to work the members and how to leverage their needs, wants, and vulnerabilities. These abilities had landed him in the office of Speaker.

The distant sound of evening chores floated in to capture his ear, but ruminations on this new path to the presidency drew him back. The more he contemplated it, the more he liked his chances. A trajectory that sent November's election to the House would make his ultimate victory, he thought, "absolutely certain."[23]

Clay's confidence grew further as he took stock of his rivals. No need to worry about William Crawford of Georgia. True, as secretary of the treasury, Crawford controlled the most lucrative posts in the nation and enjoyed the Republican establishment's anointing. But his advantages ended there, and a host of factors worked against him. Many Americans associated Crawford with the Virginia dynasty that had monopolized the presidency for the past thirty-five years, and the public increasingly scorned candidates pushed by the establishment.

Besides, an even more serious, potentially insurmountable, obstacle plagued Crawford's candidacy: The fifty-one-year-old had suffered a debilitating stroke the previous fall. For months, he had disappeared almost entirely from public view. When he returned to work, his handlers tried to stifle reports about his condition, but the pitiable reality leaked out. Crawford's stroke had left him with a thick-tongued slur, bad eyesight, and poor control of his hands. Appearing old and ill, his large size amplified the effect of his groping and unsteady movements.[24]

Originally, Clay had also dismissed General Andrew Jackson, his most odious rival. Lacking substantive political or legislative experience, Jackson had risen to prominence solely on a wave of public enthusiasm for his wartime exploits, especially his victory over the British at the Battle of New Orleans. But the general's dashing military persona distracted from his actual résumé, which overflowed with incidents of high-handed brutality that Clay believed should disqualify him in the eyes of most Americans. These troubling deeds included the hasty execution of six American militiamen, the vicious slaughter of nearly 800 Native Americans at the Battle of Horseshoe Bend, and an unauthorized foray into Florida, where he ordered the execution of two British subjects. The list included interpersonal violence, too. Jackson had killed a man in an 1806 duel and still carried a bullet in his body.[25]

Clay shuddered as he contemplated the growing popularity of this primitive and authoritarian "military chieftain." For five years, he had tried to warn the public about Jackson's arrogant disregard for the rule of law. Had Americans learned nothing from Napoleon Bonaparte's devastating romps through Europe?

Reports predicted that Jackson might siphon off some of Clay's support in the West—Ohio, Indiana, Illinois, Louisiana, Missouri, Mississippi, Alabama. But these losses, though disappointing, would not prove catastrophic. Clay knew he could beat the general handily in a House vote, where members appreciated Clay's abilities and recognized Jackson's dangers.

Clay turned his thoughts finally to John Quincy Adams. Certainly, Adams would sweep New England. Intense sectional loyalty and overflowing resentment of the Virginia dynasty would propel Adams into the top three. The former president's son claimed several other advantages as well, including a first-rate intellect, a sophisticated grasp of foreign affairs, and great power as secretary of state. But like Jackson, Adams could never beat Clay in the House. His cold demeanor aroused little personal affection, and many members continued to doubt his genuine political commitments, since he had switched parties fifteen years earlier.

Yes, Clay's path to the presidency seemed clear. He needed only enough electoral votes to finish in the top three. After that, he would ride easily to the Executive Mansion on the sturdy and affectionate shoulders of his House colleagues.

All summer and into the fall of 1824, Clay enjoyed Ashland's bucolic pleasures. He strolled its grounds, planted sycamore and catalpa trees; arranged imports of Herefords, mules, and sheep; and surveyed his fine horses. Meanwhile, he spun out optimistic predictions about the election, and his hope lengthened like Kentucky hemp.

But as November unfolded, troubling election results staggered in and roused Clay from his hazy self-delusions. The unqualified and dangerous Andrew Jackson drained even more of Clay's support in the West than expected. Jackson swept the entire elector slates of Indiana, Tennessee, Mississippi, and Alabama. Illinois's district system gave Jackson two votes, Adams, one, and Clay, none. Clay hung on only to Ohio, Missouri, and his home state of Kentucky.

He watched his presidential aspirations teeter toward a last-place finish. Yet he nourished one last hope: New York's legislature would choose its electors in late November. With even a handful of votes from that state, he could edge out the debilitated Crawford for a spot among the top three finishers and make it to the safety of the House.

But Martin Van Buren pulled the strings in New York, and the Little Magician was all in for the ailing William Crawford.

Tricked by His Own Magic

In November 1824, politically minded Americans excitedly watched New York. Results from other states placed Jackson and Adams as the clear top two finishers in the race, though neither could reach the majority threshold of 131. While everyone now knew that the House of Representatives would ultimately decide this election, would Clay or Crawford pull out a third-place finish and advance to the House? The Empire State would decide the question, and the disarray there threw the proposition entirely in the air.

New York's big prize of thirty-six electors and the state's complicated politics made it ripe for drama. Months before, Van Buren had promised all thirty-six electors for William Crawford, but he had made these assurances before his Bucktails deceived voters on the district elections issue. New Yorkers remembered this treachery and sent Bucktails packing in the fall. They threw out their Bucktail governor, ditched six Bucktail senators, and reduced Bucktail power in the House to a weak one-third minority.

A rattled Van Buren lowered his expectations and scurried to Albany to salvage a few votes for Crawford. Since the outgoing, Bucktail-dominated legislature would choose the electors, Van Buren counted on some leverage over elector selection.

But he found his Bucktails shaken, fractured, and shorn of confidence in his leadership. He watched helplessly while five days of intrigue narrowed the contest for president of the United States: The New York legislature chose twenty-five electors pledged to John Adams, seven to Henry Clay, and four to William Crawford. Those seven electors would slip Clay into the top three finishers who would advance to the House.

Van Buren reached deep into his bag of tricks. When New York's electors met to cast their votes, three Clay electors defected. The gentleman farmer from Kentucky won only four votes.

Clay watched his chance at the presidency disappear.

Van Buren's man Crawford would advance instead. The Magician had pulled a win from nowhere.

* * *

When all twenty-four states finished voting, Andrew Jackson won 99 Electoral College votes. Adams followed with 84, Crawford with 41, and Clay 37. Of the available popular vote, Jackson won that, too, with 151,000 votes to Adams's 113,000. Crawford captured nearly 41,000, while Clay finished at 47,500.

Yet the popular-vote totals indicated little, since the people in six of the twenty-four states, including New York, cast no votes in this election. A popular vote from the Empire State—with 1.5 million people, the nation's most populous—would have significantly altered the national tally.[26]

Nor did the Electoral College outcome necessarily correlate with the wishes of most Americans. Fully half the states used the general-ticket (winner-take-all) system, meaning that their Electoral College votes went entirely to the candidate with the majority in the state, skewing those wins exponentially. And no one could pretend that the outcome in New York reflected anything other than skullduggery and political games.

One additional factor, silent and mostly unremarked, shuffled the candidates' places at the finish and further highlighted the utter lack of system or principle: the Constitution's three-fifths clause that gave slave states an Electoral College "bump." Andrew Jackson benefited most from these added electors and, without them, would have finished behind Adams. William Crawford also advanced with the help of the slave-state boost. Without it, Crawford, not Clay, would have finished dead last. Only John Quincy Adams, whose votes came entirely from the Northeast, reaped no gains from this provision.

By 1824, Alexander Hamilton had lain twenty years in his grave. Had he remained alive, he would surely have repented his words of high praise for the Electoral College in *Federalist* 68. Nothing about this system fit his description of an "excellent" plan, where wise men selected the president in a climate conducive to unconstrained choices.

To the contrary, the contest reeked of arbitrariness and the arts of intrigue, a fulfillment of the framers' gravest fears and the reformers' most dire prophecies. This rotten election would soon spew its stench in the House phase as well.

THE ELECTION IN THE HOUSE

In contrast to the dark, lonely expanse of its early days, Washington City pulsed with vibrant social life by 1824, and the tempo always quickened in December when Congress began a new session. More than 250 legislators poured into the city, straining the capacity of its boardinghouses and hotels. At endless rounds of dinners, balls, card games, and receptions, they mingled with permanent residents, foreign diplomats, agency bureaucrats, society ladies, and political wives.[27]

Henry Clay relished this scene. As the city and the nation waited through December and January, he gadded about in his usual high spirits. Unbowed by defeat, his tall, elegant figure floated through receptions, mingled at dinners, and glided across the dance floor. When he encountered Adams or Jackson at these affairs, he exploited their discomfort with playful ribbing.[28]

The first phase of the election was over. Now the country waited for the votes to be read in Congress on February 9, after which the contingent procedure would unfold. Each House delegation would vote, one vote per state, as they had done in 1800. No rules bound the state delegations. They could vote in accord with the majority outcome from their state or from their own personal preferences. Even other forces might dictate their choice.[29]

Thus, underneath the patina of Washington City's parties and pleasantries, the candidates and their agents darted about to secure the thirteen votes needed to win. None had the required number in the bag.

Relieved of his own candidacy's considerable pressure, Clay rather enjoyed watching the others writhe as he entertained their obsequious overtures. Crawford's groveling operatives came first, effusing in their regard for Clay's "genuine Republican" commitments. Surely, they counseled, Clay would not damage establishment prestige and power by using his influence for any other candidate.

But Clay felt no draw to Crawford, and legitimate questions about the candidate's health made him a poor choice. Moreover, Crawford did little on his own behalf, counting instead on Martin Van Buren to resurrect his dead candidacy. True to form, Van Buren even now gathered the necessary props and assistants for another magic trick. He aimed to prevent any candidate from acquiring the majority of thirteen. Instead, he planned to engineer a tied vote, with repeated ballots that would frustrate the members and exploit their impatience. Through this means, Van Buren and his devotees hoped to coax slow, steady defections from the Jackson and Adams camps.

Jackson's agents also came to Clay, appealing to their shared western roots. Please, they begged Clay, "don't disappoint us." Meanwhile, the general loudly broadcast his own virtue, denouncing intriguers who "stalked" the candidates and vowed to attain the office only "by the free unsolicited voice of the people."[30]

These entreaties notwithstanding, Clay could never support a man who appealed so blatantly to base tribal instincts and so clearly lacked the temperament for statesmanship. He knew that Jackson's strong showing in the popular totals and his victory in eleven states fed his fantasy of representing the "voice of the people." But in Clay's view, Jackson's populist rhetoric cloaked deep authoritarian instincts. He summed up his reasoning: "I cannot believe that killing 2,500 Englishmen at New Orleans qualifies for the various, difficult, and complicated duties of the Chief Magistracy." Moreover, after decades of service to the West, Clay could not bear to boost a competitor for the region's mantle.[31]

He did not much struggle, then, to make up his mind. Though he felt no personal warmth toward the aloof John Quincy Adams, no one could deny Adams's fitness for the office. Moreover, Adams would support infrastructure improvements and other sensible policies that Clay championed. His decision hinged not on his personal likes, but on the best outcome for the country.

Considerable and long-standing bad blood between Clay and Adams would need clearing before Clay could give his unreserved support. And he deserved something in return.

Both men knew that Adams faced a steep path to the presidency. The New Englander could only count on votes from six states, and that tally would take him less than halfway to the thirteen he needed. The three states Clay won in November—Kentucky, Ohio, and Missouri—had each given a robust second-place popular-vote finish to Andrew Jackson. Jackson felt entitled to those state's votes in the House phase.

Jackson's claim on those states seemed to strengthen in January, when the Kentucky legislature instructed the state's representatives in Washington to vote for him. But since no real rules governed the congressional delegation's choice, these instructions meant little.[32]

In fact, only days later, Kentucky's congressional delegation announced that it would cast its single vote for John Quincy Adams on February 9. The Ohio delegation followed with a similar announcement.

Andrew Jackson met this news with a howl of righteous protest that reverberated from Maine to Georgia and west to the Plains. The Hero of New Orleans charged that Clay had made a deal with Adams to exchange the presidency for a prestigious cabinet appointment.

Amplifying the accusation, a Jackson-friendly newspaper in Philadelphia printed a letter from an anonymous member of Congress who claimed that Clay had entered a "corrupt bargain." "Would you believe," asked the writer, that "men professing democracy could be found base enough to lay the ax at the root of the tree of liberty?" Never, asserted the letter, would Jackson and his friends "descend to such mean barter and sale." Pro-Jackson papers picked up the letter, adding their own editorial commentary. Clay was a "Brutus," a "second Burr." Adams, a "Caesar."[33]

Clay rushed to defend his honor, but Jackson's forces had already captured the narrative.

Martin Van Buren watched the unfolding drama with glee. Now other men could suffer for their intrigues, while he feigned clean hands and a pure heart. Even better for the Little Magician, Jackson's protests and the purported Clay-Adams conspiracy drew the public's eye away from the workings of his own hands. At dinners with other members of New York's House delegation, he rehearsed the trick that would make Jackson's and Adams's strength vanish.

* * *

On clear days, the Capitol's gleaming white columns and brand-new central dome drew the eye heavenward. But mist and heavy snow enveloped the city on February 9, obscuring the Capitol's towering majesty almost completely. Snow piled up on the ramshackle huts and wooden shacks crammed between the city's better dwellings. The cold, blowing wetness emptied Pennsylvania Avenue of the beggars and orphans that often roamed there. Hucksters kept their wagons and wares under wraps, and day laborers whose employment required good weather stayed home.

Washington's better sort appreciated the storm. It prevented "foolish violence" and "riots" among the "idle people" and kept them away from proceedings at the Capitol. The best citizens could pile excitedly into their carriages and hacks and head out to watch the most thrilling show in town, unmolested by even a glimpse of the "lower citizens."[34]

Henry Clay assumed his place under the velvet-draped rostrum in the House Chamber and surveyed the huge crowd that packed the galleries. Rising above them, the sixty-foot coffered ceiling altered conversations capriciously, amplifying some sounds and muffling others. Onlookers craned their necks around magnificent green marble columns to view the congressmen at their desks.

Representatives from less populous states—Delaware, Illinois, Missouri, Mississippi—sat alone, their states' votes entirely in their own hands. New York and other states with large delegations would determine their choice by majority vote.

Each delegation's appointed tellers extended their boxes to the members, who inserted slips of paper. The tellers counted to determine each delegation's vote.

The floor and the galleries waited silently in the weak midafternoon light while the tellers brought forward the votes of the twenty-four states—many written in betrayal, sale, and exchange.

Eight delegations voted in sharp contrast to the November outcomes in their state: Kentucky and Ohio, where Clay had won with Jackson close behind, each cast a vote for John Quincy Adams; the lone representative from Missouri also voted for John Quincy Adams, though Adams had finished a distant third in the popular vote there; North Carolina's delegation ignored its citizens' preference for Andrew Jackson, selecting William Crawford instead; Louisiana forsook the Hero of New Orleans for John Adams; Maryland transformed Jackson's popularity into a single vote for Adams; Delaware's single congressman chose Crawford, though the state legislature had named Jackson electors. Illinois electors had cast two votes for Jackson in November, but now its only representative voted for Adams. New York's vote went to John Quincy Adams, by a margin of one.

In the thick stillness, the tellers added the totals in front of Daniel Webster at one table and John Randolph at another. Webster rose to announce the outcome in his stentorian baritone: John Adams, thirteen votes; Andrew Jackson, seven votes; William Crawford, four votes.

At his table, Randolph's unnatural falsetto echoed the results two octaves higher. Altering the motif slightly, he said "states" instead of "votes": John Adams, thirteen states; Andrew Jackson, seven states; William Crawford, four states.

House Speaker Henry Clay took the rostrum to announce: "John Quincy Adams, having a majority of the votes of these United States," had been elected president.

The room lay silent for a moment. As applause and cheers slowly staggered in, a low coil of hisses wound up through the chamber.[35]

* * *

That evening, Crawfordites bristled when "the villain" Clay appeared at a crowded reception, "walking about with exultation and a smiling face." One dubbed Adams a "Clay president" who would remain malleable in the hands of his maker.[36]

Andrew Jackson behaved the gentleman when he encountered Adams that evening. But his courteous veneer covered an iron determination to avenge this perceived theft. The results gave Jackson the narrative seed of a vicious campaign: Henry Clay and John Quincy Adams had stolen the election from him and from the people.

That story, of course, relied on half-truths and dubious "facts." The incomplete popular-vote total likely did not represent actual voter preferences, and the Electoral College outcome reflected "the will of the people" even less. Moreover, the House had simply followed the Constitution's rules for a contingent election—nothing dictated how members should vote. And certainly, any dealmaking that put John Quincy Adams in the presidency had extended well beyond Henry Clay.

But two days after the election, when Adams invited Clay to serve as secretary of state, Jackson's accusations received apparent confirmation. His supporters did not care to parse the details. The charges sullied Clay's reputation and permanently damaged his presidential hopes.

Determined to vindicate the "theft" of the presidency, Andrew Jackson launched his next campaign almost immediately. He resigned his Senate seat, returned to Tennessee, and gathered his forces to challenge Adams in 1828.

The Inexorable March to Winner-Take-All

Throughout the next four years, from 1828 to 1832, Jackson and his devotees reinvigorated partisan competition and drove political rancor to extraordinary heights. They beat constant refrains of the "corrupt bargain" and the "stolen election." Eleven pro-Jackson newspapers sprang up to hammer Henry Clay as the "Judas of the West," who had "foisted" Adams upon the people "against their wishes." From these fibers, the general's supporters spun an imaginative catalog of Adams's crimes: He supposedly trafficked American girls for the czar, used public monies to fund a prodigious personal gambling habit, and plotted a monarchical succession to the presidency.

Adams's supporters fought back. Through ten newspapers established solely to halt the general's momentum, they too deployed salaciously embellished allegations. With abandon, they transformed the abundant raw material of Jackson's past into outsized stories of bigamy, adultery, murder, slave trading, and deceit.[37]

The Jackson juggernaut overwhelmed Adams and his supporters. In 1828, the general overwhelmingly captured both the popular vote and the Electoral College. He won again in 1832.

The election of 1824 had fulfilled a decade of prophecies about Electoral College deficiencies, and it reeked of an unsettling arbitrariness. Confronting states' tinkering with the choice of electors, outright elector manipulation, and backroom schemes in the House phase, both the public and politicians believed the system had lost any principled rationale it might once have claimed. Who required more evidence of its failure?

Reformers in Congress immediately resumed their quest for a constitutional amendment requiring district elections. They made a case that echoed arguments now more than a decade old. Once again, proponents of change pointed out the Electoral College's vulnerability to partisan ploys. A reinvigorated Representative George McDuffie urged on his colleagues the "gross and palpable injustice of permitting" the current system to continue. The refrain of corruption carried added salience now, and McDuffie decried "the viciousness of the system" and its "tendency to pervert and change the character of those who control it." Perhaps he thought of Martin Van Buren when he complained that the Electoral College system threw "the whole power of the state into the hands of a few leading politicians of the predominant party."[38]

In an era when the "people's will" carried great rhetorical power, McDuffie contended that uniform district elections would preserve the "real will of the people, instead of the artificial will of the State." The general ticket did not adequately register the people's will, because it destroyed "the vote of the minority in the state" and even transferred the votes of that minority to the candidate they opposed.[39]

As reformers in Congress pressed for an amendment, two noted jurists joined the public conversation. Former U.S. district attorney for Pennsylvania William Rawle published *A View of the Constitution of the United States* in 1825. Rawle worried most about electors pledging their choices in advance as departures from the constitutional plan for selecting the president. Though the framers thought electors were "not likely to be swayed by party or personal bias," Rawle observed that now "the electors do not assemble in their several states for a free exercise of their own judgments, but for the purpose of electing the particular candidate who happens to be preferred by the predominant political party." "Thus," he explained, "the whole foundation of this elaborate system is destroyed."[40]

Four years later, Supreme Court justice Joseph Story quoted Rawle almost verbatim in his widely read *Commentaries on the Constitution*. Story further noted that electors' advance pledges left "nothing" for them to do, except "register votes." Exercising their "independent judgment," as Hamilton once argued the framers intended, now "would be treated, as a political usurpation, dishonorable to the individual, and a fraud upon [their] constituents."[41]

Story expressed other concerns with the system. In particular, he feared frequent efforts to throw the election to the House, where the election would not hinge on the "merits and qualifications" of the candidates. In a House election, "discords" and "corruptions" outlived a single election and "scattered their pestilential influences over all the great interests of the country."[42]

Andrew Jackson himself railed against the Electoral College, and his supporters in the Tennessee legislature forwarded a proposal for direct election of the president. Once elected in 1828, Jackson called for Electoral College reform in every annual address to Congress. He grounded these calls on the simple logic of majority rule. "To the people belongs the right of electing their Chief Magistrate. . . . Let us, then, endeavor so to amend our system that the office of chief Magistrate may not be conferred upon any citizen but in pursuance of a fair expression of the will of the majority." But Jackson's calls for reform remained vague; he never sent a concrete proposal to Congress.[43]

Proposals to reform the Electoral College flew in year after year. But unlike these efforts before the election of 1824, no constitutional amendment passed either House of Congress. Once Jackson's party achieved clear political dominance, they ceased advocating for a constitutional amendment.

Yet one extra-constitutional alteration took firm hold: The general ticket achieved near-universal use, as the fiery breath of party competition burned away every other elector selection method. Six states adopted this system after 1824, and four more changed in the next cycle. By 1836, the long era of switching methods had ended. All states used the general ticket except South Carolina.[44]

In presiding over this change, Jacksonians played a Van Buren–esque trick, often advocating one Electoral College policy at the national level while pursuing another in the states. Though their national leader championed Electoral College reform, and Jacksonians in Congress urged district elections to make the results more reflective of the people's will, at the state level they preferred winner-take-all.

Martin Van Buren led the way. Though he had once shared Henry Clay's deep disregard for Andrew Jackson, after the election of 1824, he stuck his finger in the wind, felt it blowing in Jackson's favor, and hoisted his sails. He brought his New York Bucktails into the Jacksonian fold and advocated eloquently in the Senate on behalf of district elections.[45] New York at last adopted district elections in 1828.

Tellingly, however, when Van Buren served a brief two-month stint as governor in 1829, he used this opportunity to lead the state's switch to the general ticket. Then, Van Buren happily watched Jackson capture all forty New York electors in 1832, rather than divide its electors to correspond with the more varied sentiments of New York voters. New York's general ticket ultimately benefited Van Buren himself, and he followed Jackson to the White House in 1836.

Maryland, the last state to switch from the district system to the general ticket, vividly displayed the partisan advantages at stake in winner-take-all. In 1832, the two presidential candidates finished a knife's edge apart, separated by only 14 votes out of 34,000. That year, Maryland divided its electors between the candidates, in keeping with its long-standing district elections law. But after the state adopted the general ticket for the next cycle, a candidate who lost so narrowly would not get even a single Maryland elector.[46]

* * *

As the general-ticket, winner-take-all system quickly became the near-universal norm throughout the country, voters ceased to question the practice—especially when Electoral College results only amplified the popular-vote totals in the next several elections.

Winner-take-all's perverse logic—giving a state minority's votes to the candidate they rejected—acquired the aura of a timeless principle. Surely, it seemed, the general ticket had been the intent and practice all along, owing to some superior wisdom of the framers.

Indeed, most Americans soon forgot that the men who hammered out the Constitution in Philadelphia never prescribed winner-take-all. Voters no longer remembered how many of these men—Alexander Hamilton, Gouverneur Morris, James Madison, and Rufus King—later sought to rid the system of the general ticket. The objections to winner-take-all from other American leaders, including John Marshall and Thomas Jefferson, disappeared completely from public memory.

And certainly, Americans ceased to note the vigorous and dogged movement to eliminate the general ticket in favor of an election system that more accurately reflected the people's preferences.

As winner-take-all acquired the status of original intent, Americans also forgot that partisan power ploys, not principled commitments, gave us the Electoral College that operates today.

CHAPTER 6

"The Everlasting Principle of Equal and Exact Justice"

Reconstruction's Radical Vision, the Electoral College, and the Election of 1876

FROM THE CABIN FLOOR, ELIZA PINKSTON WATCHED THE WHITE MEN drag her gagged and bleeding husband outside. Hardly noticing her own pain, she pulled herself up and listened through the door. A voice growled that if Henry wanted to vote Republican, he could do it "in hell."

Eliza threw her hands to her face. Seven gunshots broke the Louisiana night; seven times her body flinched.

In the momentary silence, she clutched her child and prayed that the men would leave. She ached to fly to Henry's side, cradle his body, and beg his soul to stay.

But grief yielded to panic as the vigilantes again flooded the cabin. They ripped the child from Eliza's arms. She reached after him, and knives slashed furiously across her face, breast, and legs. A shot rang out. Eliza crumpled to the floor, and her consciousness drained away while sounds unfolded in a jumbled sequence—curses, scurrying boots, horse hooves, and a splash as the baby's body went into the pond.[1]

The former slave woman lay in her blood on the cabin floor because of a presidential election—and fundamental questions about American democracy.

Not that anyone from Washington sent the white vigilantes to Eliza Pinkston's cabin—these men rode of their own accord. But they served up mayhem and murder in an Electoral College system that offered huge incentives for even small vote adjustments in remote places like Ouachita Parish, Louisiana. The election of 1876 vividly displayed the dangers of winner-take-all, whereby the candidate with the most votes in a state received *all* the electoral vote. This practice meant that national outcomes could hinge on a narrow margin in a single state or small group of states. In a high-stakes and intensely competitive contest, this structure incentivized fraud, corruption, and now violence. Even a small amount of voter intimidation (by Democrats) or cheating (by Republicans) could translate into huge shifts in the outcome.

All over Ouachita Parish that season, white Democrats paid visits to formerly enslaved people. Their terror campaign reduced Republican turnout to a fraction of its previous strength.[2]

These orgies of violence decimated Republican support throughout Louisiana in 1876. In East Feliciana Parish that year, no Republican won a single vote, though blacks outnumbered whites two to one, and Republicans had garnered 1,668 votes two years earlier. Other black-majority parishes showed similar shifts. As a result, Democrats claimed a victory of 7,000 votes in Louisiana, winning the state for the first time in sixteen years.[3]

Reports from South Carolina and Florida also described intimidation campaigns that kept black voters away from the polls or frightened them into choosing Democrats. These incidents capped years of terror that aimed to disenfranchise black voters, defeat Republicans, and return whites to power.

In other words, Democrats stole the presidential election of 1876 through violence and intimidation in at least three states. Republicans amassed reams of evidence to prove it, including the testimony of a scarred and permanently maimed Eliza Pinkston.

In response to Democrats' crimes, Republicans stole the election back. The Republican state officials who processed the vote threw out entire precincts where the Democratic candidate led, even from areas without fraud allegations. It mattered little how they made the numbers work, so long as they arrived at the result they wanted, needed, and thus believed to be true. They certified Florida, Louisiana, and South Carolina for their candidate, Rutherford B. Hayes.

Incredibly, still another level of potential fraud loomed. Congress confronted competing electoral certificates from these three states when it convened to count the votes as the Constitution prescribed. Lacking a mechanism to evaluate these claims, Congress could knowingly accept illegitimate certificates or reject legitimate ones. Indeed, it could steal the election in plain sight.

These election vulnerabilities converged in 1876 because so much lay at stake. The visionary historical episode known as Reconstruction had briefly delivered extraordinary federal support to black Americans seeking full citizenship after the Civil War. In isolated pockets and for a limited time, the people newly freed from slavery enjoyed a measure of legal equality, though this reality always remained precarious and embattled.

But Reconstruction required support from the federal government and from the diminishing group of self-named "Radical" Republicans who embraced the far-reaching dream of a just and equal America. By 1876, this visionary project lay at death's door. Democrats hoped to win the election and terminate Reconstruction once and for all. They leveraged the nation's deep divisions and vulnerable election system in an effort to achieve this goal.

Some Radicals' Reconstruction vision of equality included a plan for electing the president that weighted all votes the same and made all Americans equal at the ballot box. For them, rebuilding the nation on a broad egalitarian foundation meant ambitious efforts to reform the Electoral College.

Yet ironically, these dreams of a better election method perished in a presidential contest that vividly displayed the failures of the Electoral College, now but a gross caricature of the framers' plan.

The "Radical" Vision of Reconstruction

In early 1865, the Union army prosecuted the final campaigns of the Civil War. General William Tecumseh Sherman's armies had just pivoted north from Savannah, commencing a march through the Carolinas that would eclipse the devastation of his Georgia campaign. Meanwhile, less than 110 miles south of Washington, Union soldiers maintained fatiguing pressure on Confederate general Robert E. Lee's forces. Everywhere in the South, slavery crumbled, food and other supplies remained scarce, and desertions increased.

In Congress, self-proclaimed "Radical" Republicans anticipated an imminent Union victory, and they had already begun to rebuild the nation on new foundations. On the last day of January 1865, the House of Representatives took a key step toward permanently abolishing slavery by approving the Thirteenth Amendment to the Constitution.

As the clerk announced the vote totals, the chamber erupted in a jubilation that defied all decorum. Republicans on the floor sprang to their feet, tossed their hats in the air, cheered, and shook hands. In the packed galleries, a crowd that included Frederick Douglass's son Charles joined the celebration. Embracing and applauding, men catapulted from their seats while smiling ladies waved their handkerchiefs. The measure's sponsor, Republican congressman James Ashley, opened his large, burly form and raised his face heavenward, as even his abundant unconforming black curls seemed to join the exultation. The weeping, hugging, kissing, and glorying continued a full five minutes.[4]

Meanwhile, fifty-six Democrats sat stoically in their places.

Representative Ashley did not join the elated throng that celebrated afterward with President Lincoln at the White House. Instead, he dashed immediately to telegraph his hometown newspaper, the *Toledo Commercial*: "Glory to God in the Highest! Our country is free!"[5]

Ashley's message announced a truth splendidly in progress rather than fully manifest. For four years, black Americans had seized their own freedom by walking away from their masters, running behind Union lines, flooding into refugee camps, and serving in the Union army. Congressional and executive measures had sanctioned and encouraged these efforts, but none had expunged slavery finally, forever, and completely from every part of the Union. In both the Union and the disintegrating Confederacy, bondage remained a reality for many, and the amendment just passed through Congress could not take effect until ratified by three-fourths of the states.

Even so, Ashley regarded this achievement as a fulfillment of his entire life's work. He had hated slavery since his youth, when he saw boys no older than himself chained together and marched south. As a young man, he had helped escaping families navigate the southern Ohio portions of their journey. When the new Republican Party formed in 1854, Ashley eagerly helped organize it in Ohio and associated himself with its most uncompromising members. During most of his six years in Congress, he had worked with other "Radicals" to transform the war into a crusade against slavery, always pushing President Lincoln to act aggressively against the institution at the war's root.

Over the previous year, Ashley had worked tirelessly to push the Thirteenth Amendment over the two-thirds hurdle in the House. Because the seats of the eleven rebellious states remained vacant, Northerners dominated Congress. Yet even absent the slavery-besotted Southerners, passing an amendment to permanently abolish slavery presented a Herculean challenge. Northern white Democrats placed little priority on this measure, and they feared its implications. The House rejected the amendment once. Before bringing the amendment to a vote again, Ashley worked on a cluster of Democrats who might prove persuadable. He found enticements enough to bring twelve of them to "yes." Carefully timing the vote, he waited until the 1864 elections gave both Mr. Lincoln and himself a fresh mandate. Down to the wire, he fended off efforts to kill the amendment by postponing it. He called the vote this final day of January 1865.[6]

And now, pending ratification, the United States had forever expunged this blight on the nation's soul. When the seceded states rejoined the Union, they would return under a fundamentally and radically altered national compact.

Indeed, Ashley and his cohort wanted more than peace, more than reconciliation, and more than simply a return of the seceded states. They dreamed of raising a multiracial nation of equal citizens. Reading the Constitution through the lens of the Declaration of Independence, they foregrounded the claim that "all men are created equal" and are "endowed with certain unalienable rights." The Radicals championed black citizenship and voting rights. They advocated free universal public education and protections for the labor rights of all people. And they favored decisive measures by the federal government to protect and guarantee those rights.

Putting the essentials of their vision on the firmest possible footing demanded far-reaching changes in the Constitution, the nation's foundational compact. The Radicals knew they could not count on the states or on ordinary legislation to achieve their goals. These rights would be guaranteed to all Americans only if secured by the Constitution, beyond the reach of changing attitudes, partisan state legislatures, misguided courts, weak-willed executives, and a mealy Congress.

The year 1865 spun out like a whirlwind. Ten weeks after Ashley's amendment successfully passed the House, Lee surrendered at Appomattox, Virginia. Less than a week later, an assassin's bullet felled President Lincoln. By the end of 1865, the necessary three-fourths of the states had ratified the Thirteenth Amendment—Ashley's amendment—abolishing slavery. Now the hard work of reuniting and rebuilding would begin in earnest.

For Ashley and some other Radical Republicans, a truly egalitarian United States required dramatic changes in presidential elections. Ashley introduced a proposal for a national popular vote in May 1868 because he believed "our new condition as a nation"—a nation without slavery—required it. Reforming presidential elections and guaranteeing voting rights would render Americans all "one people living under a common Constitution."[7]

The demise of slavery presented new possibilities for altering the Electoral College. As long as slavery had remained, even reformers who desired sweeping election changes understood that the slave states would not relinquish the advantage they gained from the Constitution's three-fifths clause; thus, most amendment proposals to date had in some way preserved that "bump." But slavery's destruction rendered the three-fifths clause inoperative, and its Electoral College benefit evaporated. With no slave-state interests to protect, reformers believed the door had opened for a direct, national popular vote to succeed.[8]

Ashley's proposed amendment would abolish the Electoral College and create a national community of equal citizens empowered with the right to vote and to have each vote counted equally with all others, at every phase of the process. His amendment provided for a national "nominating vote" every four years. Adult citizens would vote directly for their preferred candidate in April and, months later, vote again in a runoff to decide between the top five vote-getters. The amendment also included a suffrage guarantee for all adult citizens. Ashley openly advanced the notion that citizenship and suffrage should be "synonymous." Without explicitly stating it, his amendment implied that women might also be enfranchised.[9]

In his speech introducing the measure, Ashley described both electors and party nominating committees as undesirable "interventions" between the people and their leaders. His amendment would remove citizens' votes "from the dictation and control" of middlemen who might "betray the people or defeat their choice." The Ohioan reserved special criticism for party nomination procedures. In his view, "the corrupt and unsatisfactory convention system" deprived the people of any role in choosing the candidates. The entire system was "demoralizing in its practical workings, unfair in its representation of the great body of voters, and repugnant to the principles of true democracy and republicanism."[10]

Eliminating the intermediate agency of electors and providing for a direct national vote would also end the winner-take-all system, which Ashley decried for suppressing the votes of large political minorities in each state and for its potential to produce a president who lacked majority support.

Most of all, however, Ashley railed against the existing system because it opened opportunities for "corruption and fraud." Slight adjustments in just one state's totals could dramatically impact the outcome. Winner-take-all incentivized even minor acts of cheating because small changes carried huge potential rewards. Ashley believed his amendment supplied a remedy for the "dangerous, unjust, and anti-democratic" processes of presidential elections. He swore "not to rest" until he had seen it through to success.[11]

But Ashley introduced his amendment only days after narrowly failing in his fight to impeach President Andrew Johnson. The impeachment controversy badly damaged the Ohio congressman, and voters replaced him with a Democrat in the fall of 1868. The momentum for reforming the Electoral College passed to other Republicans, who continued introducing amendments in both the House and the Senate.

Indeed, the Reconstruction era marked another period of sustained, repeated, and consistent attempts to reform the system of electing the president, though neither the volume of proposals nor the support for them matched the period of 1813–1826. In the post–Civil War era, Congress faced daunting struggles and life-and-death situations. To many, Electoral College reform seemed a luxury that could wait.

Neither Ashley's nor any other Republicans' amendments for Electoral College reform made it to a floor vote during Reconstruction. But these proposals and their connection to other Reconstruction measures demonstrated how the Radical Republicans' vision for a new nation of equal and equally empowered citizens included an equal vote for the president.[12]

The Radical Republicans did successfully champion other transformative amendments to the United States Constitution, and these included elements embedded in Ashley's Electoral College reform proposal. The Fourteenth Amendment established citizenship for those born in the United States and guaranteed equal protection under the law. The Fifteenth Amendment ranked among the era's most important achievements. It prohibited denial of the vote "on account of race, color, or previous condition of servitude" and authorized the federal government to enforce its provisions. The far-reaching amendment passed Congress in 1870, attaining the necessary two-thirds majority on strict party-line votes in each house. Not a single Democrat voted in favor of it.[13]

The Republican-dominated Congress followed these amendments with a raft of legislation aimed at making these provisions real in the freed people's lives. The Radicals aimed not just to eliminate slavery but also to elevate the freed people to full equality and to remove all obstacles toward this goal. Their measures required seceded states to write new constitutions and to ratify the Thirteenth and Fourteenth Amendments. They authorized the president to use the army to protect the rights of freed people, and they stripped former Confederate officials of their rights to vote and hold office. They empowered courts to prosecute those who committed acts of terror and violence.

For a while, the Radical agenda enjoyed significant success. Black Americans stepped eagerly into independence and full citizenship rights. They exercised their new rights to vote, to organize politically, and to hold office. Every former Confederate state sent black members to its legislature and several sent African Americans to Congress. Republicans' national coalition depended heavily on the votes of the freed people in the South.

But the Radicals' agenda soon suffered serious setbacks. Conservative and moderate Republicans became unreliable supporters, accusing their Radical colleagues of promoting "Negro domination." Instead of embracing equal voting rights unconditionally, some Republicans advocated property or literacy qualifications for the freed people, while they supported no such tests for white voters. Moreover, they objected to disenfranchising former Confederate leaders.

For their part, northern white Democrats proved extraordinarily sympathetic to their southern white brethren and served as their most effective advocates in Congress. They opposed basic protections for the freed people. In their shameful racial fearmongering, they heralded the United States as a "white man's country" and accused the Radicals of undermining that status.

After 1872, the Radical grip on leadership weakened considerably. A cascading series of corruption scandals engulfed President Ulysses S. Grant's administration and damaged the entire Republican Party. Collapsing railroad companies and banks set off a panic, followed by depression in 1873. When a specially established Freedman's Bank failed, millions of dollars in black Americans' savings disappeared.[14]

White Northerners wearied of the repeated military deployments in the South on behalf of a people for whom many felt they had done quite enough. The Democratic Party's ranks swelled with white Northerners who wanted to end measures that seemed "harsh" to white Southerners.

In the midterm elections of 1874–1875, voters dramatically demonstrated their loss of confidence in Republicans and the Reconstruction agenda. Democrats captured more than ninety House seats, gaining the majority for the first time since 1856. They stood poised to take back the presidency in 1876. For the South's black population, no result appeared more devastating.

THE WHITE SOUTHERN AGENDA: RESISTING RECONSTRUCTION

Everywhere he went in the fall of 1868, Republican congressman James Hinds saw the warnings. On a bright September morning, a coffin topped by two daggers greeted him as he opened his front door in Little Rock, Arkansas. He squatted to read the accompanying note: "We are for you, if you don't leave."[15]

As he stumped in southeast Arkansas a few days later, Hinds spied a posse of armed men following him. Though his planned itinerary included a visit to the next county, he canceled the trip for his own safety.

The blue-eyed, clean-shaven Minnesotan had settled in Arkansas just as the war ended three years earlier. Appalled at whites' vicious hatred toward the formerly enslaved people, Hinds embraced the Radical Republican agenda and plunged full-bodied into the state's politics. He helped found the Arkansas Republican Party and worked to build it with a coalition of white and black support. He addressed his crowds of white and black Arkansans as "fellow citizens." With other members of the state party, he championed free public education for both races, full enfranchisement of the freed people, and disenfranchisement of former Confederate officials. He urged his hearers to seize the moment and erect a new nation on "the granite rocks of eternal truth and justice."[16]

As the fall 1868 election approached, violence soared in Arkansas, most of it calculated to intimidate the freed people. Increasingly, however, the perpetrators also targeted white Republicans, especially government officials. Only loyal Democrats could find true safety in Reconstruction-era Arkansas.

Planning to attend a large political meeting in late October, the congressman boarded a steamer headed up Arkansas's White River, but he did not travel far. The captain discovered his identity and refused to transport a Republican "carpetbagger." He docked the boat and expelled Hinds; his traveling companion, the Reverend Joseph Brooks; and their horses.

Not knowing their own whereabouts, the two Republicans rode through a small community and asked for directions. About a mile outside of town, someone galloped up from behind them. Hinds watched in horror as the man aimed a double-barreled shotgun at Brooks, who rode a bit ahead. Shots rang out, and Brooks's body flinched. The horse bolted, with Brooks still in the saddle.

Now Hinds watched the man pull close. The barrel of the gun almost touched him. As the contents flooded his body, he fell from the saddle, and the murderer vanished without a trace.

The thirty-four-year-old lay alone on the roadside in the October afternoon as the blood gushed from his side. His thoughts flew immediately to his wife and two young daughters. With effort, he drew a pencil from his bag and scribbled a message on his hatband: "My name is James Hinds. I am shot in the body and shall live only a few minutes. My wife is at East Greenwich, N.Y. Wife, take care of Jennie and Annie."[17]

Authorities found the congressman yet alive, but he succumbed to his wounds within hours.

Hinds joined the thousands who fell victim to deadly armed violence as it convulsed the South long after Appomattox. Though the Confederate government had imploded and its army disbanded, a new era of slaughter filled the region with blood. Like the acknowledged war it followed, this new era of conflict turned on issues of race. Southern whites pursued the same goals as before, only now they used vigilantism and terror.[18]

White Southerners categorically rejected the new and equal status of the people they had once enslaved. They terrorized freed people who attempted to exercise their political rights, whether voting or running for public office; they undermined the freed people's attempt to eke out an independent economic existence; and they fought against any assertions of black Southerners' humanity and equality. Perceiving Republicans as the champions of a new racial order, they aimed squarely at party members and leaders of any race.

Between 1865 and 1877, this violence reigned episodically in every state of the former Confederacy. Very often, it targeted political figures, surged in advance of elections, or followed the withdrawal of federal troops. The violence displayed a breathtaking range and ferocity. It included episodes like the murder of James Hinds, but it also broke out as organized mob attacks, riots in southern cities, mass lynchings, and open massacres. An Alabama Freedmen's Bureau official described how roads and rivers in his state stank "with the dead bodies" of freedmen who ran afoul of whites. Calling it "the most sickening sight" he had ever witnessed, a Texan claimed it was "impossible to give the number of Negroes that have been killed." Blacks who asserted their political rights suffered beating, whipping, torture, and death. When not killed, their white supporters were terrorized into leaving or acquiescing in the newly developing racial order.[19]

Some of the worst racial terror in the country rocked Louisiana, which hosted the era's single most deadly incident of southern racial violence in the small community of Colfax on Easter Sunday, 1873. There, an army of about 300 whites attacked a building where frightened black citizens sought protection. The whites blasted the building with a cannon and set the roof on fire. When the freed people ran out to avoid being burned alive, volleys of gunfire mowed them down. The whites took about forty black men prisoner, promising to free them in the morning if they would curtail their political activity. They executed them instead.

Local black residents emerged warily in the morning to bury their dead. About 100 bodies lay about, some with their throats slit and others shot at point-blank range. Some of their faces could not be recognized for the ferocity of their wounds.[20]

Authorities never produced an accurate death toll for the Colfax massacre, but low-end estimates put the number at around 150 blacks. Three whites also lost their lives.

A year later, whites conducted a similar melee fifty-five miles away in Coushatta, and a few months after that, they pursued a massacre of comparable proportions in Vicksburg, Mississippi.

As the election of 1876 approached, blatant intimidation of black voters swelled. It surged most spectacularly in Louisiana and South Carolina, two of the three states where Republican governments remained in control, propped up by U.S. troops. The violence sought to discourage black voting and remove black politicians, while installing white

Democrats in their places. For months in advance of the election, white South Carolinians in "rifle clubs" and paramilitary groups attacked Republican political meetings and black communities throughout the state. In several Louisiana counties, this violence included nighttime raids by whites who visited black families like the Pinkstons.

This kind of violence could change the outcome of elections. All indications suggested that the election would be very close, and as reports of atrocities rolled in during the preceding weeks, the nation sat on a tinderbox.

Both parties sensed the high stakes in this presidential contest. A victory for Democrats would effectively end federal efforts on behalf of the freed people and ensure that white Southerners could return to power. For northern Republicans, retaining the executive branch meant holding an office they had possessed since 1861. Though many in the party had backed away dramatically from their commitment to black equality, those who still embraced the Radical vision wanted to preserve Reconstruction governments and the measures supporting them.

But no one possessed greater stakes in this election than the South's African Americans. For them, this election literally meant life or death, freedom or bondage.

Preventing Disaster, Advocating Reform

Almost exactly six months after the April 1865 surrender at Appomattox, Indiana governor Oliver P. Morton awoke one morning unable to move from the hips down. At forty-two years of age, the Republican stalwart had suffered a stroke and would walk only with the assistance of canes or crutches for the rest of his life. He accepted this debilitated condition with quiet resignation.[21]

Yet politically, Morton accepted nothing. Instead, he raged—against Democrats, traitors, incompetence, and insubordination. The war's end had opened unprecedented opportunities for his party, and he craved an active role in national affairs. Less than sixteen months after the onset of his paralysis, the Hoosier sat at his new desk in the U.S. Senate chamber, his energy and commanding presence seemly undiminished by the canes at his side.

In the Senate, Morton advanced a vision of Reconstruction much like the one articulated by his Radical House colleagues James Ashley and James Hinds. For Radicals like Morton, the post–Civil War era presented an opportunity to rebuild the nation on foundations firmer than before. Morton urged his colleagues to "go down to the eternal rock, and there upon the basis of the everlasting principle of equal and exact justice to all men . . . [plant] the column of reconstruction." In his mind, the founders had failed to lay a broad enough foundation, but this generation now had a chance "to begin the world over again." They would make right what the framers had neglected, creating a new nation on "principles of humanity . . . justice [and] equal rights, principles that appeal to the hearts and consciences of men."[22]

In this context, Morton clearly understood the purpose of the South's rampant violence. Unrepentant Confederates did not want a new nation raised on principles of equal justice—they liked the old system of white domination just fine. Morton laid it out: White Southerners hoped to reduce "the colored people to a condition of *quasi* slavery." Despite the Thirteenth Amendment's decisive abolition of human bondage, white Southerners wanted continued access to exploitable labor. To achieve this end, they forced formerly enslaved people into labor contracts with draconian conditions and expectations, subjected them to arrest under the most facile pretenses, and denied them all rights to advocate for themselves. Former Confederates bolstered these schemes with orgiastic violence against both the federal government and the freed people. To many white Southerners, the war begun in 1861 yet continued, and their objectives regarding peoples of African descent had not changed.[23]

Morton knew that oppressive white rule would overtake the South completely if he and his Radical colleagues did not hold firm. As more and more southern states forced out Republican leaders and replaced them with Democrats, including former Confederates, Morton worried that the profound human suffering and cataclysmic upheavals of the war might come to naught. He did not blame white Southerners exclusively. They succeeded only with support from their Democratic allies in the North and the weak-kneed moderates in his own party. In the harshest terms, Morton castigated his wishy-washy colleagues for their submission

to "inhuman" and "heathenish" ideals. They trafficked in "appeals to prej-
udice" and set "race against race." He found "nothing noble . . . nothing
generous . . . nothing lovely, in that policy or that appeal."[24]

Morton watched Democrats capture the House majority during
1874–1875 and recognized that only the presidency remained as a bas-
tion of defense for the freed people. In all but the three southern states
controlled by Republicans, white rule had returned on wings of terror and
intimidation. Buttressed by the presence of U.S. troops, black Americans
in Florida, Louisiana, and South Carolina clung precariously to their
rights.

Morton foresaw great hazards awaiting in the 1876 presidential
election. For that reason, when he presented a proposal to reform the
Electoral College in January 1875, he accompanied it with a grave, prophetic warning. "Great dangers impend," he admonished, in the system
for electing the president. Moreover, these threats were "greater now
than they have ever been before in the history of the country and will
increase."[25]

In the first half of his speech, Morton echoed motifs that reformers before him had sounded, and he amplified themes other Radicals
had taken up. The Electoral College no longer operated as the framers designed it. Electors had long since ceased to act independently
but, rather, pledged themselves in advance to specific candidates.
Winner-take-all completely disenfranchised the political minority in
every state, potentially enabling "a small minority of the people" to elect
a president. Morton bolstered this last point with a mathematical illus-
tration of winner-take-all's distorting impact. Surveying the previous
eight presidential elections, Morton demonstrated that the popular and
electoral vote always differed by at least 10 percent, but several times had
not come even as close as 30 percent.[26]

Morton favored a national popular vote, but he did not believe such
a measure could succeed in the brittle, hyper-partisan climate. He would
be satisfied to "bring the election home to the people" through district
elections. Morton's amendment, then, retained each state's weight in the
Electoral College, but eliminated electors and allowed for a direct vote

of the people in districts, much like other amendments that members of Congress had repeatedly proposed since 1813.[27]

Then Morton pivoted from these details to impress on his Senate colleagues the extraordinary potential for fraud in the nation's presidential elections system. Electoral College outcomes often hinged on the results in only one or two states. Because small adjustments in a single state could significantly change national outcomes, the system offered a strong incentive to cheat. Bad operators could manipulate votes in an isolated locale far more easily than they could manufacture the hundreds of thousands of votes that usually separated national-popular-vote outcomes. Indeed, Morton pointedly accused New York City Democrats of regularly gaining votes through fraud, vote buying, and ballot stuffing. By such corrupt measures, these urban operators regularly overwhelmed the Republican vote in the rest of the state and captured the entire elector slate for their candidate. In a close election, small fraud in an elector-rich state like New York could tip the outcome.[28]

Morton turned from local voter manipulation strategies to another arena where danger lurked: Congress could defraud the people in plain sight. This possibility grew from the ambiguity of the Constitution's Article II, which dictated that "the President of the Senate shall, in the presence of the Senate and House of Representatives, open all the certificates and the votes shall then be counted." The phrase gave no instruction as to exactly *who* should do the counting. Moreover, the Constitution's text did not describe what made a state's electoral certificate legitimate nor indicate who possessed the right to make that determination. If a state submitted two competing slates of electors, how would the Senate president know which set to count? Congress could steal an election in full public view by knowingly accepting fake certificates or disqualifying legitimate certificates.[29]

Indeed, in zeroing in on this flaw in the Constitution, Morton described a problem that leading political thinkers and scholars had identified decades earlier. James Madison had cautioned about this problem. Jurists James Kent and Joseph Story each witnessed ugly, partisan ballot-counting disputes at the state level. Each went on to publish well-respected commentaries on American law and the Constitution, and both raised concerns about the possibilities of contested ballots resulting in a disputed national election. Kent suggested that only some sort of impartial tribunal could fairly adjudicate in such cases. But in a hyper-partisan climate, an impartial tribunal seemed an impossible dream.[30]

In recent years, Congress had, in fact, struggled repeatedly just to count the vote. In 1857, Congress spent three days considering whether to reject or accept Wisconsin's votes, since a snowstorm had prevented the state's electors from meeting on the required day. Vote-counting issues plagued the election of 1864 as well. These concerns had surfaced again in the most recent election, 1872, when the Senate rejected certificates from Arkansas and Louisiana on technicalities, and "in twenty minutes . . . disenfranchised about 600,000 people." In each case, the election outcome had not hinged on the disallowed votes, but Morton cautioned that 1876 might end this series of "happy accidents."[31]

Because the Constitution provided that an inconclusive election would go to the House—as in 1800 and 1824—Morton saw a train wreck looming. By rejecting electoral certificates on a technicality, Congressional conspirators could contrive to send the election to the House. Since Democrats enjoyed a substantial majority there, they would seize the opportunity to place their candidate in the Executive Mansion. The dream of Reconstruction, already on life support, would die.

Morton's plan to reform presidential elections, then, included a provision for Congress to establish tribunals that could rule on questions about the legitimacy of electoral certificates. Only with such a mechanism could Congress count the vote without opening the door for partisan operators to defraud the American people—in plain view.

But Congress did not act on Morton's proposal. And though other Republicans also proposed different sorts of tribunals, Congress failed to act on those as well.

The Disputed Election of 1876

Senator Morton's predictions of election mayhem required no special prophetic gift. As reports of violence billowed from the South, any alert observer could see an impending election disaster.

Election night, November 7, 1876, ended inconclusively, though much more hopefully for Democrats. Their candidate, New York governor Samuel Tilden, garnered 184 solid electoral votes. He needed only one more to win a majority of 185. With only 165 votes securely in his column, Republican Rutherford B. Hayes's prospects looked grim.[32]

The indeterminate outcome lay in precisely those three southern states where Republican administrations remained in charge and where election-related violence had ticked up: Florida, Louisiana, and South Carolina. Questions about the legitimacy of a single Oregon elector further complicated the result. While Democrat Tilden would win if he captured even a single additional elector from these states, Republican Hayes would need a perfect sweep to win.

Representatives of both candidates poured into the contested states. Within five days, armies of senators, former governors, generals, newspaper editors, state officials, and attorneys of both parties swamped hotels in Tallahassee, Columbia, and New Orleans. Ostensibly, none of them could change the outcome—they came merely to "observe" and "assure a fair count." But Democrats hunted the single electoral vote they needed, and Republican election officials thwarted them as they canvassed and counted the results.

A fair and honest count lay out of reach in all three states. The appalling violence and intimidation in South Carolina and Louisiana—all inflicted by white Democrats—exacted a toll no one could measure. Republicans cried foul at these tactics, but then fraudulently counted the ballots to balance matters out. A journalist covering the Florida count observed, "The truth of the matter is, both parties are at sea. Neither knows exactly what to do, and yet is bewildered by the fear that the other will do it first." A Republican operative noted that "money and intimidation can obtain the oath of a white man as well as black to any required statement. A ton of affidavits could be carted in . . . and not a word of truth in them."[33]

The three contested states sent competing sets of electors to Congress, triggering exactly the crisis of legitimacy Morton had predicted. Lacking any mechanism to rule on the validity of the certificates,

Congress's usual February formality of counting the vote promised to become a partisan fiasco.

Intense pressure bore down on Congress as it scrambled to establish a special Electoral Commission satisfactory to all. The commission's fifteen members—five Democrats, five Republicans, and five Supreme Court justices—would rule on the validity of the electoral certificates of the disputed states. The commission began its work in early February 1877 and, together with Congress, consumed nearly the entire month considering and ruling on the competing elector slates. In each case, the commission returned an 8–7 decision that favored the Republican candidate, Rutherford B. Hayes, giving him all twenty disputed electoral votes. The commission awarded not a single disputed elector to Democrat Samuel Tilden, who on election night three months earlier had stood only one vote shy of victory.

The work of the commission, then, would give the presidency to Republican Rutherford B. Hayes.

Meanwhile, behind the scenes and on another track entirely, a group of journalists and operatives secured a separate deal to put Hayes in the White House. Hayes had indicated to an intermediary that he hoped to "treat the South kindly," by which he meant the *white* South. More than anything, the white South wanted Reconstruction finally to end, which meant withdrawing the last federal troops that propped up Republican administrations in Florida, Louisiana, and South Carolina. Once the troops vacated those states, nothing would remain to protect the freed people in the rights guaranteed to them by the hard-won Thirteenth, Fourteenth, and Fifteenth amendments.[34]

Southern legislators wanted other things as well—infrastructure investments in the South, a Democrat in the president's cabinet, and patronage jobs for Democrats.

As the vote counting—aided by the Special Electoral Commission— neared its termination in Congress, a handful of Democrats pursued a last-ditch effort to prevent its completion, hoping to push a final tally past March 4 and provoke a crisis they could exploit. But they succeeded only in reducing the proceedings to a farce and delaying a final resolution until 4:00 a.m. on March 2—only two days before outgoing president Ulysses S. Grant's term expired.[35]

Early that morning on board his train for Washington, Republican Rutherford B. Hayes learned that he had won the Electoral College by a single vote, 185–184. The nation had waited four months to know that outcome.

FORSAKING RECONSTRUCTION

Fulfilling his promise to the Democrats who helped him attain the White House, President Hayes very quickly removed the troops from Louisiana and South Carolina. Immediately, the Republican governors in those states yielded their offices to Democrats. The entire South had been, in their own language, "redeemed." A former Confederate colonel who had helped negotiate for Hayes's election rejoiced to see the end "of the night of the Reconstruction Period."[36]

Hayes also supported important southern infrastructure projects, appointed a Democrat to his cabinet, and gave patronage jobs to Democrats.

Senator Oliver Morton continued to promote a constitutional amendment that would alter the Electoral College. He argued his case in national opinion journals and urged its necessity in speeches. But a second stroke felled the senator less than a year after the election of 1876, and he died in his Indiana home at the age of fifty-four.[37]

Over the next fifteen years, southern white leaders achieved exactly what Senator Morton and his colleagues had struggled so mightily to prevent. They pulled down the pillars of the more equal and just society that Radical Republicans had erected. They ruthlessly commandeered black labor through systems of sharecropping, tenancy, debt peonage, and convict leasing. They reestablished systems of social degradation by demanding segregation in public transportation and accommodations. They squelched black ambition by sequestering African American children in grossly underfunded and inadequate schools. Underpinning it all, they decimated black political power with poll taxes and literacy tests. Giving all these efforts a legal gloss, they wrote state constitutions that enshrined these measures and won high-profile court decisions that legitimated their efforts.

By the end of the nineteenth century, white Southerners had accomplished the victory they sought. Though slavery had vanished, a new system very like it had taken its place. Just as before the Civil War, white Southerners sat atop a social and political hierarchy sustained by the toil and suffering of African Americans, who could find few paths out of these confines.

Ironically, in this new era that rose after 1877 and achieved full expression by 1895, white Southerners gained a boost in the Electoral College more significant than the obsolete three-fifths cause had ever conferred. After slavery's end, for the first time, the freed people counted fully—not merely as three-fifths—in the population for purposes of representation in Congress and the Electoral College. This new population calculus increased the South's congressional delegations and the number of its electors. Yet, once black Southerners completely lost the vote and the last black congressman went home in 1901, they had no actual representation in Congress nor in presidential elections. As since the nation's founding, African Americans' mere presence enhanced the political power of the very people who oppressed them.

Thus the nation postponed a meaningful reckoning with the aftermath of slavery for almost a century. Not until the civil rights struggle of the mid-twentieth century did the United States endeavor again to "go down to the eternal rock . . . the everlasting principle of equal and exact justice to all men" and fulfill the vision that the freed people and their congressional supporters—men like James Ashley, James Hinds, and Oliver Morton—so passionately extolled.

* * *

To be clear, the Electoral College did not cause the end of Reconstruction.

Even before the election of 1876, many white Americans had already forsaken that once-hopeful vision. Southern violence raised the social, psychological, and political cost of protecting the freed people, and many white Northerners proved more sympathetic to former Confederates than to those once enslaved. In eight of the eleven former Confederate states, Reconstruction had already been abandoned well before the election of 1876. Once elected, Hayes simply completed the work in Florida, Louisiana, and South Carolina. Though he extracted promises that the new regimes would protect the rights of freed people, these governments reneged on their word.

Moreover, the election of Democrat Samuel Tilden would have terminated the last vestiges of Reconstruction even more decisively.

Yet the Electoral College played a role in the way these events unfolded. In the high-stakes atmosphere, winner-take-all incentivized the rampant election violence and motivated the fraud that placed the results in doubt and sabotaged any presidential mandate. Hayes's dubious Electoral College win brought him to office with a weak hand and a cloud of illegitimacy, forcing him to make more immediate and far-reaching concessions on Reconstruction than he might otherwise have done.

Moreover, in giving Congress the final task of deciding the election, the system guaranteed that the outcome would carry a stench, no matter how honestly that body ruled. Democrats continued to believe the election had been stolen, and they reinforced the narrative of Republican treachery each time they referred to the president as "Rutherfraud" or "His Fraudulency." After an election driven by partisan animosity, this outcome further deepened mistrust.

The contest of 1876 exposed the serious and dangerous issue of disputed ballots that had lurked in the Constitution's design all along, but still Congress failed to rectify the problem. For the remainder of the nineteenth century, elections remained remarkably close. Congress finally passed an Electoral Count Act in 1887 that aimed to provide clear guidance in cases where states sent competing returns. But the legislation only opened more questions, and its ambiguous language would have offered little help, had Congress needed it.

While any presidential election method would interact with the nation's deepest problems and the darkest human impulses, some methods play more tantalizingly to these forces than others. Unsurprisingly, the American system for choosing the president—born in 1787 from the Constitutional Convention's political realities and molded over intervening decades to the demands of party optimization—became a tool that both political parties used to advance their power.

* * *

Radical Republicans' Reconstruction efforts to rebuild the country on more solid foundations opened a new chapter in the struggle to reform the Electoral College. Proponents of change had framed a national popular vote as necessary to create a nation of equal citizens, where all votes count equally. When the nation took up this challenge again nearly a century later, it called for "equal and exact justice" in language similar to Reconstruction's visionaries.

The nation has moved much, much closer to the ideal of equal citizenship for all, but that goal remains elusive in fundamental ways. Certainly, Americans are not equal until each citizen casts an equal vote for president.

CHAPTER 7

"Samson with His Locks yet Unshorn"

The White South, the Electoral College, and the Civil Rights Movement

ALL THAT DAY IN JULY 1948, THE RALLY AT THE BIRMINGHAM MUNIC-
ipal Auditorium oscillated between "orderly scene" and "mob demon-
stration." Speaker after speaker castigated the national Democratic Party
for "stabbing the South in the back." The audience leapt repeatedly to its
feet, rebel-yelling and applauding at the most combative lines. "We've got
to do something to save ourselves," cried one convention-goer. During
the frenzied climax, audience members "snake-danced" around the
auditorium and across the stage, while a seventy-seven-year-old woman
burst into a jig and male students from Ole Miss chanted "To Hell with
Truman!"

The organizers had tried to give the gathering a national appeal, with
American flags on the stage and red, white, and blue bunting hanging
throughout the hall. But the 6,000-member crowd preferred southern
symbols. They waved Confederate flags, hoisted portraits of General
Robert E. Lee, and warmed to the band's repertoire of "Dixie," "Carry Me
Back to Old Virginny," and "My Old Kentucky Home." The *Birmingham
News* described the affair as a "rip-snorting, Confederate-flag-waving
convention" with "revival-like fever."

From the stage, South Carolina governor Strom Thurmond watched
the raucous, all-white, mostly male crowd, many wearing shirtsleeves in

the July heat. Large fans provided some relief, but the governor felt warm in his wide-lapeled, double-breasted suit.

The forty-five-year-old Thurmond stole a quick glance to his left, where his pretty, twenty-two-year-old wife Jean made a pleasing contrast to the aging men around her. Thurmond had married her only seven months earlier, less than a year after he became governor and she became his secretary. A man running for president of the United States needed a pretty wife as well as a fashionable suit.

Thurmond took the podium and began his speech haltingly, body and voice a bit stilted, eyes cast down at his notes. Under segregation, he insisted, black Southerners had benefited greatly from "the kindness of the good southern people."

He could feel how the crowd loved that line.

Continuing, he warned that Truman's civil rights policies would lead to a police state. "It won't be long until there are bayonets around your ballot boxes."

The audience urged him on.

Thurmond broke free from his notes. His body relaxed, and his gestures moved more easily. With his high-pitched, nasal voice rising and deep southern accent lubricating each word, he skewered President Truman and the national Democratic Party. They had taken the South for granted, but they needed to understand that "the South was not in the bag." His pointed index finger punched the syllables. Finally, Thurmond let loose a line in the best tradition of southern defiance: "There's not enough troops in the army to force the southern people to break down segregation and admit the nigger race into our theaters, into our swimming pools, into our homes, and into our churches."

The audience leapt in applause, and Thurmond glowed, his raised hands absorbing the adulation.

When newspapers quoted Thurmond afterward, most substituted the more polite word "Negro" for the epithet he had used. Back at the headquarters hotel, someone hung a dummy from a balcony. A sign across the effigy's body said, "Truman—killed by civil rights."[1]

Thurmond and his State's Rights Democratic Party—Dixiecrats, most called them—did not really angle to take the presidency. Only in a reality-detached scenario could they win even as many as 150 electoral votes, and victory required 266. Nonetheless, with just a handful of electors, they could prevent either major party candidate from reaching a majority and thus throw the election to the House. In a House vote, Thurmond's Dixiecrats could leverage their strength to extract the concession that animated this entire endeavor: a halt to civil rights initiatives.

Indeed, the Dixiecrats planned open and purposeful manipulation of the Electoral College to "safeguard" the South's system of segregation, black disenfranchisement, and labor exploitation. Mississippi governor Fielding Wright described the movement as an "electoral college fight to save the South."[2]

The demand for black equality gained a compelling momentum in the middle decades of the twentieth century, and white Southerners sought every available tool to stop it. In the Dixiecrat Revolt and during the twenty years following, Deep South political leaders repeatedly looked to the Electoral College as one of these tools.

At the same time, the Civil Rights Movement helped ignite the most vigorous effort to date for a direct national popular vote, since full political equality could only mean that every vote should count equally in every part of the nation.

With broad public support, an amendment to create a national popular vote very nearly succeeded. But, unsurprisingly, the white South's segregationist leaders, including Strom Thurmond, stopped this effort in its tracks.

JIM CROW AND THE ELECTORAL COLLEGE

The Electoral College's intimate connection with white supremacy did not vanish with slavery's abolition in 1865. Reconstruction briefly secured the freed people's rights, but as its protections crumbled, the South gradually and systematically disenfranchised its black citizens. This system of Jim Crow magnified the white South's Electoral College power, rendering the region "a political giant . . . [a] Samson with his locks yet unshorn," in the words of a southern apologist.[3]

This augmented Electoral College power arose from precisely the same source identified in the Constitution's three-fifths clause: the region's "all other persons." Before 1865, the politically powerless enslaved population counted at the rate of three-fifths for congressional and Electoral College representation. In the "New South," however, the black population gave whites an even greater advantage, since they counted at *full* value, rather than merely three-fifths, while remaining utterly disenfranchised. Indeed, the South enjoyed a de facto "five-fifths clause."[4]

The presence of disenfranchised African Americans made a national popular vote unthinkable to white Southerners in the Jim Crow era, just as their presence had helped prevent the Constitutional Convention from adopting a popular vote for the president more than a century before. James Madison had observed during the 1787 Convention that, with a popular vote, the South "could have no influence in the election on the score of the Negroes." In eerily similar language, a North Carolina judge noted in a 1917 essay that white Southerners would not favor a national popular vote because they "would not consent to a system which would deprive them of representation by reason of the negroes."[5]

In the first decade of the twentieth century, 7 million black citizens boosted the white South's representation in the House of Representatives and the Electoral College. Based on the 1900 census, this disenfranchised population gave the states of the former Confederacy an added thirty-five House seats and thirty-five electors. In Georgia, for example, very few of the 1 million black citizens could vote, yet their presence increased the state's representation in both Congress and the Electoral College by five. Similarly, Mississippi owed four seats and four electors to its disenfranchised blacks who made up 58 percent of its population.[6]

The effects of disenfranchisement rippled beyond the African Americans targeted by discriminatory state constitutions and voting laws. In a region where poverty and illiteracy ravaged both races, poll taxes and literacy tests also ensnared many whites. Consequently, often as little as 3 or 4 percent of the population voted in some southern states. This political exclusion, coupled with the region's commitment to one-party Democratic rule, enabled a small group of powerful whites to punch high above their weight in national politics.[7]

These factors dramatically increased inherent disparities in Electoral College voting power. In 1904, the nearly equal populations of

Mississippi and California gave each state ten electoral votes. Yet, because of voter disenfranchisement, only 58,383 Mississippians chose those ten electors, while 324,165 Californians voted for the same number. The *New York Times* referenced exactly these kinds of inequities when it observed in 1916 that "the South most certainly does possess an unfair advantage in having its nonvoters counted as voters, so that a handful of Southerners are more potent than a great number of northerners."[8]

Beginning in 1911 and through the rest of the twentieth century, reformers introduced proposals to alter the Electoral College in every single Congress, except one. In some years, Congress entertained multiple proposals, receiving nine such amendment resolutions in 1916, and ten in 1947. Some of these amendments would abolish the Electoral College in favor of a direct, national popular vote. Others sought district elections or allocating a state's electoral votes proportionally to the state's popular vote, while a few aimed only to eliminate electors and automatically assign electoral votes based on winner-take-all.[9]

Interest in Electoral College reform surged in late 1916, after President Woodrow Wilson narrowly escaped an Electoral College defeat, despite a hefty popular-vote advantage. An informal survey that November revealed southern leaders' solid opposition to Electoral College reform. No southern politician mentioned how the current system inflated their political power. Instead, they couched their preferences for the Electoral College in high-minded, principled language. A Texas senator regarded current operations of the Electoral College as "essential to the prosperity and the existence of the republic." The notorious race-baiting Mississippi governor, Theodore Bilbo, insisted that a popular vote "would destroy the last vestige of states' rights."[10]

Northern and western leaders expressed far more mixed opinions about Electoral College reform, but some demonstrated clear awareness that white Southerners drew Electoral College power from those they disenfranchised. As one midwestern representative who abhorred such inequities put it, "One vote in Alabama has as much to say . . . as ten votes in Kansas."[11]

Newspaper editors chimed in on this debate as well. The *New York Herald* described the Electoral College as "an anachronism . . . a public evil, and a public danger." The *Philadelphia Inquirer* argued that "the weather-beaten, out-of-date, and even dangerous electoral system should be abolished." The *Washington Herald* suggested that practical considerations, not a simple reverence for the Constitution, should dictate an evaluation of the system's merits: "If the Constitution had provided candles for lighting purposes, we would not be using candles today instead of electricity. In electing our Presidents today, however, we are using a candle-powered system."[12]

Unsurprisingly, then, the thirty-four proposals for a national popular vote introduced between 1911 and 1948 came overwhelmingly from midwestern and northern congressmen. Only a single congressman from the former Confederacy advocated discarding the Electoral College in this period. Representative Richmond Pearson Hobson of Alabama introduced a national-popular-vote proposal six times between 1911 and 1913. But the independent-minded Hobson lost a bid for the Senate in 1916 in a campaign where his support for abolishing the Electoral College figured as an issue. Though he tried, the war hero never could resurrect his political career.[13]

Equally unsurprising, the South used its added Electoral College weight to preserve the system of racial oppression against any efforts to dismantle it.

"A Man Just Like You"

As the Greyhound bus rolled northeast from Augusta, Georgia, into South Carolina on a February night in 1946, U.S. Army sergeant Isaac Woodard settled into his seat. After three transformative years, the twenty-six-year-old looked forward to going home. He had earned a battle star for unloading ships under enemy fire in the Pacific theater, and his bravery, discipline, and competence equaled any white man's. He wondered if the folks in Winnsboro would observe the new confidence in his carriage and demeanor.

Like other newly discharged black servicemen, Woodard expected America—especially South Carolina—to change with him. Surely, after this all-out fight against the Nazis' racist ideology, the nation would recognize and remove the same evil at home. Woodard planned to stop behaving toward whites with the groveling subservience they expected.

He patted the breast pocket of his standard-issue jacket and felt the outlines of his mustering-out check. The $649.73 would give him a solid start in civilian life. Best of all, each mile that disappeared under the wheels brought him closer to his roots in Winnsboro and to his wife. He would arrive there in a matter of hours. The future looked bright.

The bus ambled through stops in small towns between Aiken and Columbia. Woodard wanted to get off and use the bathroom. But when the driver objected to his request and cursed him, Woodard cursed him back, adding, "I am a man, just like you." At the next stop, only sixty miles from Woodard's home, the driver exited the bus, fetched the local police chief, and ordered Woodard off.

Outside the bus, Woodard stood face-to-face with Batesville, South Carolina's 200-pound police chief, Lynwood Shull. As the young veteran began to recount his disagreement with the driver, the chief's nightstick landed abruptly on his head. Woodard felt Shull jerk his arm behind his back, turn him sharply, and thrust him down the street and away from the watching eyes of passengers on the bus.

Woodard moved through Batesville's dim streets, pushed and prodded by Shull. He replied "Yes" to questions about his military service. That is, he replied "Yes," without the customary "Sir."

The officer's blows fell fast and heavy. Woodard's consciousness faded.

Now Shull was pulling him to his feet. More blows. Then, Woodard felt the metal-reinforced end of that baton penetrating deep into his eye sockets.

His bright future went black.

Woodard never saw again. Doctors later confirmed that his eyeballs had been ruptured.

Months later, an all-white South Carolina jury deliberated less than thirty minutes before acquitting Lynwood Shull of all charges.[14]

President Harry Truman generally avoided civil rights issues, following the lead of his predecessor, Franklin Delano Roosevelt. As Democrats, both men understood that the white South formed their party's major constituency, and alienating those voters could cost them an election. Moreover, they needed the Southerners who chaired powerful committees to steer their agenda through Congress. Just as problematic, southern Senate Democrats killed every civil rights proposal with the filibuster, including even anti-lynching and anti–poll tax measures that Americans overwhelmingly supported. Roosevelt and Truman saw little sense in expending political capital only to meet defeat.

But Truman had come under increasing pressure since taking office in April 1945. The labor wing of the Democratic Party increasingly pushed civil rights initiatives, and the North's urban areas swelled with black migrants from the South who voted, organized, and publicized the evils of white supremacy.

Meanwhile, the white South horrified the nation with its brutality toward black citizens. The blinding of Isaac Woodard stood out as only one incident in a thick catalog of violent crimes against black veterans that year. When President Truman heard a recitation of these episodes, which included details of the Woodard blinding, he responded with horror and incredulity.[15]

The president convened a commission on civil rights, and that commission issued its report, *To Secure These Rights*, in October 1947. The report documented in detail the violence and inequities black Americans faced under Jim Crow. It advanced a moral, economic, and international case for dismantling segregation and recommended sweeping civil rights measures that included federal anti-lynching, anti–poll tax, and fair employment legislation. The president followed with a special message on civil rights to Congress in February 1948, urging it to pursue the measures in the report.[16]

In July, Democrats from all over the country streamed to Philadelphia and packed the city's Convention Hall to nominate Harry Truman as their presidential candidate. As the roll-call vote began, Handy Ellis of the Alabama delegation took the microphone to denounce the party's new and forthright civil rights stance. With other Southerners pressed eagerly about him, Ellis declared that his state could not, on principle, "further participate" in this convention. "We bid you good-bye," he announced. Turning on his heels, he marched out of the hall, with thirteen Alabamians and all twenty-six Mississippi delegates filing behind.

Those southern delegations who remained cast protest votes against President Truman's nomination.[17]

The Dixiecrat plan to "save" the South had begun.

THE DIXIECRAT REVOLT

Most days, Charles Wallace Collins puttered around Harmony Hall, his sixty-six-acre, eighteenth-century Maryland estate. From the small porch on back of the elegant Georgian-style mansion, he could see Broad Creek in the distance and beyond it the wooded banks of the Potomac River. Mount Vernon, the historic home of President George Washington, lay just a few miles downriver on the Virginia side. These environs suited Collins's self-estimation. A white lawyer and economist who had his suits tailored in London, he had been born on a cotton plantation in Alabama's black belt in 1879.[18]

On a typewriter at his gentleman's retreat, Collins banged out his manifesto, *Whither Solid South? A Study in Politics and Race Relations*. Published in 1947, the book aimed to "arouse orthodox southerners to action in the face of organized hostility toward the southern states." This hostility arose, he claimed, from "new racial theories" of human equality and a novel, loosely employed slogan of "democracy." It emanated from a constellation of forces—the northern Democratic Party, left-leaning Republicans, religious groups both Jewish and Christian, labor unions, intellectuals, and above all, black Americans themselves. This "Negro movement" sought "to make the Negro equal to the white man economically, politically, and socially."[19]

Collins believed that the "Negro legislative program" would destroy the "southern way of life." Peoples of African descent, he maintained, belonged to a "primitive and undeveloped" race, and the South had arranged its social and labor system around this central fact. Collins described the region's black population as ignorant, carefree, and irresponsible—but "happy" living under the guidance of whites.[20]

Collins laid out a strategy focused on the Electoral College as a key tool for protecting white supremacy. Through its outsized power in the Electoral College, the region could deny the presidency to a "misguided" candidate like Truman. By purposefully throwing the election to the

House, the South could force one of two desirable outcomes. The best solution would be "a northern deadlock" that "could lead to the election of a southern President." As another possibility, "the South would hold the balance of power and the bargaining power that goes with it." Indeed, with that leverage, the Solid South could exchange its support for a complete halt to civil rights initiatives.[21]

The Electoral College formed the cornerstone of Collins's plan, but he also recommended two other strategies to help white Southerners preserve their dominance. One tactic involved uniting with conservative Republicans outside the region. Their ideologies of small government and economic conservatism fit more naturally, he believed, with the program of southern segregationists.[22]

Second, the filibuster also gave the white South an important tool for preventing "dangerous" bills from coming to a vote. In the Senate, Southerners used marathon speeches and other stalling tactics that members could stop only by a two-thirds "cloture"—closure—vote. By the time of Collins's publication, the South's political leaders had successfully killed civil rights measures with the filibuster for three decades.[23]

From his idyllic Potomac perch, Collins corresponded extensively with the Deep South's key political leaders. He mailed copies of *Whither Solid South?* to legislators, politicians, and attorneys across the region. And the Dixiecrat movement eagerly embraced his message, revering *Whither Solid South?* as both blueprint and bible. U.S. senator James Eastland of Mississippi claimed to keep a copy on his desk. Eastland and Mississippi governor Fielding Wright helped distribute the book to other southern leaders. When Strom Thurmond addressed the crowd that July 1948 night in Birmingham, Charles Wallace Collins glowed approvingly in the audience.[24]

The Deep South's Dixiecrat ploy implemented Collins's strategy. The Democratic parties of Mississippi, Alabama, Louisiana, and South Carolina chose elector slates pledged to Strom Thurmond, rather than President Truman. In Alabama, Truman did not appear on the ballot at all. The Alabama Democratic Party added to its traditional rooster symbol a feature that would guide any uncertain voters: a banner with the words "White supremacy—for the right."[25]

The Dixiecrat plan threatened to upend the 1948 presidential election. It divided the Democratic Party and weakened Harry Truman's already poor prospects for reelection. Most observers thought Truman would join the ranks of John Tyler, Millard Fillmore, and Chester Arthur—presidents who finished out the terms of others and then vanished into obscurity. Political prognosticators predicted a decisive win for Republican Thomas Dewey.

On election night, Dixiecrats swept four Deep South states—Mississippi, Louisiana, Alabama, and South Carolina. Strom Thurmond won every single county in Mississippi and Alabama, taking more than 87 percent of the vote in the Magnolia State. These four states and one faithless elector from Tennessee translated to thirty-nine electoral votes.[26]

But President Truman performed so well nationally that the Dixiecrat gambit failed to impact the outcome. The incumbent Democrat beat Dewey decisively, winning 303 electoral votes to Dewey's 189 and carrying the popular vote by 4.5 percent.

Tellingly, areas of Dixiecrat success mapped neatly onto regions where whites lived with high concentrations of disenfranchised blacks. A higher percentage of African Americans lived in the four Dixiecrat states than anywhere else in the country. In his home state of South Carolina, Thurmond lost the mostly white upland counties, while winning big in the ten counties with black populations more than 60 percent.[27]

The Dixiecrat revolt marked the beginning of a long transition that ultimately realized one of Collins's recommendations: a southern white alliance with conservative Republicans, rather than Democrats, outside the region. Indeed, in the remaining twelve presidential contests of the twentieth century, the Deep South states of Mississippi and Alabama would only vote three more times with their traditional Democratic allies.

The Deep South's white political leaders would also try two more times to protect the racial hierarchy by manipulating the Electoral College.

NEAR SUCCESS: THE LODGE-GOSSETT AMENDMENT

The Dixiecrat ploy rattled the political establishment, and Congress responded by nearly passing an amendment to alter the system for electing the president. The amendment effort also addressed rising public support for abolishing the Electoral College. A 1944 Gallup poll had indicated that 65 percent of Americans wanted to do away with it. That number rose to 70 percent in 1947.[28]

The plan—the Lodge-Gossett Amendment—preserved each state's Electoral College weight, but it eliminated electors and automatically allocated electoral votes proportionally to the popular vote in each state. This proposal appealed in several respects: It eliminated unnecessary electors, ended winner-take-all, and gave each state's political minority proportional weight in the Electoral College. Yet by preserving the basic Electoral College formula, Lodge-Gossett satisfied those disinclined toward more far-reaching change.

As always for the white South's political leaders, concerns about race dictated their response to this proposal. They remained quite confident that they could continue to deprive blacks of the vote in their own back-yard. But most white Southerners also believed Lodge-Gossett would limit the influence of northern black voters and thus undermine black influence in their party—the Democratic Party. South Carolina's Senator Olin Johnston indignantly but falsely claimed that, under the Electoral College, "the vote of a Negro [in Harlem] is worth a hundred times as much on the national political scene as the vote of a white man from South Carolina." That problem would go away with Lodge-Gossett, which "would lessen the power of organized minorities in the North and East," according to an Alabama commentator.[29]

Moreover, Lodge-Gossett would not impact the South, which could easily preserve its long-standing one-party white rule in the region. But it would introduce political competition in the North, making the north-ern wing of the party more dependent on the South and less responsive to northern black voters. Just like that, Lodge-Gossett would solve the South's difficulty with the national Democratic Party.

On February 1, 1950, Lodge-Gossett easily won the necessary two-thirds majority in the Senate with overwhelming support from its southern members. However, the plan died in committee when it went to the House. Presidential elections would continue on the same path they had followed for a century and a half.

THE FREE ELECTOR MOVEMENT: SOUTHERN BOLTERS TRY AGAIN

Now a U.S. senator, Strom Thurmond looked up from his papers to gaze at the empty desks in the chamber. He did not consult his watch, but he knew the hour was well past midnight. His eyes burned, and sleep beckoned like a seductress. At fifty-four, Thurmond still prized his physical prowess, and he had built stamina through regular use of barbells and a faithful morning push-up regime. He summoned that strength on this night to continue releasing a torrent of words.

The senator nibbled on a bit of pumpernickel bread and purposefully shifted focus from his fatigue to his future. This filibuster against civil rights legislation would garner glowing praise in South Carolina. The white voters there and throughout the South would laud him as their champion, the one man to battle for a state's right to conduct its elections as it saw fit. In the future, he could point to this night, when he alone among twenty-two southern senators had courageously defended the white South.

It was 1957, nine years after Thurmond's Dixiecrat run for president. That strategy had earned him a reputation in the South as a fighter for principle, and it had taught him the value of constantly burnishing those credentials. Though he had failed in the 1948 presidential bid and would lose tonight as well, voters rarely remembered the results. They only recalled the fight.

In these wee hours, the empty Senate Chamber seemed especially cavernous. Thurmond had been at it since almost 9:00 p.m. the previous evening. He occupied the time by reading aloud from Washington's Farewell Address, the Bill of Rights, state election statutes, and other documents. Occasionally he swigged orange juice, milk, or water. Clarence Mitchell of the National Association for the Advancement of Colored People watched from the gallery. Jean Thurmond perched there as well, nicely turned out in a short-sleeved navy suit, pearl earrings, and a double-strand pearl necklace. A third, unidentified man snored quietly. The three constituted Thurmond's total audience for much of the night.

As the late-August dawn broke outside, a few senators and staff straggled in. Most watched Thurmond's theatrics only briefly from the doorway. Southern colleagues shot angry looks at Thurmond—they had all agreed *not* to filibuster, since their opponents clearly had the votes to pass this bill. Thurmond had betrayed his caucus and launched this performance just to raise his own political capital, knowing full well that pointless grandstanding wasted everyone's time.

That afternoon, Thurmond's voice grew barely audible. Jean replenished him with bits of the steak she had cooked beforehand. He sucked on lozenges and popped malted milk tablets, told stories, and read from more documents.

At 9:12 p.m. that evening, Strom Thurmond finally relinquished the floor, having talked for twenty-four hours and sixteen minutes, the longest single speech in Senate history. Reporters thronged him in the hallway. Jean ran down from the gallery to kiss his cheek and praise his principles: "He has done a wonderful job of telling the country how important this is."[30]

Thurmond had wasted twenty-four hours opposing a relatively weak civil rights bill. Two hours after he quit talking, it passed overwhelmingly.

Thurmond's high-profile antics responded entirely to black Americans' recent string of pivotal victories. Activists had filed suit in court for equal access in education, and the High Court had answered with its *Brown v. Board of Education* decision, a stunning blow to segregation. Eighteen months later, African American citizens in Montgomery, Alabama, began a yearlong boycott of city buses. Inflicting severe economic pain on the bus company, the activists won their quest for equal treatment on city buses. Less than thirty days after Thurmond's record-breaking 1957 all-nighter, nine black students successfully integrated Little Rock's Central High School under the protection of the National Guard.

Black Americans' insistent demand for dignity and equality raised the stakes in the presidential election of 1960. Southern whites did not trust either national political party to help them preserve white supremacy. Dusting off their copies of *Whither Solid South?*, they followed Charles Wallace Collins's playbook once again. As in 1948, they sought to leverage the region's inflated Electoral College strength to extract concessions that protected southern white rule.

This time, however, the defiant Southerners did not run their own candidate. Rather, they put "unpledged electors" on the ballots—electors not attached to any presidential candidate. These electors would be free to vote for any candidate when casting their ballots in December. By March 1960, it appeared that seven southern states with a total of sixty-nine electors might participate in this plan. Just like the Dixiecrat ploy, the move highlighted the Electoral College's vulnerability to dysfunction and manipulation by dark political impulses.

As the election rolled into its final ten weeks, the race appeared extraordinarily tight. John F. Kennedy needed the Democratic Party's traditional southern base, and no one could predict how far the unpledged elector scheme would go. Mississippi was fully on board, as was most of Alabama. Other southern states seemed equivocal in their support for Kennedy.[31]

The November 8 vote produced one of the closest results in American presidential history. By midnight, returns showed Kennedy with a popular-vote lead of 2 million from Democratic strongholds in the East. But as the night unfolded and totals poured in from the Midwest and the West, Kennedy's advantage faded. He won only a few states in the West, and these only by the tiniest margins. Illinois's twenty-seven electors hinged on a margin of just .2 percent, and New Mexico's only .01. Hawaii decided for Kennedy by a scant .0009 percent margin.[32]

Kennedy's decisive Electoral College victory of 303–219 illustrated how winner-take-all converted tiny margins at the state level to big Electoral College wins. His popular vote lead amounted only to 112,827 votes, or .17 percent of the total.[33]

But the outcome would have changed dramatically if just thirty-five southern electors—fewer than had peeled away in 1948—had defected from Kennedy. In that case, the vote would have landed in the House, and the *Whither Solid South?* playbook would have proved its genius. As it turned out, the free elector scheme deprived Kennedy of only fifteen electoral votes: eight from Mississippi, six from Alabama, and one faithless elector from Oklahoma.

One Person, One Vote: The Second Reconstruction and the Electoral College

In 1964, a chill, late-February wind whipped the 260 local black residents standing outside the Madison County Courthouse in Canton, Mississippi. The elderly among them moved with the assistance of canes and their younger companions. Some had dressed for the occasion in suits and ties, while others wore workman's garb underneath hats and coats. The line of people streamed down the walkway leading to the century-old Greek-revival brick courthouse. It snaked under the large magnolia tress that overspread the sidewalks, wound through the wrought-iron gate, and piled up along its matching fence.

A black-clad sheriff's deputy paced the line with a gun in one hand and a billy club swinging from his hip. Police officers toted guns and nightsticks while they barked orders at the crosswalks and moved the growing line around. FBI agents, clergymen from the National Council of Churches, photographers, and journalists milled watchfully about the grounds as well. Meanwhile, a heavy parade of law enforcement vehicles patrolled the streets.

Men, women, old and young, stood there most of the day, barely advancing. The registrar admitted only one person at a time and, over two days, only seven people made it inside to take the complicated test on the Mississippi Constitution. Aspiring registrants filed through a glass door sporting the rebel-flag decal of the Citizens' Council, a white-supremacist organization devoted to preserving racial segregation in all areas of southern life.

African Americans accounted for 72 percent of Madison County's population, though only 1.1 percent of them were registered to vote, while 97 percent of the county's white citizens were registered. That spring, black residents of other Mississippi towns acted on their hunger for the vote and turned out to register in similar displays. But these initiatives produced little in the way of immediate results.[34]

These 1964 "Freedom Days" capped years of frustrating work by black Mississippians. Especially telling, after three years of painstaking and methodical labor, organizations devoted to registering black Mississippians had invested $50,000 and registered fewer than 4,000 voters statewide. Organizing in Leflore County, for example, had produced only thirteen new registrants in two years. The meager results stemmed from the fierce resistance of local whites, who punished would-be voters by getting them fired and withholding federal food relief from their impoverished communities. White supremacists bombed the homes of some who tried to register. They flogged others and killed at least five in one three-county area alone.[35]

As Canton's black citizens sought the vote in the late winter of 1964, the state lay on the cusp of turmoil that would mark it for years. That summer, white supremacists burned twenty African American churches and killed civil rights workers, while white churches in downtown Jackson turned away black worshippers. As the nation watched these events, Mississippi and other Deep South states seemed like pariahs in a nation ready to dismantle the legal apparatus of black subordination.

The Twenty-Fourth Amendment, rendering poll taxes unconstitutional in federal elections, went into effect only five weeks before the Canton drive. Tellingly, Mississippi rejected it outright, while most southern state legislatures did not even entertain it.

And while Canton's citizens risked their lives to register to vote, major civil rights legislation wended its way through Congress. The groundbreaking Civil Rights Act of 1964 promised sweeping impact. Prohibiting segregation and discrimination in public accommodations, employment, and federal programs, this legislation included enforcement mechanisms to make these provisions a reality. It boasted broad bipartisan support, as well as President Lyndon Baines Johnson's eager advocacy.

Yet, southern senators tried to send this groundbreaking legislation to the filibuster grave they reserved for civil rights measures. As so often in his long Senate career, Strom Thurmond stood out as the bill's most eager executioner. Americans watched in frustration as less than two dozen powerful southern men joined him to prevent a vote on a measure that claimed 70 percent public approval. Predicting that its passage "would mark one of the darkest days in history," Thurmond and his coconspirators made repeated and meaningless requests for amendments, read long articles into the record, and asked for pointless roll calls. Extraordinary maneuvering by the bill's sponsors finally brought the 1964 Civil Rights

Act to a vote after sixty working days, ending one of the longest filibusters in Senate history and marking the first time the Senate had ever broken a filibuster on civil rights legislation.

Black Americans forced the nation to reassess its values. This Second Reconstruction sought sweeping changes through constitutional amendments, court decisions, and landmark legislation. It forced the nation to reckon with the meaning of equality and provoked a reconsideration of the method for electing the president of the United States.

A year after black citizens in Canton, Mississippi stood for two days, hoping without success to register to vote, Congress passed the Voting Rights Act of 1965. The language of the legislation explicitly connected its provisions to the Fifteenth Amendment, ratified during Reconstruction ninety-five years earlier and forbidding denial of the right to vote "on the basis of race, color, or previous condition of servitude." As if making good on an uncashed check that black Americans had carried for ninety-five years, the Voting Rights Act authorized federal enforcement mechanisms to protect citizens' access to the polls.

Civil rights initiatives called attention to the many ways voting equality could be denied. One example included the Supreme Court's *Gray v. Sanders* decision, which produced Justice William O. Douglas's pointed explanation that political equality "can mean only one thing— one person, one vote." The case stemmed from a Georgia complaint that the state primary system conferred outsized electoral weight on low-population rural counties. In 1963, the High Court ruled eight-to-one that Georgia's system violated the Equal Protection Clause of the Fourteenth Amendment.[36]

The logic of "one person, one vote" seeped quickly into American life. Three years after *Gray*, the state of Delaware applied its conclusions in a lawsuit aimed at the Electoral College practice of winner-take-all. The Delaware suit maintained that winner-take-all, like Georgia's county-unit system, violated its citizens' rights to equal protection under the Fourteenth Amendment. The case used language employed by opponents of the general ticket for more than 100 years: The general ticket "arbitrarily cancel[ed]" the votes of political minorities and gave their votes to "candidates whom they oppose." The Supreme Court declined to hear the case, but the suit demonstrated that many Americans wanted remedies for the irrevocably flawed Electoral College.[37]

Frustration with the Electoral College seemed to permeate the air and even spring from unlikely quarters. In 1966, the U.S. Chamber of Commerce's Board of Directors called its membership's attention to "the weakness" of Electoral College operations. The board asked its 4,000 nationwide affiliates to respond to a poll, indicating whether they preferred a district election system or a national popular vote: 91.5 percent of returned ballots favored a national popular vote.[38]

In a sweeping report a year later, the American Bar Association (ABA) called the Electoral College "archaic, undemocratic, complex, ambiguous, indirect, and dangerous." The ABA advocated abolishing it in favor of a national popular vote. Zeroing in on winner-take-all, the report noted that the system "grants all of a state's electoral votes to the winner of the most popular votes in the state, thereby cancelling all minority votes cast in the state."[39]

Gallup polls tracked public support for abolishing the Electoral College at 65 percent in 1967. That year, thirty-five resolutions to alter the system poured into Congress. Eleven of these measures called for a direct popular vote.[40]

The moment seemed right, but political leaders needed an extra push. The presidential election of 1968 spooked both parties into action.

THE SOUTH'S FINAL GAMBIT: 1968
After Sam Smith and his five-piece Alabama combo warmed up the crowd with "Your Cheatin' Heart" and "Ring of Fire," Mona and Lisa Taylor scurried to the mics to sing "Them Old Cotton Fields Back Home." In matching dresses and blonde bouffant hairdos, the sisters from Jasper, Alabama, belted out the southern favorite. Meanwhile, well-groomed "Wallace girls" wearing plastic boaters passed buckets through the aisles for contributions.

The mood shifted from playful southern fun to earnest national reverence, as the crowd stood for the national anthem. Someone pronounced a benediction and led them all in the Lord's Prayer. Tears flowed as 6,000 voices sang "God Bless America."

The crowd lingered in the heavy sweetness of the moment. They had come for this very feeling—to capture the sense of the America they knew, loved, and feared they had lost.

The Taylor sisters broke the spell as they scampered back to the stage singing "Are You from Dixie?" The audience eagerly joined the clapping, then whooped and hollered as the sisters changed the lyrics to "Are You for Wallace?"

This rally was in Milwaukee.

As if from heaven, a voice boomed over the loudspeaker: "Ladies and Gentlemen, the next president of the United States," and George Wallace bounded onto the stage. The band amped up its lively picking, as Wallace's short and agile form sprang stage left and snapped a salute, then bounced stage right to salute again. He saluted the folks in the balcony and the policemen in the aisles as the crowd applauded, yelled, and cheered for several minutes. Stepping behind the bullet-proof podium, he raised his hands to quiet them.

The former Alabama governor wrapped his opening in classic populist garb: "Those over-educated ivory tower folks look down their noses at you and me, and call us rednecks, peckerwoods, pea-pickers, and crackers," he intoned. But "there sure are a lot of rednecks in Milwaukee!" The crowd roared its delight.[41]

Wallace gloried in the national appeal of his campaign. He also denied the racist overtones in his message. Yet, many at the meeting on this 1968 summer night might have remembered the governor's defiant lines of seven years earlier: "I draw the line in the dust and toss the gauntlet before the feet of tyranny, and I say segregation now, segregation tomorrow, segregation forever." They might also have remembered how Wallace stood in the schoolhouse door at the University of Alabama in 1963, turning away the U.S. deputy attorney general who came to register two black students.

Perhaps few remembered, however, that the two students registered anyway, without incident and away from the cameras just a few hours later.

Wallace had since softened his racist appeals. Now he rephrased them, promising to "turn the schools back to local control" and to end forced school busing programs designed to achieve integration. He promoted "states rights," railed against open housing laws, and swore to silence the bureaucrats "who tell you whom you have to bathe with in the factory shower" and want "to pay somebody not to burn down the country." He promised to promote law and order.[42]

Even more telling, a survey of campaign staff and of electors pledged to him revealed a thick overlap with known anti-Semites, members of the segregationist Citizens' Councils and other far-right groups like the John Birch Society, and even the Ku Klux Klan.[43]

Supporters explained their enthusiasm in simple terms: "We're sick and tired of the way things are going in this country." Others liked his plain-spoken, folksy style: "I can understand George Wallace better than any candidate I've ever heard." Certainly, crowds responded approvingly to Wallace's tough lines promising to shoot looters, and they delighted in the belittling zingers he lobbed at hecklers.[44]

The appeal to law and order resonated with white, middle-class Americans who had watched waves of rioting, burning, and looting in their cities that year. One such episode had erupted after the assassination of civil rights leader Martin Luther King Jr. in April. Another followed two months later, after a gunman murdered Democratic presidential hopeful Robert Kennedy Jr. By the fall of 1968, similar incidents had plagued America's cities for three years, and many wondered why the country's recent sweeping civil rights measures had not fully righted the country's 350-year record of racial wrongs.

Charles Wallace Collins had died in 1964 at the age of eighty-five. Clearly, the blueprint he laid out in *Whither Solid South?* had not stopped the Civil Rights Movement. But before the white South's die-hard segregationists completely surrendered, they would try Collins's plan one final time, more than twenty years after he conceived it in his manor on the Potomac.

Unlike Strom Thurmond twenty years earlier, George Wallace managed to get on the ballot in all fifty states. He drew large crowds not only in the South but also in the Midwest, West, and urban North. A few weeks before the election, 16,000 admirers at New York's Madison Square Garden erupted wildly for twenty minutes when he came to the podium. Prognosticators believed Wallace might capture as many as 177 electoral votes. Though not enough to win, those numbers could tip the election to the House and put Wallace in a solid position to stymie further civil rights legislation. Moreover, the strong showing might offer the necessary foundation for a 1972 comeback.[45]

More than any of the South's two previous Electoral College ploys, the Wallace spectacle sent fear through the major political parties. At first the Republican camp of Richard Nixon regarded the Alabamian as a threat only among the Deep South's whites, who continued to resist integration and to vote on racial issues. Though Nixon generally avoided direct discussions of race, he offered a more dignified version of Wallace's law-and-order talking points, and he also promised to halt school busing. As the campaign entered its final weeks, Nixon aides feared a potential Wallace sweep of the entire South, including the border states of Kentucky and West Virginia.

Wallace's campaign also sent shivers through Democrat Hubert Humphrey's ranks. In particular, the Alabama phenom carved measurably into Democrats' traditional bases of support among northern union members.

At the polls in November, Wallace demonstrated his genuine strength. His clear dominance in five southern states won him forty-five electoral votes, more than any of the previous southern bolts. Tellingly, more than 40 percent of his 9.9 million popular votes came from outside the South. Wallace even ended his campaign with more money on hand than when he started.

Nixon's Electoral College margin of 301 to Humphrey's 191 masked a razor-thin popular-vote victory of only 500,000 votes—less than a single percentage point.

The year 1968 marked the third time in twenty years that anti–civil rights forces had sought to exploit the Electoral College's idiosyncrasies and leverage the South's strength to preserve white supremacy. In the final weeks of the campaign, polls showed support for abolishing the Electoral College ticking up sharply, to 80 percent.

Wallace's candidacy frightened both parties into finally addressing the Electoral College, and Americans seemed eager for them to do it.

Defending the "Safeguard"

On September 18, 1969, House members rose to their feet, cheering and applauding as New York congressman Emanuel Celler walked from the well to his seat. The eighty-one-year-old had just shepherded to passage a historic amendment for direct popular election of the president. Close to the end of his career after more than forty-five years in the House, Celler felt his own emotions rising at this "crowning achievement of [his] life."[46]

The decisive vote stunned members and observers alike. A whopping 338 representatives voted yes, while only 70 voted no, giving the amendment an 83 percent approval from the House and 66 votes more than needed for the two-thirds majority threshold. Moreover, the vote revealed broad support from leaders as well as the rank and file of both parties, from large and small states, and from most regions of the country. The overwhelming vote demonstrated wide agreement with Representative Celler's assessment of the Electoral College as a "historical blunder . . . unsporting . . . dangerous . . . and downright uncivilized."[47]

Yet a closer analysis of the vote revealed weak support for the amendment in the Deep South. The entire delegations of Mississippi and South Carolina voted against it. Six of Louisiana's eight-member delegation and five of Alabama's eight representatives voted no. Notably, in those four states, African Americans formed a higher percentage of the population than anywhere else in the country. Of the total seventy votes against the amendment, forty-seven of them—67 percent—came from the South.[48]

Even after this overwhelming approval by the House, the amendment still faced the hurdle of passage in the Senate and ratification by three-fourths of the states. But its high level of public support made its chances seem strong.

Yet opposition rose immediately from southern senators, who pursued delay tactics that postponed Senate consideration of the amendment for a full year.

In the meantime, the South lost a final battle to preserve school segregation. In late 1969, the Supreme Court's *Alexander v. Holmes County Board of Education* decision forced an end to the southern delay tactics that had stalled meaningful school integration for fifteen years. A few months later, 200 white parents in Lamar, South Carolina, brought axe handles and bricks to attack and overturn two school buses carrying black children.[49]

Ten days after the ugly Lamar incident, the Senate voted to renew the 1965 Voting Rights Act. They overwhelmingly extended this pivotal legislation, but the vote revealed the Deep South's continued opposition to its provisions. All twelve of the "no" votes on extension came from the South, with every senator from eight southern states voting no or failing to vote.

While the Senate stalled on the national-popular-vote amendment, Deep South senators explained their opposition to abolishing the Electoral College. A most telling objection came from U.S. senator Jim Allen of Alabama. Having served four years as George Wallace's lieutenant governor, Allen had ridden the Wallace wave to Washington in 1968. In justifying his opposition to popular election, Allen mimicked his mentor by using carefully chosen euphemisms for race. Three times, he referenced the "bloc vote," a term that frequently substituted for its near homophone, "black vote." Allen favored keeping the Electoral College because, he maintained, it reduced the weight of black voters in northern cities. Yet he failed to note that winner-take-all guaranteed continued practical disenfranchisement of Alabama's blacks in presidential elections.[50]

Finally, in mid-September 1970, the amendment's sponsor, Senator Birch Bayh of Indiana, brought it to the floor. Southern senators immediately gave it the civil rights treatment. When Strom Thurmond joined this filibuster, he cited high-minded principles like "preserving the federal system," while lacing his speech with references to race, both overt and implicit. On the one hand, Thurmond presented himself as a champion of minority rights by arguing that the Electoral College advantaged "traditional voting blocs as the Negro vote and the Jewish vote," referring to large northern cities. Thurmond, like Allen, remained silent about the disenfranchising impact of winner-take-all on black Southerners. He even reminisced fondly about his 1948 Dixiecrat run for president, without noting that the Dixiecrat Bolt aimed to stop civil rights measures.[51]

Over the next two weeks, Thurmond called on his considerable filibuster experience to form a trio of obstruction with senators Sam Ervin of North Carolina and James Eastland of Mississippi.

They sustained the filibuster for three weeks and through two cloture votes with the aid of other southern senators and a small handful of Republicans from outside the region. The failed vote to end the filibuster reflected regional lines, not partisan divisions. Direct election of the president looked a great deal like a civil rights measure.

The amendment's sponsors declined to pursue the matter further after they could not close the filibuster on the second try.

Black citizens and their allies had wrought significant changes in the South's racial structure over the previous fifteen years. The Electoral College remained one final place where white Southerners could preserve their dominance. Because the African American population did not rise above 37 percent in any state, the Electoral College's winner-take-all mechanism guaranteed that black Southerners would remain voiceless in presidential elections, despite their rising presence at the polls. Indeed, the white South could at least preserve racial dominance in presidential elections.

As so many times before, the efforts of a small band of willful Southerners killed the dream of true and far-reaching political equality. One person, one vote would not prevail in the election of president of the United States.

Champions of a national popular vote did not give up. They brought thirty-three amendments for a national popular vote in 1971 and the same number in 1973. Indeed, amendments on direct elections streamed in for the rest of the decade. In 1979, the Senate once again voted on a national-popular-vote amendment, only to see it fall short of the necessary two-thirds majority for passage. For the rest of the century, not a single Congress closed without a member introducing a proposal for direct popular election of the president. Yet, no Electoral College amendment has come to a vote since 1979.[52]

* * *

Throughout the twentieth century, the system for choosing the president demonstrated its extraordinary malleability in the hands of small groups of politicians dedicated to a singular purpose. This system remains exploitable by any movement that represents only a small base. White supremacist goals motivated attempts in the twentieth century, but other equally nefarious goals could inform efforts to throw a presidential election to the House and hold an election hostage to ignoble aims. As long as the Electoral College continues in its present form, Americans no doubt have not seen the last of such ploys.

Importantly, the Electoral College's connections to America's racial realities have persisted long past the era of slaveholding. If slavery played a role in creating the Electoral College and in dictating its precise form, an enduring dedication to white supremacy helped prevent changes that would allow all Americans an equal say in electing their president.

Ironically, America's accidental Electoral College system—stumbled on by the framers, forged in a necessary concession to slaveholding states, and molded to the will of subsequent generations—continues its disenfranchising work today. Winner-take-all suppresses the votes of political minorities in every state, and in much of the South, that political minority remains a racial minority. Thus, despite great gains, many African American voters in southern states have no voice in presidential elections. Only once since 1900 have black citizens in Mississippi, Alabama, Louisiana, and South Carolina had a say in the election of the president—in 1976, when black and white Southerners agreed in their preference for Democrat Jimmy Carter.

Indeed, the promise of equal and exact justice, of one person, one vote, awaits us still.

PART III

THE ELECTORAL COLLEGE TODAY

PART I OF THIS BOOK EXPLAINED HOW THE FRAMERS CREATED AN ELECtoral College for practical reasons, rather than from principled commitments. Having run out of time, patience, and other options, they devised a plan of proxy election. The people would choose wise individuals—those with knowledge of potential candidates—to vote for president on their behalf. These discerning electors would exercise a choice in an environment designed to elicit good judgment and to minimize corrupting influences.

But actual Electoral College operations quickly departed from this vision and continued to change throughout more than two centuries of innovations—the story of part II. Today, our election processes bear little resemblance to the concept sketched out by James Madison in early September 1787. This system has repeatedly malfunctioned, returning problematic and contested results. Moreover, destructive regional factions have used it, hoping to extract concessions in exchange for the presidency. All the while, Americans have sought repeatedly to alter or abolish the Electoral College.

In this book's third and final section, we examine the Electoral College's impact on the United States today. If this mechanism serves us well in the present, by all means, let's keep using it to choose our presidents. But if it fails our national needs and violates our cherished principles, we ought to work for change.

The real test of an election system is how it works on political processes. Are its operations simple and transparent? Does it produce good candidates and competent leaders who have broad popular support? Does it promote a healthy political culture?

Most of all, do all citizens have an equal voice in this process?

Let's examine how today's Electoral College meets these challenges.

CHAPTER 8

Deceptions, Distortions, Dangers, and Dysfunction

The Electoral College Today

Carolyn Dupont and Stephen Clements

WRITING AT LENGTH IN 1816, THOMAS JEFFERSON ARGUED THAT CONstitutions should change over time. "Laws and institutions must go hand in hand with the progress of the human mind," he explained, capturing this idea in an apt metaphor: "We might as well require a man to wear still the coat which fitted him when a boy, as civilized society to remain ever under the regimen of their barbarous ancestors."[1]

When it comes to the electoral college, the coat never did fit properly, and the United States has changed in ways that make us even more poorly suited to its confines. Our body politic has stuffed itself into an institution that cannot accommodate the democratically minded nation we have become. In the process, we've distorted the coat's fabric, pulled it out of shape, and split the seams. In some ways, the mismatch between our democratic ideals and our method of presidential selection seems merely weird and even a bit comical. In other ways, it's downright unhealthy and dangerous. This chapter unpacks the many ways today's Electoral College flies in the face of our values and threatens our national health and stability.

Our Ballots: Obscuring the Process

The United States holds the "real" presidential election every fourth December, when 538 electors convene in their respective state capitals and the District of Columbia and vote. This election determines the winner, as described in and required by the Constitution's Article II. In uncomplicated cycles, this day passes with little note or fanfare, and it seems a mostly ceremonial process whose outcome everyone already knows.

By contrast, Americans focus breathlessly on the election six weeks earlier, when we stream to the polls on the first Tuesday in November. Yet, the Constitution neither prescribes nor protects this process, and our votes that day do not actually select the president.

We misunderstand the events of these two days because our ballots obscure, rather than reflect, several key realities. When a citizen darkens the dot next to their presidential choice, that vote gets credited to the candidate's entire slate of state electors. Thus in 2020, a single vote for, say, Joe Biden in Arkansas translated to a vote for the six electors preselected by the Democratic Party of Arkansas and pledged to vote for its candidate. Likewise, a Donald Trump vote in the same state was credited to the six electors preselected by the state's Republican Party. These hypothetical Arkansas voters likely did not realize that they voted for six people whose names they probably did not know.[2]

Adding to the strangeness, not every vote translates to the same number of electors. A Montanan votes for three electors, while in 2020 a Californian voted for fifty-five. A Texan chose thirty-eight electors, a Georgian sixteen, and a Minnesotan ten.

Ballots did not always obscure election realities this way. Before 1920, all ballots showed electors' names. Some states printed the candidates' names and likenesses atop a column, with their electors identified below. Sometimes electors' names appeared with no party or candidate identified. Either way, a voter chose actual electors. This process accurately represented the workings of American presidential elections, but the task of checking twenty, thirty, or even forty boxes filled presidential selection with tedium and resulted in frequent error.[3]

In the middle decades of the twentieth century, states gradually shifted to using the "short ballot" that eliminated electors' names. Accompanying this change, state laws required votes for candidates to count as votes for their electors. As late as 1969, eighteen states still identified electors on their ballots; today, only six states use ballots that include electors' names.[4]

The need for simplicity and error reduction drove the twentieth-century switch to the short ballot. But in obscuring how our presidential elections work, this move furthered the gap between citizens' perceptions and the actual process. It seems an odd system indeed when each citizen votes for a different number of electors, does so without knowing their names, and uses a ballot that misrepresents this reality.

This ballot obfuscation hides still more strange and troubling aspects of our presidential elections. Consider the role of electors. In the Electoral College's original conception, electors made actual decisions based on their discernment and knowledge of potential candidates. Yet, in essence, today's state laws and public expectations forbid electors' independent judgment. Twenty-nine states plus the District of Columbia require electors to vote in accordance with the state's popular-vote outcome. Others rely on elector pledges and public expectations. These devices render electors entirely superfluous and potentially dangerous, as we'll explore in the next chapter.[5]

Along with those changes described in earlier chapters, these adjustments have altered our presidential election system at its very core, transforming it from a proxy election by experienced and knowledgeable persons into a mathematical formula. The process no longer needs real human electors who show up in state capitals; it only requires math. We are left with an algorithm that accepts a variable from each voter, but then weights these variables very differently.

Nonetheless, we talk about choosing the president as if it's a straightforward democratic process without these obfuscations and distortions. We hear and repeat the rhetorically powerful "let the American people decide." But that phrase fails to reckon with the truth of our system. "We should have the people choose electors whose names they don't know and then let our algorithm decide" lands poorly as a line to inspire public confidence.

These oddities have arisen because we've kept the Electoral College structure while trying to cram modern American democratic sensibilities into it. Like Jefferson's grown man wearing a young boy's coat, our presidential selection process is awkward, irritating, and not very appealing.

But, in fact, our method for choosing the president is much worse than that. As the remainder of this chapter demonstrates, the Electoral College algorithm distorts our votes to a shocking degree. It wildly inflates some votes while utterly erasing others, mocks the ideal of political equality, and has serious consequences for the health of our country.

DISTORTING OUR VOTES

The Electoral College does not directly translate voters' preferences as registered at the ballot box. Rather, it passes our votes through two distorting prisms, warping the results like a fun-house mirror.

The inequality begins with the number of electors allotted to each state. A state's allocation of electors equals its representation in Congress, making our votes unequal in this very first step. For example, in 2020, every 193,000 people in Wyoming got an elector, as opposed to Californians, who got one elector per 717,000 residents. Nebraskans got one elector for every 385,000 people, while Texans got one for 753,000.[6]

If electors were allocated proportionally to population, each state would have received one elector for every 607,000 people in the 2020 election. That year, fifteen states were "underrepresented" in the Electoral College, meaning that they had fewer electors than a strictly proportional distribution would provide. Large states were most underrepresented, with California having ten fewer electors and Texas getting nine fewer than under a proportional allocation.[7]

This underrepresentation arises, in part, from Congress's 1929 decision to permanently cap the House of Representatives at 435 members. As our population grows, large states with more rapidly growing populations—California, Texas, and Florida—cannot gain a proportional increase in the House of Representatives. Thus, the disparity in electoral vote allocation between the smallest states and the largest has increased since 1929, and this inequality will likely continue to grow.

Meanwhile, twenty-nine states and the District of Columbia were overrepresented in 2020—they had more electors than under a proportional representation. Nine of these overrepresented small states received double or triple the number of electors that proportional representation would confer. Only six states were allocated a number of electors roughly equal to one for every 607,000 people.[8]

Thus, each American's vote assumes a wildly different weight in choosing the president. Yet, incredibly, the process then further compounds the disparities with another extraordinarily distorting layer. Winner-take-all, the practice of awarding a state's entire slate of electors to its popular-vote winner, takes American voting inequality to new heights. This feature silences the voice of all Americans who did not vote with the majority in their state, and in fact, gives their votes to electors for the candidate they did not choose.

Most states have allotted their electors this way for well over a century, a development detailed in chapters 4 and 5. The practice remains so deeply engrained today that it has long since acquired the aura of timeless principle. But it bears reminding that the framers did not create this mechanism, and none ever sanctioned it. Several condemned it outright as it came into use, and a generation of early political leaders fought vigorously against it. Electoral college defenders frequently paper over the extra-constitutional and embattled origins of winner-take-all.

The gross inequities of winner-take-all often escape public attention. Election maps often rely on its logic to display a patchwork of "solidly" Red or Blue states (as in the results from 2020, the most recent presidential election, depicted in figure 8.1). These depictions obscure the real and vibrant political diversity in each state. A county-based map (figure 8.2, also from 2020) offers a more accurate representation, displaying large swathes of blue in "Red" states, and significant patches of red in "Blue" states.[9]

A comparison of the two maps demonstrates how winner-take-all obscures, flattens, and distorts America's political realities. Figure 8.1 would suggest, for example, that every single voter in Mississippi and Alabama chose Republican Donald Trump in 2020. But the more

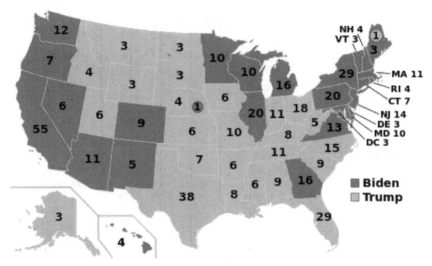

Figure 8.1. Traditional electoral map (2020). *Wikimedia Commons*

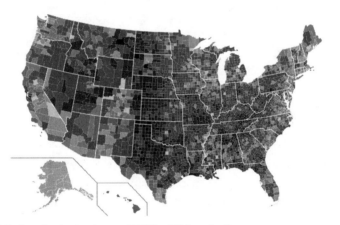

Figure 8.2. County electoral map (2020). *Wikimedia Commons*

detailed figure 8.2 reveals that many counties in these two states leaned heavily toward the Democratic candidate, Joe Biden. (Readers will see America's political diversity illustrated even more vividly by exploring the many colorful online maps that show county and even precinct-level results from 2020.)

This flattening of our political diversity translates to an egregious distortion of citizens' votes. Despite Mississippi's and Alabama's many and large blue splotches, only Donald Trump won any electoral votes from those two states. The 41 percent of Mississippi voters and 37 percent of Alabamians who cast Democratic ballots lost any say at all in the actual presidential election. Even more troubling, their votes went to Donald Trump—the candidate they did not want to win. Figure 8.3 offers a close-up view of Mississippi and Alabama's counties.

We find similar distortions throughout the country. Most Americans are shocked to learn, for example, that in 2020 Donald Trump won more votes in California than in any other state. They find it incredible that

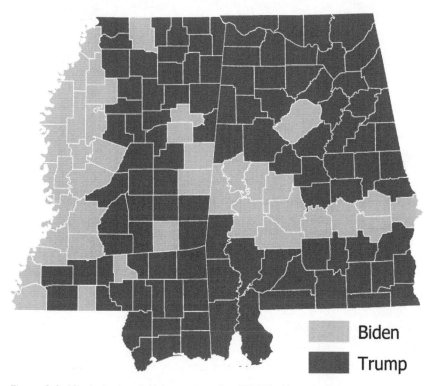

Figure 8.3. Mississippi and Alabama counties (2020). *Maps by Ryan Kelly, compiled with data from "2020 United States Presidential Election in Alabama," Wikipedia, https://en.wikipedia.org/wiki/2020_United_States_presidential_election_in_Alabama, and "2020 United States Presidential Election in Mississippi," Wikipedia, https://en.wikipedia.org/wiki/2020_United_States_presidential_election_in_Mississippi*

2020 Presidential Election
Purple America

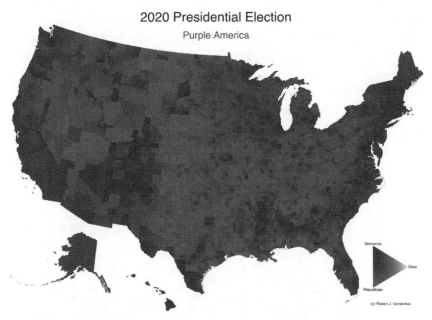

Figure 8.4. Color-spectrum political map of the United States (2020). *Courtesy of Robert J. Vanderbei, https://vanderbei.princeton.edu/JAVA/election2020/*

more Texans voted for Joe Biden than did New Yorkers. Of course, those Trump voters in California got no electors and could not help their candidate. Neither could the Biden voters in Texas.

America's real political diversity and the accompanying winner-take-all distortions also reveal themselves in figure 8.4. This map expresses county election results through a red-blue color spectrum. Tellingly, much of the map appears purple (the darkest shading), demonstrating that very similar numbers of Republicans and Democrats turn out in many areas of the country. Close examination of this map yields significant surprises. Much of California, for example, shows up quite purple. The Deep South appears far less ruby-red (the lighter shading) than traditional electoral maps lead us to believe.[10]

One more set of visuals highlights the political realities and gross distortions that winner-take-all obscures. Table 8.1 shows final 2020 outcomes in each of the twenty-seven states where the winner garnered less than 59 percent of the vote. Follow the right-hand column down, and

Table 8.1. States Where the Winner Finished with Less Than 59 Percent of the Vote (2020)

State	Winning Candidate Percentage	Losing Candidate Percentage
AK	52.8	42.8
CO	55.4	41.9
DE	58.7	39.8
CT	59.3	39.2
FL	51.2	47.9
IL	57.5	40.6
IN	57.0	41.0
IA	51.01	44.9
KS	56.1	41.5
LA	58.5	39.9
ME	53.1	44.0
MN	52.4	45.3
MS	57.5	41.0
MO	56.8	41.4
MT	56.9	45.0
NE	58.2	39.2
NH	52.7	45.4
NJ	57.1	41.4
NM	54.3	43.5
OH	53.3	45.2
OR	56.5	40.4
RI	59.4	38.6
SC	55.1	43.4
TX	52.1	46.5
UT	58.1	37.6
VA	54.1	44.0
WA	58.0	38.8

SOURCE: TABLE CREATED BY THE AUTHOR; DATA COMPILED FROM THE AMERICAN PRESIDENCY PROJECT, UNIVERSITY OF CALIFORNIA, SANTA BARBARA, HTTPS://WWW.PRESIDENCY.UCSB.EDU/ STATISTICS/ELECTIONS/2020.

Table 8.2. Battleground States' Margins of Victory

State	Winning Candidate Percentage	Losing Candidate Percentage
AZ	49.4	49.0
GA	49.5	49.2
MI	50.6	47.8
NC	49.9	48.6
NV	50.1	47.7
PA	50.0	48.8
WI	49.4	48.8

SOURCE: TABLE CREATED BY THE AUTHOR; DATA COMPILED FROM THE AMERICAN PRESIDENCY PROJECT, UNIVERSITY OF CALIFORNIA, SANTA BARBARA, HTTPS://WWW.PRESIDENCY.UCSB.EDU/STATISTICS/ELECTIONS/2020.

you'll see the large share of each state's vote—more than 40 percent in most cases—silenced by winner-take-all.

The large number of Americans routinely disenfranchised in presidential races appears even more starkly in the seven additional states—the notorious "swing" states—where the 2020 winner finished by a razor-thin margin (see table 8.2). In two of these, Democrat Joe Biden won with a margin of less than .4 percentage points. Yet, the distorting prism of winner-take-all sends these significant minorities away empty-handed and hands the entire slate of electors to the majority who won, no matter the size of their lead. It's hard to justify an election system that routinely silences so many citizens.

Contrasting the total popular and electoral vote outcomes from these seven states illustrates how winner-take-all's gross distortions increase exponentially in closely contested states. While Biden won only 49.66 percent of the total popular vote from these seven states, he got 84 percent of the Electoral College votes. By contrast, Donald Trump won 48.74 percent of the popular vote but only 16 percent of these states' electoral votes.

Other comparisons illustrate the arbitrary slicing and dicing of the vote that winner-take-all achieves. Six million Californians voted for

Donald Trump in 2020, yet they received *zero* voice in the Electoral College. Meanwhile, winner-take-all awarded seventeen Electoral College votes to 1.7 million Joe Biden voters across five small states. Most Americans struggle to find fairness in a system that gives 0 votes to 6 million citizens, while crediting seventeen votes to 1.7 million people. A distortion of this degree in a race for any other office—governor, senator, or county sheriff—would spark outrage, and justly so.[11]

As another way to describe the distortions of winner-take-all, those 6 million California Republicans cast about 3.75 percent of the nationwide popular vote, but they could not help their candidate at all. Yet, the 1.7 million small-state Biden voters, who cast less than 1 percent of the popular vote, gave their candidate more than 6 percent of the electoral votes he needed to win.

As another illuminating example, consider a rural, Red-leaning Illinois voter who lives a mere ten yards from the Indiana state line. He can hear the dogs barking and the roosters crowing on the Indiana side. He peers up at the same night sky as his neighbor in the next state, and the two share a cultural world. When they discuss politics, they find themselves quite agreed. But their votes for president carry vastly different weights. The right-leaning Hoosier will be represented in his state's Electoral College, while the Illinois conservative gets no voice at all. The accidents of ten yards and a state line make their votes unequal.

This arbitrary distortion happens in every state, in every presidential election. Take the 26,780 Trump voters in Augusta, Georgia, unrepresented in their state's 2020 Electoral College. Had they lived and voted just across the river in North Augusta, South Carolina, their votes would have counted. Likewise, 328,151 Joe Biden voters in St. Louis County, Missouri, had their votes given to the candidate they did not choose. Their votes would have mattered if they lived in East St. Louis, Illinois, on the other side of the Mississippi River.[12]

Isolated data points can demonstrate disadvantages and advantages for voters in small and large as well as Red and Blue states. All told, the Electoral College overrepresents voters in small states, and at present, the geographic distribution of the parties gives Republicans an easier path to an Electoral College win without an accompanying popular-vote majority. However, we should not get bogged down in an analysis of *which* voters this system advantages or disadvantages. Voting patterns shift over time, and the party disadvantaged today may be the advantaged party of tomorrow.

Rather, we should ask this question: By what logic or fundamental values should an election system disenfranchise *any* American, or weight *any* votes more heavily than others?

Indeed, most Americans would prefer a system based on the straightforward and widely shared principle of political equality.[13]

DISTORTING CAMPAIGNS

A traveler from reliably Red Kentucky arrives at Tampa International Airport during the last week of October 2016. During the thirty-five-minute shuttle ride to her Clearwater Beach hotel, the driver plays the radio, and its blaring transforms the thirty-five-minute trip into a special kind of aural hell. Back home in Kentucky, radio ads feature only state and local races. But the ugliness and constancy of presidential ads in the Sunshine State vex and dispirit our Kentucky traveler. One ad highlighting Donald Trump's childish incompetence follows quickly after another denouncing Hillary Clinton's greedy corruption. The ads come so thick and fast that the listener memorizes them all, and then tunes them out.

The election season contrast between Kentucky and Florida's airwaves highlights how the Electoral College distorts American presidential campaigns. Candidates have long since accommodated their strategies to the system's realities. Presidential campaigns completely ignore voters in "solidly" Blue or Red states, while concentrating their resources in the increasingly tiny handful of "swing" states. Why waste money or a candidate's time in states they cannot win, or in those they are sure to win?

Much empirical evidence demonstrates this phenomenon as an enduring pattern for at least the last half century. In 2016, Donald Trump campaigned personally in nineteen states, while Hillary Clinton appeared in only thirteen. Half of the states got no campaign visit by either candidate. Similarly, in 2012 President Obama and Mitt Romney personally campaigned in only ten states.[14]

Campaign spending follows the same pattern. In 2008, campaigns poured 99.75 percent of political advertising dollars into eighteen states, leaving a paltry .25 percent for the remaining thirty-two states. Similarly, they spent two-thirds of their 2012 resources in only four swing states: Ohio, Florida, Virginia, and Iowa.[15]

In close elections, strategies around resources may decide outcomes. In 2016, Hillary Clinton's campaign famously took for granted the "Blue wall" of Michigan, Wisconsin, and Pennsylvania. She made almost no appearances there until she realized her peril in the campaign's final weeks. Clinton paid dearly for this miscalculation, as Trump won a surprise upset in those very states by slender margins, sending him to an Electoral College win.

The outsized importance of a single swing state can propel local issues to national significance. In 2000, the election-night map left both George W. Bush and Al Gore dependent on the final disposition of Florida's twenty-five electoral votes. After nearly six weeks of recounts, court intervention, and obsessive national focus on hanging "chads," the vote came down to a tiny margin of 537, giving the state and the presidency to Bush.

But events earlier that spring involving a small Cuban boy and one Florida community may have determined the election's outcome. When a boat carrying five-year-old Elián González and his mother from Cuba capsized at sea, the mother drowned, but the child was taken to relatives in Miami. Most Americans believed González should return to his father in Cuba, but Cuban Americans in Florida insisted he remain in the United States.[16] Democratic candidate and then vice president Al Gore desperately needed a Florida win and feared alienating this key constituency in the state. Gore carefully parsed the issue, distancing himself from the Clinton administration and often appearing equivocal. Nonetheless, after the Clinton administration seized the boy and reunited him with his father, Cuban Americans in Miami-Dade County punished the Democratic Party, voting overwhelmingly for Republican George W. Bush. Absent this ordeal, Gore would likely have won from Miami-Dade alone far more than the 537 Florida votes he needed. Voters in a tiny corner of South Florida may have dictated the outcome for the entire nation.[17]

According to one analyst, the 2024 election will hinge on just four key states. With forty-three electoral votes between them, Arizona, Georgia, Nevada, and Wisconsin will get the lion's share of media attention, campaign spending, and candidate visits. Residents of those states should prepare themselves with a bag of ear plugs and a television mute button in good working order.[18]

As for the rest of us? We're already "in the bag."

THE DANGERS OF A MINORITY VOTE WINNER

Dr. Judith Best, a political scientist who published extensively on the Electoral College, emerged as one of the staunchest scholarly defenders of the Electoral College in the later decades of the twentieth century. Best's congressional testimony helped persuade key Senate leaders like Orin Hatch and Daniel Patrick Moynihan to reject a constitutional amendment for a national popular vote. Among other arguments, Best maintained that this system rarely put a candidate in office without an accompanying popular-vote victory. Indeed, at the time of her testimonies in the 1970s and 1990s, a popular-vote loser had not won the Electoral College since 1888, and for most of the twentieth century, the Electoral College results typically magnified popular-vote victories. Best's fierce advocacy for the Electoral College notwithstanding, she conceded that an electoral system that routinely elevated a minority-vote winner to office would be "simply indefensible."[19]

America has arrived at this moment of the Electoral College's indefensibility. In recent elections, this system has routinely undone or threatened to undo the majority's will. In 2000, the Electoral College sent George W. Bush to the White House with 271 electoral votes, though he lost the popular vote to Al Gore by just over 500,000 votes. Then in 2016, this system produced an even more shocking result: Donald Trump lost the popular election to Hillary Clinton by a whopping 3 million votes and yet still won a 304–227 Electoral College victory. These two anomalous outcomes came twice in just five election cycles.

The Electoral College also came perilously close to "misfiring" two other times in recent elections. In 2004, Bush won reelection with a 286–251 victory. Despite John Kerry's popular-vote loss of 3 million, he would have won the Electoral College if a mere 1 percent of Ohio voters—60,000—had shifted. And in 2020, Joe Biden would have lost if fewer than 50,000 voters in Georgia, Arizona, and Wisconsin had gone for Trump, even though Biden's popular-vote margin topped 7 million. Notably, the near-misses of 2004 and 2020 did not come in elections with close popular-vote margins. Rather, the Electoral College algorithm threatened to undo wide and decisive popular-vote wins.[20]

Thus, the Electoral College result has differed dramatically from popular-vote outcomes in four of the last six elections. Given the country's current partisan geography, these kinds of misfires may well threaten elections in the foreseeable future. Blue voters are increasingly concentrated "inefficiently" in urban and coastal areas, while a handful of sparsely populated and overrepresented midwestern states lean heavily Red. The number of truly competitive swing states has narrowed, so that elections will increasingly hinge on outcomes in fewer states and, often, only tiny margins in those states.

Minority-vote winners lack the broad legitimacy to govern effectively. George W. Bush and Donald Trump, the two twenty-first-century presidents elected without a popular-vote win, took office with the highest disapproval ratings since polling began. Though the invasion of Iraq gave Bush a temporary boost sufficient to win reelection, his approval plummeted again in his second term. For his part, Trump never attained even as much as a 50 percent approval rating during his entire four years, and his average approval represented record lows. Political polarization blossomed under both presidential tenures.[21]

Presidents who represent only minority factions struggle to garner public support for their policies and cannot build necessary coalitions in Congress. President Trump, for example, could not pass the signature policies that propelled his candidacy: He never repealed the Affordable Care Act nor achieved immigration reform, including a fully funded border wall with Mexico. The machinery of American democracy grinds slowly, but a president with no mandate can bring the wheels of government to a screeching halt, sapping respect and confidence from American institutions.

Most nations suffer occasional instability. In such times, broad support for political leaders proves harder than ever to win. Yet in precisely these times, public confidence and legitimacy matter most. The wider the gap between electoral and popular-vote outcomes, the more citizens struggle to embrace the winner. Polarization, turbulence, and turmoil soar to new heights.

Only a person who has lived under a rock for the last ten years fails to appreciate the United States' extraordinary political fragility at this precise moment. How might another minority-vote winner send us on paths we should all fear to contemplate?

The United States needs a system for choosing the president that puts a person in the White House with broad public confidence, every single time.

PROMOTING DYSFUNCTION: OUR TWO-PARTY SYSTEM

The framers wrote the Constitution and approved a system of electors with no party system in mind. But as chapter 4 demonstrates, the mutually hostile political parties that rose in the nation's early years shaped and even warped the electoral system to extract its maximum partisan benefit. Unsurprisingly, the electoral features forged in political antagonism prop up today's troubled party structure and nourish its dysfunction.

Electoral college operations embed our elections tightly with the two major political parties. Much of this entanglement comes from state statutes, which authorize the state Democratic and Republican parties to name the electors in advance, usually through a party convention or nominating committee. Both parties choose electors as a reward for loyalty, service, and generous contribution records. (Note that these qualifications stand almost in exact opposition to those Hamilton named in 1788: "discernment" and freedom from "sinister bias.") In most states, the law obligates electors to support their party's nominee.

At the national level, too, our system empowers the major parties. Most significantly, party machinery monopolizes the choice of candidates to whom the electors must pledge. The national parties decide which states will vote in early primaries and caucuses. Since the most zealous party loyalists vote more heavily in primaries and caucuses, the task of winnowing the candidate pool falls to extreme partisans in a handful of states. By the time most Americans vote in their state's primaries, the choices have narrowed significantly and, often, distastefully to large numbers of voters. Moreover, in many states the parties permit only their own registered voters to vote in primaries, excluding Independents and third-party registrants from the process. Further discounting the people's voice, national party operatives and leaders often work behind the scenes to boost preferred candidates to the top. It's a process not likely to produce centrist candidates with broad support, and, for many, the results often mock the notion of a real choice for president.

The Electoral College math of getting to 270 further props up our two-party system. Since third-party choices threaten to siphon away electoral votes sufficient to prevent the major candidates from reaching 270, the parties work to nip these challenges in the bud. Thus much-needed options that voters crave face extraordinarily high hurdles to success. State election laws make it hard for third-party candidates to get on the ballot. Moreover, voters continue to incline toward even unappealing major-party candidates, since third-party options often feel like "wasted" votes.

It's easy to see that our system can't be changed without upsetting the party system. But perhaps that wouldn't be so bad.

It's no secret that these days large numbers of Americans dislike both political parties. Many citizens feel "politically homeless"—unrepresented by the policies, rhetoric, and candidates of either party. This dissatisfaction reveals itself in the more than 40 percent of Americans who identify as political Independents, growing numbers who choose third-party candidates, and in the many citizens who vote for down-ballot races without casting a vote for president. In the past several cycles, many Americans yearned deeply for other options but, in the end, cast a vote they considered "the lesser of two evils."[22]

It's a disheartening commentary. In some eras past, America's two large parties functioned more positively. When a two-party system works well, each side negotiates across the interests of its coalition. The parties compromise and promote centrism, tamp down extremism, and elicit pragmatic behavior from party leaders. These dynamics should produce candidates that represent a broad swath of the electorate.

Both parties once displayed an ideological fluidity that helped them build broad coalitions and work toward consensus. From the late 1940s through the 1990s, Americans often voted across party lines.

But our two parties have changed dramatically in recent decades, driven by geographic and demographic shifts, a purposefully polarizing media landscape, and changes in each party's constituencies.

Given the bright, clean lines that currently divide our parties, Americans rarely vote across party lines these days. Most of us vote *against* the opposing party—whom we regard as out to destroy the country—rather than *for* a candidate whose character, experience, and policies resonate with our values. Our political parties increasingly thrive on doctrinaire ideological rigidity, and they frequently pander to extremists, especially in state-level primaries. The accompanying bitter polarization threatens our cohesion and political stability.[23]

Under current conditions, the Electoral College incentivizes this polarization. It offers multiple paths to the presidency with only a minority of voters. Why should a party appeal to the broad center when a candidate can win with small numbers of voters in just a few states? By promoting political polarization, the Electoral College plays a key role in our ugly, dysfunctional partisan landscape.

Consider for a moment the absurdity of two rigid parties in a country of 158 million voters. Is it really possible that all Americans fit neatly into one of two boxes? Hardly. Yet, our system forces exactly that choice. Voters prioritize one or two issues and then accept the party package for the remaining ones. What's a fiscal conservative with socially liberal inclinations to do? Or a pro-life voter who also believes passionately in protecting the environment?

Moreover, today's political polarization actually makes us more poorly informed. We consume media that presents only the facts we want to know, rather than getting information that unpacks the real complexity of our most vexing problems. With our tribal identities on hyper-alert, we cannot objectively consider arguments and process information. Making this situation even worse, we tend to live close to and interact regularly only with others of our "tribe." These social silos reinforce our skewed political understandings and our intense political prejudices. As a nation, we are growing meaner and dumber.[24]

We need a more fluid configuration that responds effectively to the electorate, promotes policies with broad consensus, and pushes our leaders toward solutions. This more flexible arrangement could offer multiple parties, or it might simply transform our existing parties into healthier and less brittle coalitions that shift slowly but responsively over time. A more positive and productive scenario would offer Americans real options, rather than promote rigid categories and produce candidates that appeal only to the extremes.

By itself, the Electoral College has not caused America's political dysfunction. Dismantling it will not completely solve this problem. Yet as long as we keep the Electoral College, we prop up our current rigid arrangements and foreclose desperately needed paths out of this mess.

* * *

This is the United States: a major world superpower with a deceptive, distorting, dangerous, and dysfunctional system for choosing its leader.

We've limped along under this arrangement for 235 years. As the country has changed, we've crammed our new sensibilities into this old suit. But the seams have torn in many places. It's too short in the arms, and our shoulders can barely move. It's time to put these old clothes in a museum where they belong and fashion a system that fits our democratic values.

CHAPTER 9

An Indefensible System

By what rationale can we justify the Electoral College as the best way to elect the president of the United States? At its core, the question asks whether we can justify gross and widespread political inequality.

Yet, Electoral College champions try mightily to defend this system. They speak of today's algorithm with the reverence of original intent, papering over the gap between the framers' plan and our present-day system. Their rhetoric ignores, minimizes, or repackages the vast inequities this mechanism creates. They describe the Electoral College as a brilliant device that fosters positive outcomes.

But these advocates rely almost entirely on rhetoric and assertions and rarely offer data to back up their claims. And why would they? Easily obtainable evidence undermines every pillar in their argument and leaves us to confront one startling truth: Our current system for electing the president reflects no valuable principle, confers no benefits, and endangers our republic.

Let's examine the Electoral College defenders' case.

LARGE-STATE AND URBAN DOMINANCE

Electoral college defenders argue that this system prevents voters in more heavily populated regions of the country from dominating elections. As a writer on this topic recently argued, "The core function of the Electoral College is to require presidential candidates to appeal to the voters of a sufficient number of large and smaller states, rather than just try to run up big margins in a handful of the biggest states, cities, or regions."[1] The underlying assumption is that under a direct popular vote, a candidate could win with support only from large states or even only from urban areas.

We hear this claim expressed in several ways. Pundits insist that "without the electoral college, California and New York will decide elections." Other times, the argument highlights the heavy concentration of voters in cities, suggesting that "Los Angeles and New York will dominate our elections without the electoral college." A similar concern shows up in statements like "the electoral college gives rural Americans a voice."[2]

These claims sound scary. They aim to stoke conservative fears of domination by large, left-leaning states. (No one ever says, for example, "without the electoral college, Texas and Florida will decide elections.") For right-of-center voters in America's heartland, alarm bells ring at the idea of wild-eyed liberal elites from Hollywood and Wall Street controlling the presidency.

Eliciting fear may be exactly the point, because none of these claims is true. Take the allegation that a few populous states would dominate presidential elections under a national popular vote (NPV). It's an easily testable assertion, though data of any kind rarely accompanies these claims. About 154.6 million Americans voted in the 2020 presidential election. Under an NPV, it would have taken 77.3 million (plus one) votes to win.

Even if *every single voter* in the nine largest states voted for the *same* candidate in 2020, that person would have fallen short of the majority needed to win the presidency.

Of course, every single voter in a state doesn't vote the same way, and they never will. But this hypothetical example illustrates how fear of large-state domination rests on the false assumption that citizens of a state vote as a monolith—it's the logic of winner-take-all dominating our thinking. The false argument ignores the real political diversity of Americans in every part of the country.

A better test of the claim about large-state domination relies on Americans' actual votes. Table 9.1 lists 37 states by population, from highest to lowest, along with Democrat Joe Biden's 2020 popular-vote

Table 9.1. 2020 Biden Popular-Vote Totals in 37 States

State	Biden Votes	Cumulative Total
CA	11,110,250	11,110,250
TX	5,259,126	16,369,376
FL	5,297,045	21,666,421
NY	5,230,985	26,897,406
PA	3,458,229	30,355,635
IL	3,471,915	33,827,550
OH	2,679,165	36,506,715
GA	2,473,633	38,980,348
NC	2,684,292	41,664,640
MI	2,804,040	44,468,680
NJ	2,608,335	47,077,015
VA	2,413,568	49,490,583
WA	2,369,612	51,860,195
AZ	1,672,143	53,532,338
MA	2,382,202	55,914,540
TN	1,143,711	57,058,251
IN	1,242,416	58,300,667
MD	1,985,023	60,285,690
MO	1,253,014	61,538,704
CO	1,804,352	63,343,056
WI	1,630,866	64,973,922
MN	1,717,077	66,690,999
SC	1,091,541	67,782,540
AL	849,624	68,632,164
LA	856,034	69,488,198
KY	772,474	70,260,672
OR	1,340,383	71,601,055
OK	503,890	72,104,945
CT	1,080,680	73,185,625

UT	560,282	73,745,907
IA	759,061	74,504,968
NV	703,486	75,208,454
AR	423,932	75,632,386
MS	539,398	76,171,784
KS	570,323	76,742,107
NM	501,614	77,243,721
NE	374,583	77,618,304

SOURCE: TABLE CREATED BY THE AUTHOR; DATA COMPILED FROM THE AMERICAN PRESIDENCY PROJECT, UNIVERSITY OF CALIFORNIA, SANTA BARBARA, HTTPS://WWW.PRESIDENCY.UCSB.EDU/STATISTICS/ELECTIONS/2020.

total from each state. The right-hand column tracks the cumulative totals. Run your eyes down this column and see whether Biden got 77.3 million popular votes from only large states. The table reveals that he did not reach this number from even the twenty-five most populous states. Nor did votes from as many as the thirty-five most populous states seal that critical "win" number.

In the final analysis, it took votes from each of the thirty-seven most populous states to get Joe Biden to the winning threshold of 77.3 million. Such a win hardly represents dominance "by a few large states."

Compare the need, in this scenario, for votes from thirty-seven states under an NPV, with Biden's Electoral College win, which relied on just twenty-five states, plus the District of Columbia.

Which method of counting the vote requires support from more citizens in more varied regions of the country?

In fact, it's the Electoral College that allows domination by a small group of large states, and such a scenario is not at all far-fetched. Under the distribution of electors in 2020, a candidate could have accrued 270 electoral votes by winning only tiny margins in the eleven largest states, as table 9.2 shows. Partisan tendencies in these states have prevented such a lop-sided victory, but small shifts could make this scenario a reality. In fact, based on 2020 results, Democrats would need only to increase votes in Texas by about 631,000 and by even smaller margins in

Table 9.2. 2020 Electoral Votes of the Eleven Largest States

State	Electoral Votes	Cumulative Total
CA	55	55
TX	38	93
FL	29	122
NY	29	151
PA	20	171
IL	20	191
OH	18	209
MI	16	225
GA	16	241
NC	15	256
NJ	14	270

SOURCE: TABLE CREATED BY THE AUTHOR.

three other states—Florida, Ohio, and North Carolina—to accumulate the magic 270 electoral votes with only the eleven largest states.

The 2020 census slightly shifted the allocation of electors, but even under the 2024 Electoral College distribution, a candidate can win with only twelve states.

Does a candidate ever win all the large states? Indeed, they do. Ronald Reagan won a sweeping 489–49 Electoral College victory in 1980, one of the largest ever. Tellingly, however, his greater than 90 percent margin in the Electoral College masked a much slimmer popular vote of only 50.7 percent. Reagan got to the crucial 270 win number by capturing the twelve largest states. It made no difference that he ultimately won a total of forty-four states—the twelve largest would have put him in the White House. The distorting math of winner-take-all inflated his 50.7 percent popular-vote margin by almost 40 percent, and we recall Reagan's 90.9 percent Electoral College victory as one of the greatest landslides in American presidential history.[3]

In 2008, Barack Obama nearly accomplished the same feat as Ronald Reagan. He won ten of the eleven largest states. He achieved the critical threshold of 270 with the votes of only fourteen of the seventeen largest states, demonstrating yet again how the Electoral College can permit large-state domination. To be clear, Obama's win, like Reagan's, did not rely on this narrow base alone. He went on to a victory in twenty-eight states, adding Washington, DC, and two additional electoral votes from Nebraska. His ultimate Electoral College win was 365–173, and he won a popular-vote victory of 52.8 percent. Yet, had his wins stopped at fourteen of the seventeen largest states, he would have captured the presidency—thanks to the idiosyncratic skewing of the Electoral College system.[4]

Every American should tremble at the staggering arbitrariness that would permit a victory drawn from only twelve large states—no matter who the candidate. Such a win would represent the worst sort of minority rule.[5]

Contrary to the common claim, then, that the Electoral College prevents domination by the large states, it actually *facilitates* wins by a small number of voters in select regions of the country. The threshold for a popular-vote majority is much, much higher and requires a much broader distribution of votes in a far greater number of states.

The related assertion that the Electoral College "gives rural Americans a voice" is also demonstrably untrue. Like the "large-state domination" myth, this claim reverses an important fact: The Electoral College, with its winner-take-all system, silences millions of rural voters in every presidential election. Vote totals from "liberal" California demonstrate this truth. Recall from the last chapter that 34 percent of California voters—more than 6 million people, many in rural parts of the state—pulled the lever for Donald Trump in 2020. Yet, winner-take-all effectively gave these 6 million votes to Joe Biden in the form of fifty-five electoral votes. In that cycle, winner-take-all also silenced millions of conservative rural voters in New York, Illinois, Georgia, Maryland, Pennsylvania, and Nevada, to name a few. It threw out more liberal votes from Texas's Rio Grande Valley; from the Mississippi River corridor in Mississippi, Arkansas, and Louisiana; and across a large swath of central Alabama. Voters in rural areas surrounding the Great Lakes also lost their voices, as did those in the Pacific Northwest interior and the Shenandoah Valley of Virginia.

Only a direct, national popular vote would prevent domination by voters in a handful of states and force candidates to pursue support from every region of the country.

Protecting the Small States

The Electoral College gives disproportionate weight to voters in the small states. As noted in the previous chapter, by the 2020 elector distribution, each elector from Wyoming represents 193,000 people, while California got one elector for every 717,000 people. The 9,697,498 people living in the ten smallest states have thirty-three electors. Almost the exact same number of people live in New Jersey, but New Jerseyans get only fourteen electors.

Electoral college defenders don't deny this fact, though they rarely note it explicitly. Rather, they suggest that these states deserve this boost. Without this plan, these apologists maintain, small states could not defend their interests from domination by the large states. This assertion plays on the theme presented above, but it merits separate attention.

Do small states, in fact, have an interest that requires protection on account of their size? In other words, does state size dictate a set of policy concerns, with small-state residents voting one way and large-state citizens voting another?

Certainly, a state's geographic location, whether in the South, North, Great Plains, mountains, or coasts, may impact its citizens' interests. A state's unique economy, natural resources, demographic patterns, religious culture, and history may shape its citizens' political ideology and voting habits. But the mere fact that a state has a relatively small population, in and of itself, creates no identifiable interest that leads residents to choose one candidate over another. In other words, state size dictates neither policy positions nor ideological leanings.

Data from small states confirm that size does not predict voting patterns. Small-state citizens generally vote with the same diversity as do all other states. As table 9.3 shows, in 2020, five of the ten least-populous states favored the Democratic candidate and five favored the Republican.

Table 9.3. 2020 Vote Totals in the Ten Smallest States

State	Population	Democratic	Republican
NH	1,395,647	**424,937** (52.76%)	365,660 (45.36%)
ME	1,372,559	**435,072** (53.09%)	360,737 (44.02%)
MT	1,112,668	244,786 (40.55%)	**343,602** (56.92%)
RI	1,110,822	**307,486** (59.39%)	199,922 (38.61%)
DE	1,017,551	**296,268** (58.74%)	200,603 (39.77%)
SD	908,414	150,471 (35.61%)	**261,043** (61.77%)
ND	811,044	114,902 (31.76%)	**235,595** (65.11%)
AK	740,339	153,778 (42.77%)	**189,951** (52.83%)
VT	648,279	**242,820** (66.09%)	112,704 (30.67%)
WY	580,175	73,491 (26.55%)	**193,559** (69.94%)
TOTAL		2,444,401	2,463,376

SOURCE: TABLE CREATED BY THE AUTHOR; DATA COMPILED FROM THE AMERICAN PRESIDENCY PROJECT, HTTPS://WWW.PRESIDENCY.UCSB.EDU/STATISTICS/ELECTIONS/2020.

Even more telling, taken as a group, these states gave nearly the exact same number of popular votes to each candidate: about 2,450,000.[6]

Additional data points demonstrate the lack of any unifying small-state interest. The two smallest states, Vermont and Wyoming, differ in population by a mere 68,000 people, but their citizens voted almost as mirror opposites: Vermont cast 242,820, or 66 percent, of its votes for the Democratic presidential candidate, while Wyoming gave 193,559, or nearly 70 percent, of its votes to the Republican candidate.

Put another way, size really does not matter.

Americans are quick to decry artificial and arbitrary political advantages, and most of us believe that everyone deserves an equal opportunity. It seems a doomed argument, then, that some Americans deserve a voting-power "boost" based on where they live.

Federalism

A recent X (formerly Twitter) posting expressed the popular argument about "federalism" in a dire form: "The National Popular Vote would erase state lines. America would no longer be a federation of states."[7]

Can you say "hyperbole"?

The term "federalism" rings with the overtones of a high-minded and esoteric principle worth preserving at all costs. Yet, the word simply expresses the notion of concurrent sovereignties: The United States is a union of *people* and of *the states* at the same time. The federal government acts on both the states and individuals. Moreover, our Constitution carefully identifies and erects boundaries between federal authority and state jurisdictions.

To be clear, states are important. They serve vital functions that best remain in their purview. For many purposes, fifty sets of distinctive institutions, cultures, and regulations is a positive aspect of our system.

But abolishing the Electoral College will not alter our federal arrangement. The Constitution's division of powers between federal and state governments would remain fully intact under an NPV. So would the Senate, which represents each state equally in Congress.

An NPV would not wipe out state borders, state constitutions, governors, state legislatures, state courts, state budgets, state police, or any other of the many agencies in states. These jurisdictions and the powers reserved to them would remain firm. The Electoral College plays no role in any of these.

States could continue to run our presidential elections under an NPV. And states would continue to adhere to minimum federal election standards.

An Electoral College defender who recently used this argument in an op-ed titled "The Electoral College: Last Defense of Federalism" stated his case in typical form: "The Electoral College was designed to both protect the interests of the states and the people."[8]

What does it mean to "protect the interests of the states"? An important discussion during the Constitution's creation illuminates why a distinction between the states and the people doesn't always make sense. James Madison and his allies understood that advocates for states' interests often overstated their claims, especially when balanced against the rights of individuals. "Can we forget for whom we are forming a government?" asked James Wilson. "Is it for men, or for the imaginary beings called states?" Alexander Hamilton joined the fray, asking, "[because] the states are a collection of individual men, which ought we to respect most: the rights of the people composing [the states], or of the artificial beings resulting from the composition?"[9]

Do "states" have interests separate from their people's needs and concerns? Americans vote as citizens of both a state and a nation, but they don't chuck one identity or the other when they choose a president.

Moreover, as discussed earlier, the "interests of a state" are neither clear cut nor monolithic. Indeed, citizens of a state vote its interests in many, often divergent, ways. West Virginia, for example, has a clear interest in extractive mining. Some West Virginians want a pro-coal president; they will enthusiastically support a candidate promising to revitalize that industry. But West Virginians also vote coal interests in the opposite direction. Some prioritize the industry's environmental and human costs when they vote, pulling the lever for a more environmentally conscious candidate.

Consider a state like Texas, with its heavy reliance on oil and natural gas. High gas prices benefit the state's oil producers, create jobs in this industry, and boost the state's economy. Yet low gas prices help the state's 30 million residents manage their budgets and make ends meet. Which scenario do Texans want? Turns out, they don't seem to agree. Texans' vibrant political diversity reveals itself in the less than six-percentage-point gap between the Republican and Democratic candidates in 2020. Winner-take-all and the false argument of "federalism" would have us believe this diversity does not exist.

The people of any state do not speak with unity on any policy question or candidate. Certainly, all voices in every state deserve an equal say in selecting the president.

In the same conversation recorded above, Hamilton posed a telling rhetorical question: "Will the people of Delaware be less free if each citizen has an equal vote with each citizen of Pennsylvania?"[10]

Let's rephrase his question for our context: Will the people of any state accrue harm if all Americans have an equal vote for president?

Weigh that answer against the considerable damage that arises when millions of citizens go into the voting booth with more voting power than others—indeed, when millions of citizens must watch their votes effectively given to the candidate they did not choose.

"Federalism" sounds high minded and principled, but the Electoral College plays no meaningful role in our federal system. In reality, this claim offers but an abstract and thin justification for a system that tramples Americans' rights to equal treatment.

Preventing Fraud

At the time of this writing, a former president of the United States faces criminal charges for the first time in history. According to an indictment filed in Georgia, then-president Donald J. Trump conspired with others to remain in power, even though he lost the 2020 election, as confirmed by his own attorney general, by recounts in several contested states, and by a branch of his own Homeland Security Department. As part of the alleged scheme, fake electors in seven states convened, signed electoral certificates, and sent these documents to the National Archives. Notably, the fake-elector plan unfolded in states where the outcome hinged on tiny margins—Arizona, Georgia, Michigan, Nevada, New Mexico, Pennsylvania, and Wisconsin. The plan involved eighty-four people willing to serve as fraudulent electors, as well as others who helped coordinate the scheme.[11]

Defenders of the Electoral College maintain that it prevents fraud by making it easier to discover and isolate. Like almost all Electoral College myths, the claim ignores a truth that hides in plain sight: Bad actors can more easily manipulate votes in a single pivotal state or group of states than coordinate fraud and theft across millions of votes in many locales. Moreover, with its several complex stages, the Electoral College offers repeated openings for manipulating a presidential election.

The Electoral College's inducements to fraud appear in the historical record. Readers will recall the shocking events recounted in chapter 6, when Democrats pursued appalling violence aimed to influence the 1876 election results in three key states. Republicans in those states committed fraud to steal the election back. Today, anyone hoping to uncover the truth about that election must wade through layer upon layer of corruption and deceit, and, to this day, scholars argue about who rightfully won.

Manipulating votes in a few key locales can tip an entire election, and this structure offers one opening for fraud under the Electoral College system. Yet another opportunity presents itself when the electors assemble to cast their votes in December. We've already explained how electors now serve no real purpose, but because they are human beings, they present a vulnerability in the system. For this reason, the alleged Trump scheme focused on electors willing to falsely certify a win for him in their respective states.

But fraud and vote-manipulation opportunities don't end there. Chapter 6 described how Congress can steal an election in full public view when it counts the vote. Indeed, Congress has disallowed electoral certificates on several occasions, most in the nineteenth century. On mere technicalities, it has blatantly disenfranchised hundreds of thousands of Americans. Congress rejected Arkansas's electoral certificates in 1872, for example, because the state used the wrong seal. Congress may have stolen the election of 1876 when it awarded a series of disputed certificates to Republican Rutherford B. Hayes. Trump's alleged plan also extended to this stage. He pressured Vice President Mike Pence to refuse to certify the results, and the president's supporters in Congress tried to bolster the scheme by objecting to certificates from several contested states.

Indeed, the Electoral College offers multiple stages and far greater opportunity to steal an election than would an NPV. Fraud and cheating happen in every election, but isolated and uncoordinated incidents can't tip results that hinge on large numbers of votes. However, give a power-hungry leader some savvy lawyers and the multiple openings available in our Electoral College process, and you've got an invitation to steal the presidency.

* * *

Collectively, these myths make some outrageous suggestions: that the current disenfranchisement of millions of Americans and the gross inequality of our votes is of no account; that states deserve greater consideration than the people who compose them; and that the framers purposefully created paths for minority rule.

Above all, these claims reinvent the Electoral College as a brilliantly pristine device that somehow "knows" when the minority choice would be wisest.

Americans in large numbers have long intuited the Electoral College's poor compatibility with the United States' democratic values, and most prefer an equal vote with all other citizens. Gallup began tracking public opinion on the Electoral College in 1944. Since that year, preference for abolishing it in favor of an NPV has hovered slightly above 60 percent, occasionally reaching into the 70 percent range and shooting up briefly to 80 percent after the 1968 election. Only once has Gallup taken a poll in which fewer than 50 percent of Americans favored abolishing the Electoral College: Immediately after the November 2016 election, only 49 percent of Americans favored this change. Since then, the percentage of Americans favoring an NPV has risen again, reaching 61 percent in 2020.[12]

One notable development has accompanied these trends. Whereas roughly equal percentages of Republicans and Democrats supported abolishing the Electoral College before 2000, partisan opinion on the issue has diverged significantly since then. Today, 89 percent of Democrats favor electing the president by an NPV, while only 21 percent of Republicans want to discard the Electoral College.[13]

The reason for this partisan distinction seems clear: Only once since 1988 has a Republican presidential candidate won support from the majority of Americans—in 2004, when George W. Bush was reelected. On two other occasions, in 2000 and 2016, the Republican Party captured the White House through the Electoral College, without an accompanying popular-vote win. Increasingly, the party relies on Electoral College distortions to elect a candidate whom most Americans have rejected. Most troubling, they have crafted a series of paper-thin arguments to justify this mechanism.

Representative government rests on the foundational principle that the people choose leaders who reflect their values, priorities, and policy preferences. When majorities win elections, democratic accountability works to require responsiveness to the people's will. In theory, electoral majorities punish officials who stray from the people's wishes by voting them out. But when a system offers access to power while rejecting the majority's choice, democratic accountability disappears. Parties and candidates have little motivation to adapt to the public's demands.

The Electoral College offers just such avenues for minority victories. The party and its candidates are never forced to adapt to a changing electorate.

From our origins, the best American thinkers have insisted that minority rights require protection. But none of our constitutional architects claimed that minorities should govern.

Electoral college defenders seek to disguise this path to minority rule under high-minded rhetoric. But let's be clear: These rationales all stem from a hope to subvert the will of the majority.

A BETTER PLAN

Americans have wanted to elect the president directly for a very long time, but the Constitution's extraordinarily high bar for amendments has frustrated efforts for change.

At least one group has abandoned efforts at a constitutional amendment and now promotes a work-around to current Electoral College operations. Their plan would guarantee the presidency to the winner of the national popular vote, without a constitutional amendment. This effort, the National Popular Vote Interstate Compact (NPVIC), asks state legislatures to pledge their electoral votes to the winner of the national popular vote, rather than the winner of a state's popular vote. By its own terms, the compact will go into effect when sufficient states representing 270 electoral votes have signed on. To date, thirteen states representing 205 electoral votes have adopted this plan, and the compact is pending in six more with a total of 63 electoral votes. If passed in all six states, the compact would have states comprising only 268 electoral votes, two short of the 270 needed.

Despite the NPVIC's laudable intentions to secure a victory for the winner of the NPV, this plan suffers several fundamental shortcomings. Perhaps most significantly, under current political conditions it seems unlikely to prevail in enough states to take effect.

The NPVIC may also suffer legal and constitutional obstacles. Opponents could make successful challenges under the Constitution's interstate compact clause, which forbids states from entering into agreements or compacts with other states. Moreover, courts could feasibly construe the NPVIC as disenfranchising a state's citizens if the state-wide popular vote were to settle on one candidate and the legislature gave its electors to another.

Finally, this plan could produce a president dogged by the same claims of illegitimacy that plague a minority-vote winner now. As long as the Electoral College remains intact, however problematic, many Americans could reasonably condemn a process that opens a constitutionally questionable path of victory.

A constitutional amendment allowing the people to directly elect the president remains the best solution.

Our nation needs a plan that will require a winner to garner support from a clear majority—greater than 50 percent—of voters. Such a plan would likely require a run-off between two candidates, since races with more candidates reduce the odds that more than 50 percent of voters will settle on a single person.

While we are about the business of revamping our system for selecting the president, why not give the people greater say in selecting the candidates? As Congressman James Ashley argued in 1868, a better plan would remove as many interventions as possible between the people and their leaders, and today's closed party primaries constitute a problematic layer of intrusion. A simultaneous, nationwide, open primary would undermine the inordinate power our political parties wield over candidate selection, and this process would push moderate candidates with broad centrist appeal to the top.

Such a primary outcome might select two Democrats who would face off against one another in the run-off. Maybe two Republicans would emerge as the final candidates. More likely, we'd get a final choice between two quality candidates with slightly different philosophies and practical, nuanced policy positions. Best of all, this open primary would eliminate extremists and force the parties to accommodate to the will of the majority—a foundational principle of democratic accountability. If, rather than propping up morally bankrupt parties, this system hastened their dissolution and made way for new, more flexible and practical alliances, so much the better.

* * *

The principle of political equality has run like a subterranean river under our republic's history. Our most visionary thinkers, some of them well known and prominent but others more obscure, have urged this idea as utterly foundational. We've never enacted it comprehensively, though we've inched toward equality, bit by bit, over more than two centuries.

Thomas Jefferson believed deeply in political equality and regarded it as an essential principle. To be sure, his gendered assumptions and deep financial interests in slaveholding prevented his following the implications of political equality to their logical conclusions. Yet, he elaborated this idea more fully than many of his contemporaries. Jefferson laid out this notion in elegant simplicity in an 1816 letter about revising Virginia's first state constitution, crafted forty years earlier. This same letter featured his metaphor for an outdated constitution—"a man [wearing] still the coat which fitted him when a boy"—that informed the previous chapter.[14]

Retired from public life and benefiting from long experience in public service, Jefferson emphasized repeatedly that a good constitution would result only from a solid foundation. Constitution writers, he urged, should "lay down true principles, and adhere to them inflexibly." Identifying one particular idea as the "mother-principle," Jefferson maintained, "governments are republican only in proportion as they embody the will of their people and execute it." Returning to the theme many lines later, he urged a test for every constitutional provision: "see if it hangs directly on the will of the people."[15]

Jefferson argued that the will of the people found expression only when they had an equal say. He explicitly recast "republicanism" to emphasize the point: "A government is republican in proportion as every member composing it has his equal voice in the direction of its concerns." Moving on, he called "inequality of representation" a "republican heresy." As to specific applications, he recommended direct popular election of the state's chief executive, popular election of judges, and equal representation of all citizens equally in the legislature.[16]

Virginians did not fulfill Jefferson's wishes in 1816, nor did they do so in 1830 when they crafted a new constitution, nor even in their next constitution, ratified in 1851. Virginia finally erected a community of legally equal citizens in its 1971 constitution.[17]

The same year that Jefferson wrote the words above, Senator Abner Lacock of Pennsylvania stood in the temporary Senate chamber in Washington, DC, and introduced the first amendment to the Constitution that called for direct, popular election of the president.

Five decades later, another generation of Americans also sought good foundations as they rebuilt the country after a gruesome civil war. They struggled mightily to remake the United States Constitution on the principles Jefferson advanced, extending his ideas into the racial arena, where the sage of Monticello had not ventured. These visionary Reconstruction architects sounded a great deal like the author of the Declaration of Independence, as they pressed their congressional colleagues to erect a government on "the eternal rock . . . the everlasting principle of equal and exact justice." For many of these leaders, "equal and exact justice" dictated an equal and direct say in choosing the nation's chief executive. They tried again to revise the Constitution and make this vision a reality.[18]

Yet again in the 1960s, the nation pursued another mighty effort to write equality—finally and fully—into our Constitution. The Supreme Court affirmed the principle of "one person, one vote," and a constitutional amendment abolished poll taxes. Important legislation secured rights to equality of education, employment, and voting access. But the principle of equality still came up short, as southern segregationists defeated a widely embraced amendment to eliminate the Electoral College.

These segregationists aimed mostly to deprive black Americans of their voice in presidential elections. Yet, their actions squashed political equality for every American, not just those of African descent. This inglorious defeat of an equal vote for all underscores how inextricably all our fates are bound together.

Most Americans look to the heroic days of the 1960s and assume that the decade's civil rights victories finally sealed our true equality as citizens. But we are not there, not quite yet. The struggle for an equal voice in the choice of our national leader has taken a back seat to other concerns for many decades now. Moreover, the voting inequities embedded in the Electoral College are often taken for granted, minimized, and masked by rhetoric that praises this system.

But the need for equal and exact justice remains. Enacting a constitutional amendment for a direct, national vote for president presents an urgent arena for struggle. Let us take another step toward equality and justice and build our government on this eternal rock.

CONCLUSION

"The Earth Belongs Always to the Living Generation"

"TRUST THE FOUNDERS," INSTRUCTS THE MEME. "KEEP THE ELECTORAL College."[1] Since we no longer use the Electoral College that the framers established, this glib admonition makes no sense. Appealing to widespread cultural reverence for the Constitution, it plays artfully on a series of mistaken beliefs and ignores the 235-year history that has substantively altered the plan from its original form. Indeed, this message commits the cardinal sin against history: reading the present into the past.

This book's early chapters show that the framers adopted a system of electors primarily because they did not want to place presidential selection in Congress's sullying hands. Designed by Madison in the Convention's final days, their plan for electors proved the only alternative on which they could agree and thus complete their work. This method of proxy election did not emerge from a high-minded political philosophy or pristine principle but, rather, as a practical, last-ditch solution that helped frustrated men bring their four-month labors to a conclusion.

It makes little sense to revere a flawed device born of practical necessity as a sacrosanct and elevated institution.[2]

Further undermining any sublime notion of the Electoral College, the system quickly departed from the idea conceived by Madison and elaborated by Hamilton in *Federalist* 68. Partisans shaped it to their will. They captured control of electors and forsook the intent that wise men, free of "sinister bias," would exercise independent judgment in an influence-free environment. They instituted winner-take-all to maximize partisan advantage and silence their opponents in every state. Taken together, these changes transformed the original design for proxy election into a distorting and disenfranchising algorithm.

Throughout its 235-year history, this system has frequently performed poorly. Many times, the Electoral College has produced inconclusive and contested results, as in the election of Thomas Jefferson in 1800, John Quincy Adams in 1824, and Rutherford B. Hayes in 1876. Its structure has incentivized fraud in at least two notorious elections (1876 and 2020).

Moreover, the Electoral College has been consistently intertwined with the country's sordid racial history. Prior to the Civil War, it disproportionately magnified the political power of slaveholding states, giving them far more clout in presidential elections than they would otherwise have possessed. After the demise of Reconstruction, the Electoral College endowed the whites of the former Confederacy with an even greater boost than before. The population of black Southerners, though stripped by Jim Crow of all political power, bumped up the region's Electoral College weight significantly. In turn, white leaders from these states deployed this outsized strength in their fight against black dignity and humanity in the civil rights era.

Electoral college outcomes do not always correlate well with the expressed will of the people. Most often the results have vastly inflated the popular-vote results, sometimes by even as much as 40 percent. The landslide Electoral College victories of Woodrow Wilson and Ronald Reagan (first term) disguise quite modest popular-vote margins. On six other occasions, the Electoral College algorithm has magnified popular-vote wins by more than 30 percent.[3] But more consequentially, misfires that produce minority-vote winners, including two times in the last six cycles (2000, 2016), have denied presidents a popular mandate, hobbled presidential effectiveness, and polarized the body politic.

Add to this history the public's perennial dissatisfaction with our method of selecting the president, as expressed in a flood of amendment proposals, seven occasions when one Congressional Chamber approved a far-reaching amendment, and persistent majority support for a national popular vote, as demonstrated by polling.

No, history—our experience as a nation—has not vindicated the Electoral College.

The Electoral College also fails the test of clarity and simplicity. Every four years, the United States conducts a presidential election, even as its citizens remain largely unaware of the gap between their voting activity and the original design. We perform the Constitution's pre-scribed rituals without the purposes, functions, and meanings they once possessed. As we cast ballots that obscure our election realities, we enjoy the activity, rhetoric, and appearance of participatory democracy, but not the full substance of it.

This odd and obfuscating system floods American political life with damage. It distorts political campaigns and drives our political dysfunc-tion and polarization to new heights. At the current unique moment, as our nation suffers under unusual instability, conditions are ripe for repeated Electoral College misfires that undo the will of the majority.

Perhaps most significantly of all, the Electoral College cannot be justified morally.

Americans express their political values in a variety of ways: "all men are created equal," "equality before the law," "democracy," "republicanism," "the will of the people," "equality of opportunity," "the consent of the governed," and "one person, one vote," capture some of the ways we talk about the principles we cherish.

We embrace these principles because we regard them as right and just. We understand that people deprived of their equal political power with others—whether in the courts or in the voting booth—lack the ability to protect themselves and their livelihoods, families, and property.

It's safe to say that very few Americans, other than followers of extremist groups, would blatantly embrace inequality in any form. Indeed, we universally decry unequal treatment on the basis of race, sex, national origin, age, physical ability, sexual orientation, or ideology.

Let us, then, confront the reality that today's Electoral College amounts to blatant and extreme political inequality, based on a citizen's arbitrary state of residence. It's out of step with American values and with our most widely shared convictions about what it means to govern ourselves.

* * *

The framers widely acknowledged the Constitution's imperfections. The day he signed it, Benjamin Franklin confessed that "there are several parts of this constitution which I do not at present approve." The ink of his signature had been dry but one week when George Washington expressed his "wish [that] the Constitution offered had been made more perfect." Six weeks after the delegates ended their work, James Madison fired off a long letter to Thomas Jefferson explaining the Constitution's shortcomings, and George Mason circulated a list of its faults. Franklin, Washington, and Madison endorsed the Constitution not because they approved it on all points, but because it promised a more effective government than the Articles of Confederation. Moreover, under the Convention's realities, they believed it was the best they could achieve at that moment.[4]

The Constitution's supporters asserted that its inevitable flaws should cause no alarm, because the document provided for amendments. "The seeds of reformation are sown in the work itself," noted a North Carolina champion of the Constitution. "There is express provision made for amendments, when its defects and imperfections shall be discovered in its operation." As Americans put the Constitution into practice and discovered its defects, they could fix them. Madison seemed to suggest as much when he noted of the Electoral College, "that mode which was judged most expedient was adopted, till experience should point out one more eligible."[5]

Reality has not unfolded exactly as the framers hoped.

The framers did not reckon with the very difficult path they created for constitutional amendments. Because the Articles of Confederation required unanimous consent of all thirteen states to pass an amendment, the Constitution's lower bar likely seemed reasonable. But consider that one method for amendment requires two-thirds approval from both houses of Congress, followed by ratification by three-quarters of the states. Alternatively, two-thirds of the states can call for a convention to suggest amendments, but this process has never been used.

These constraints have made amendments difficult and almost hopeless in eras of great political polarization. Apart from the Bill of Rights,

Americans have amended the Constitution only seventeen times in 230 years. As of this writing, it has not been amended for three decades.

At the time of its origins, the U.S. Constitution created the most representative—indeed, most democratic—government in the world, despite its several undemocratic features. Other nations used our system as a model when they erected their own governments; some, particularly South American republics, even copied our plan to choose their chief executive through an Electoral College.

Yet few of these subsequent constitutions created hurdles for amendments so high as those in the U.S. Constitution. Consequently, as ideas and culture have changed, many of these countries have adapted their governments more readily. Not only have many other nations eliminated or mitigated features that foster minority rule, but they have also more easily broadened their electorates and guaranteed a more sweeping range of individual rights. According to some scholars, by several metrics, the United States now lags behind rather than leads the way as a standard-bearer for democracy.

Under these global democratizing trends, electoral colleges have not fared well. Between 1910 and 1994, Argentina, Brazil, Chile, Colombia, and Paraguay all eliminated their systems of indirect election. In the 1950s, France tried an electoral college in a single election—and then discarded it. Notably, Kentucky's first constitution in 1792 provided for an electoral college to choose its governor. But when the state wrote a new constitution six years later, its framers ditched that system in favor of direct election.[6]

The U.S. Constitution's difficult amendment process, unfortunately, renders it less pliable and flexible than our dynamic and vibrant nation needs. Its high hurdles have repeatedly frustrated important and beneficial reforms.

In the case of the Electoral College, Americans have continually sought to elect their president by a "more eligible" method. More amendments on this topic have been introduced in Congress than on any other. Seven times, one house has passed an amendment, only for it to fail in the other. The 1969 amendment that garnered such high hopes and promise was stymied by yet another anti-majoritarian practice, the filibuster.

The small number of changes to the Constitution also implicitly promotes notions of its sacred status and reinforces our reluctance to amend it. If experience has taught us that we cannot change it, deep cultural reverence renders us reluctant even to begin to identify its flaws. Thus, the admonition to "Trust the founders. Keep the Electoral College" resounds convincingly for Americans schooled in how they should *feel* about the Constitution. But fuzzy emotions mean little if not underpinned by knowledge of the Constitution's actual provisions, history, and effects.

The founders themselves did not want subsequent generations to feel so rigidly bound to their provisions, nor to regard their work as untouchable. Jefferson expressed this idea in 1789, just months after the U.S. Constitution went into effect. In Paris, Jefferson watched the French people struggle for their rights in a failing monarchy many centuries old. The events spiraling around him prompted him to reflect at length on the relationship between inherited forms of government and the rights of each living generation. He penned a long letter to his friend James Madison on these themes. "No society can make a perpetual constitution, or even a perpetual law," observed Jefferson. "The earth belongs always to the living generation. They may manage it then, and what proceeds from it, as they please."[7]

Jefferson returned to the same idea twenty-seven years later, in the same 1816 "coat" letter we visited in the two preceding chapters. Bringing that remarkable missive to a conclusion, Jefferson mused, "Some men look at Constitutions with sanctimonious reverence and deem them, like the ark of the covenant, too sacred to be touched. They ascribe to the men of the preceding age a wisdom more than human and suppose what they did to be beyond amendment." Jefferson urged his reader not to "weakly believe that one generation is not as capable as another of taking care of itself and of ordering its own affairs." He continued, "each generation is . . . independent of the one preceding . . . it has then, like them, a right to choose for itself the form of government it believes most promotive of its own happiness."[8]

Societies work best when they preserve venerated traditions but adapt and mold them to their present values and understandings. Indeed, every generation should regard itself not merely as inheritors of institutions handed down to them, but also as creators of forms that suit their present needs and values.

"Trust the founders"? Yes. But slavish reverence for the work of past generations undermines faith in our own experience and judgment about how best to govern ourselves. Years of founder veneration have taught us to trust their wisdom. We have forgotten that they also trusted ours.

ACKNOWLEDGMENTS

In the process of writing this book, I have accumulated too many debts to enumerate. But I want to identify and thank a few people who were especially helpful.

Steve Clements and I had countless discussions about this material, and my thinking about the electoral college has benefited significantly from his comments and caveats.

Adam Prince helped me break free of academic writing, pushed me to tell stories, and helped me tell them better. His intervention made this a profoundly different book than it might otherwise have been.

I deeply appreciate David Bratt and Laura Bardolph of BBH Literary for their faith in this project and for their guidance along the way.

Throughout this journey, I imposed on quite a few friends who read chapters and offered feedback. Conversations with Bert and Connie Grayson, David Burt, Larry Prinssen, and Tip Moody have vastly improved these pages.

Similarly, I asked academic colleagues for the benefit of their analysis on select chapters. Jeff Freyman, Richard Taylor, David Swartz, Brad Wood, and Josh Lynn all read generously and responded insightfully. My dear friend and colleague Tom Appleton read every word, and I am deeply grateful for his attention to detail and kind encouragement—gifts he has offered not only with this manuscript but also throughout my career.

My brother Vincent Dupont, one of my favorite intellectual sparring partners, read much of the manuscript, urged me to rein in "metaphorical excess," and asked thoughtful questions that helped me fine-tune these pages.

I inflicted parts of early drafts on other family members as well, including my dear sister-in-law, Mary Nan Theissen. I corralled my adult children, Daniel Dupont, Julianne Norman, and Elise Partain, into reading portions. All proved to be tough and discerning critics.

Finally, I owe so much to my husband, Greg Partain. We both lost count long ago of how many drafts he read. I have no sharper critic, no more patient reader, no better analyst, and no more persistent supporter in writing and in life.

NOTES

INTRODUCTION: ELECTILE DYSFUNCTION

1. Kierra Fazier, "Jan. 6 Sentences Are Piling Up. Here's a Look at Some of the Longest Handed Down," *Politico*, May 30, 2023, https://www.politico.com/news/2023/05/30/january-6-arrest-sentencing-00099158.

2. Jennifer Agiesta and Ariel Edwards-Levy, "CNN Poll: Percentage of Republicans Who Think Biden's 2020 Win Was Illegitimate Ticks Back Up Near 70 Percent," CNN, August 3, 2023, https://www.cnn.com/2023/08/03/politics/cnn-poll-republicans-think-2020-election-illegitimate/index.html.

3. See "Do You Understand the Electoral College?," PragerU, May 17, 2015 (video), https://www.prageru.com/video/do-you-understand-the-electoral-college.

4. Three of my favorites include George C. Edwards III, *Why the Electoral College Is Bad for America*, 3rd ed. (New Haven, CT: Yale University Press, 2019); Alexander Keyssar, *Why Do We Still Have the Electoral College?* (Cambridge, MA: Harvard University Press, 2020); and Jesse Wegman, *Let the People Pick the President: The Case for Abolishing the Electoral College* (New York: St. Martin's, 2020). Keyssar, I should note, is a fine historian. A well-argued piece by a legal scholar is Katherine Shaw, "'A Mystifying and Distorting Factor': The Electoral College and American Democracy," *Michigan Law Review* 120, no. 6 (2022): 1285–1306.

5. "II. Thomas Jefferson to James Madison, 6 September 1789," Founders Online, National Archives, https://founders.archives.gov/documents/Jefferson/01-15-02-0375-0003 (original source: Julian P. Boyd, ed., *The Papers of Thomas Jefferson*, vol. 15, 27 March 1789–30 November 1789 [Princeton, NJ: Princeton University Press, 1958], 392–98).

CHAPTER 1: PHILADELPHIA, 1787: FUMBLING THEIR WAY

1. Madison described and analyzed the problems created by the Articles of Confederation in his "Vices of the Political System of the United States, April 1787," Founders Online, National Archives, https://founders.archives.gov/documents/Madison/01-09-02-0187 (original source: Robert A. Rutland and William M. E. Rachal, eds., *The Papers of James Madison*, vol. 9, 9 April 1786–24 May 1787 and Supplement 1781–1784 [Chicago: University of Chicago Press, 1975], 345–58). Madison also elaborated many of these problems in his preface to the first edition of his *Notes of Debates in the Federal*

Convention of 1787 (New York: Norton, 1987), 3–19 (originally published in Henry Gilpin, ed., *The Papers of James Madison*, vols. 2–3 [Washington, DC: Langtree & O'Sullivan, 1840]).

2. The story of the Newburgh Conspiracy is ably told in Richard H. Kohn, "The Inside History of the Newburgh Conspiracy: America and the Coup d'Etat," *William and Mary Quarterly* 27, no. 2 (April 1970): 187–220. For Madison's description of the soldiers surrounding Congress at Independence Hall, see "Notes on Debates, 21 June 1783," Founders Online, National Archives, https://founders.archives.gov/documents/Madison/01-07-02-0102 (original source: William T. Hutchinson and William M. E. Rachal, eds., *The Papers of James Madison*, vol. 7, 3 May 1783–20 February 1784 [Chicago: University of Chicago Press, 1971], 176–80). "To George Washington from Henry Knox, 17 December 1786," Founders Online, National Archives, https://founders.archives.gov/documents/Washington/04-04-02-0396 (original source: W. W. Abbot, ed., *The Papers of George Washington*, Confederation Series, vol. 4, 2 April 1786–31 January 1787 [Charlottesville: University Press of Virginia, 1995], 460–62).

3. "From James Madison to James Madison Sr., 1 April 1787," Founders Online, National Archives, https://founders.archives.gov/documents/Madison/01-09-02-0188 (original source: Rutland and Rachal, *The Papers of James Madison*, 9:358–61).

4. "From James Madison to Edmund Randolph, 8 April 1787," Founders Online, National Archives, https://founders.archives.gov/documents/Madison/01-09-02-0197 (original source: Rutland and Rachal, *The Papers of James Madison*, 9:368–71).

5. "To George Washington from James Madison, 16 April 1787," Founders Online, National Archives, https://founders.archives.gov/documents/Washington/04-05-02-0139 (original source: W. W. Abbot, ed., *The Papers of George Washington*, Confederation Series, vol. 5, 1 February 1787–31 December 1787 [Charlottesville: University Press of Virginia, 1997], 144–50).

6. Madison described the scene stoically, "On That Day a Small Number Only Had Assembled." Madison, *Notes*, 23.

7. He described his sense of "despair" using exactly that phrase in "From James Madison to Edmund Pendleton, 22 April 1787," Founders Online, National Archives, https://founders.archives.gov/documents/Madison/01-09-02-0215 (original source: Rutland and Rachal, *The Papers of James Madison*, 9:394–96).

8. See William Pierce's description of Madison, in William Pierce, "Character Sketches of Delegates to the Federal Convention," Consource.org, accessed February 29, 2024, https://consource.org/document/william-pierce-character-sketches-of-delegates-to-the-federal-convention/20130122082412/ (original source: William Pierce, "Letter to the Federal Convention," in *The Records of the Federal Convention of 1787*, vol. 3, ed. Max Farrand [New Haven, CT: Yale University Press, 1911]).

9. See William Pierce's description of Randolph in Pierce, "Character Sketches," as well as Richard Beeman's in *Plain, Honest Men: The Making of the American Constitution* (New York: Random House, 2009), 87–88.

10. Beeman, *Plain, Honest Men*, 61, describes the interior of Independence Hall. Madison described his seat at the front in the preface to his *Notes*, 17.

11. The Delaware delegation had come to the Convention under instructions not to agree to any measure that would change the existing arrangement of each state having one vote. See Madison, *Notes*, 37.

12. Madison recorded Randolph's speech and the fifteen resolutions of the Virginia Plan in *Notes*, 28–33.

13. Madison, *Notes*, 46.

14. For a description of James Wilson, see Pierce, "Character Sketches," as well as Beeman, *Plain, Honest Men*, 49–51.

15. Madison, *Notes*, 48.

16. Madison, *Notes*, 50–51. See Pierce's description of Gerry in Pierce, "Character Sketches"; Beeman, *Plain, Honest Men*, 111–14.

17. Madison, *Notes*, 50.

18. Madison, *Notes*, 51.

19. Madison, *Notes*, 50–51.

20. Madison, *Notes*, 51.

21. Madison, *Notes*, 93, 94.

22. For a character sketch of William Paterson, see Beeman, *Plain, Honest Men*, 146–49. See also John E. O'Conner, *William Paterson: Lawyer and Statesman, 1745–1806* (New Brunswick, NJ: Rutgers University Press, 1979).

23. This description is based on Beeman, *Plain, Honest Men*, 74–75.

24. Paterson made his initial speech on this topic on June 9; it is recorded in Madison, *Notes*, 96–97. He offered a more elaborated alternative to the Virginia Plan on June 15; see Madison, *Notes*, 118–21.

25. Madison's main speech answering Paterson's plan can be found in Madison, *Notes*, 140–48. Quotes in *Notes*, 214, 148.

26. Madison, *Notes*, 148.

27. Madison, *Notes*, 239.

28. Martin's speech and Madison's comments on it in Madison, *Notes*, 201–4.

29. Madison, *Notes*, 162. This vote was on a question to change the language of the clause on vesting legislative power. Lansing proposed the phrase in "the United States in Congress" rather than in "the national Legislature," signaling the country would be a union of states and not people.

30. Madison, *Notes*, 221 (Wilson); Madison, *Notes*, 228 (King); Madison, *Notes*, 215 (Hamilton).

31. Madison, *Notes*, 230.

32. Madison, *Notes*, 214 (Madison); Madison, *Notes*, 215–16 (Hamilton); Madison, *Notes*, 241 (Morris); and Madison, *Notes*, 209–11 (Franklin).

33. "To George Washington from Alexander Hamilton, 3 July 1787," Founders Online, National Archives, https://founders.archives.gov/documents/Washington/04-05-02-0228 (original source: Abbot, *The Papers of George Washington*, 5:244–45).

34. The debate on counting enslaved people in the formula for representation can be followed in Madison, *Notes*, 256–82. James Wilson suggested that counting slaves in the population, even at a rate of three-fifths, would "give disgust" to the people of Pennsylvania. Madison, *Notes*, 275.

35. Madison, *Notes*, 278 (Davie); Madison, *Notes*, 286 (Morris).

36. "From George Washington to Alexander Hamilton, 10 July 1787," Founders Online, National Archives, https://founders.archives.gov/documents/Washington/04-05 -02-0236 (original source: Abbot, *The Papers of George Washington*, 5:257).

37. Madison described this meeting in *Notes*, 301.

38. Madison, *Notes*, 282.

39. The figures presented here are based on the census taken three years later, in 1790. *Return of the Whole Number of Persons within the Several Districts of the United States* (Philadelphia: Childs and Swaine, 1791), 3, https://www2.census.gov/library/publications/decennial/1790/number-of-persons.pdf.

40. Pierce, "Character Sketches."

41. Madison, *Notes*, 306–8.

42. Madison, *Notes*, 306 (Sherman); Madison, *Notes*, 308–9 (Mason).

43. Madison, *Notes*, 309.

44. Madison, *Notes*, 309.

45. Madison, *Notes*, 328.

46. Madison, *Notes*, 347.

47. Madison, *Notes*, 355.

48. Madison, *Notes*, 355.

49. Madison, *Notes*, 356–57.

50. Madison's speech is recorded in *Notes*, 363–66.

51. Madison, *Notes*, 365–66.

52. Madison, *Notes*, 368.

53. Madison, *Notes*, 368–69.

54. Madison, *Notes*, 359.

55. For a description of the activities of the various delegates during the recess, see Beeman, *Plain, Honest Men*, 258–76.

56. Article X of this draft constitution provided for election of the chief executive by Congress. The draft constitution is copied in Madison, *Notes*, 392.

CHAPTER 2: THE BEST ATTAINABLE SOLUTION

1. The description of Morris is largely based on Richard Beeman, *Plain, Honest Men: The Making of the American Constitution* (New York: Random House, 2009), 46–49. John Jay's statement is in Richard B. Morris, ed., "John Jay to Robert Morris, Sept. 16, 1780," in *The Papers of John Jay* (New York: Harper & Row, 1975), 2:821; quoted in Beeman, *Plain, Honest Men*, 48. Emphasis in the original. For Morris's extensive sexual dalliances, see Thomas Foster, "Reconsidering Libertines and Early Modern Heterosexuality: Sex and American Founder Gouverneur Morris," *Journal of the History of Sexuality* 22, no. 1 (2013): 65–84, http://www.jstor.org/stable/23322034.

2. This conversation on the slave trade was most vigorous on August 8, 21, and 22. See James Madison, *Notes of Debates in the Federal Convention of 1787* (New York: Norton, 1987), 409–12, 502–8 (originally published in Henry Gilpin, ed., *The Papers of James Madison*, vols. 2–3 [Washington, DC: Langtree & O'Sullivan, 1840]). For Mason's denunciation of slavery, see Madison, *Notes*, 504.

3. Among them, Gouverneur Morris pointed out that the three-fifths clause gave an inducement to the importation of slaves (Madison, *Notes*, 411–12). Luther Martin of Maryland pointed this out as well (Madison, *Notes,* 502).

4. Madison, *Notes,* 502.

5. Madison, *Notes,* 530.

6. Madison, *Notes,* 566 (Gerry and Mason); Madison, *Notes,* 551 (Randolph).

7. Madison, *Notes,* 524.

8. Madison, *Notes,* 526.

9. Madison, *Notes,* 642.

10. Madison, *Notes,* 567.

11. Madison, *Notes,* 567.

12 . "John Dickinson to George Logan, Jan. 16, 1802," in *Supplement to Max Farrand's The Records of the Federal Convention of 1787*, ed. James H. Hutson (New Haven, CT: Yale University Press, 1987), 300–301.

13. John Dickinson to George Logan, in Hutson, *Supplement*, 300–301.

14. Madison, *Notes,* 576.

15. Madison, *Notes,* 591 (Spaight). The objections of the South Carolina members, including Rutledge, are recorded in Madison, *Notes,* 577, 582.

16. Madison, *Notes,* 577.

17. Madison, *Notes,* 584 (Randolph); Madison, *Notes,* 588 (Wilson).

18. Madison, *Notes,* 630.

19. "James Madison to Jared Sparks, 8 April 1831," Founders Online, National Archives, https://founders.archives.gov/documents/Madison/99-02-02-2323. (This is an Early Access document from *The Papers of James Madison*. It is not an authoritative final version.)

20. Madison, *Notes,* 651 (Mason); Madison, *Notes,* 653 (Franklin).

21. These conversations on the day of signing are recorded in Madison, *Notes,* 652–59.

22. Merrill Jensen, John P. Kaminski, and Gaspare Saladino, eds., *Documentary History of the Ratification of the Constitution* (Madison: Wisconsin Historical Society Press, 1976), 10:1412. Subsequent references to this work will be cited as *DHRC*. "From James Madison to George Hay, 23 August 1823," Founders Online, National Archives, https://founders.archives.gov/documents/Madison/04-03-02-0109 (original source: David B. Mattern, J. C. A. Stagg, Mary Parke Johnson, and Katherine E. Harbury, eds., *The Papers of James Madison, Retirement Series*, vol. 3, 1 March 1823–24 February 1826 [Charlottesville: University of Virginia Press, 2016], 108–11).

23. Pauline Maier's *Ratification: The People Debate the Constitution, 1787–1788* (New York: Simon & Schuster, 2010) is the best history of ratification.

24. "Diary Entry: 19 September 1787," Founders Online, National Archives, https://founders.archives.gov/documents/Washington/01-05-02-0002-0009-0019 (original source: Donald Jackson and Dorothy Twohig, eds., *The Diaries of George Washington*, vol. 5, 1 July 1786–31 December 1789 [Charlottesville: University Press of Virginia, 1979], 186).

25. "To George Washington from George Mason, 7 October 1787," Founders Online, National Archives, https://founders.archives.gov/documents/Washington/04-05-02-0331 (original source: W. W. Abbot, ed., *The Papers of George Washington, Confederation*

Series, vol. 5, 1 February 1787–31 December 1787 [Charlottesville: University Press of Virginia, 1997], 355–58).

26. "From George Washington to Benjamin Harrison, 24 September 1787," Founders Online, National Archives, https://founders.archives.gov/documents/Washington/04-05 -02-0316 (original source: Abbot, *The Papers of George Washington*, 5:339–40).

27. Mason's struggle to make changes and the Convention's hurried rejection of them can be followed in Madison, *Notes*, 640–42. "From James Madison to Thomas Jefferson, 24 October 1787," Founders Online, National Archives, https://founders.archives.gov /documents/Madison/01-10-02-0151 (original source: Robert A. Rutland, Charles F. Hobson, William M. E. Rachal, and Frederika J. Teute, eds., *The Papers of James Madison*, vol. 10, 27 May 1787–3 March 1788 [Chicago: University of Chicago Press, 1977], 205–20).

28. "To George Washington from George Mason, 7 October 1787."

29. "From James Madison to Thomas Jefferson, 6 September 1787," Founders Online, National Archives, https://founders.archives.gov/documents/Madison/01-10-02-0115 (original source: Rutland, Hobson, Rachal, and Teute, *The Papers of James Madison*, 10:163–65); "From James Madison to Thomas Jefferson, 24 October 1787," Founders Online, National Archives, https://founders.archives.gov/documents/Madison/01-10-02 -0151 (original source: Rutland, Hobson, Rachal, and Teute, *The Papers of James Madison*, 10:205–20).

30. Randolph's remarks on the final day of the Convention, recorded in Madison's *Notes*, 655–57, demonstrate his ambivalence. Maier summarizes his objections well in Maier, *Ratification*, 89 –90.

31. "To George Washington from James Madison, 30 September 1787," Founders Online, National Archives, https://founders.archives.gov/documents/Washington/04 -05-02-0322 (original source: Abbot, *The Papers of George Washington*, 5:345–48); "From George Washington to James Madison, 10 October 1787," Founders Online, National Archives, https://founders.archives.gov/documents/Washington/04-05-02-0334 (original source: Abbot, *The Papers of George Washington*, 5:366–68).

32. Maier, *Ratification*, 26.

33. "Washington to Madison, 10 October 1787."

34. This description is based on Maier, *Ratification*, 256.

35. "Reminiscences of Patrick Henry's Thunderstorm Speech," in Jensen, Kaminski, and Saladino, *DHRC*, 10:1511–12; "From Thomas Jefferson to William Wirt, 4 August 1805," Founders Online, National Archives, https://founders.archives.gov/documents/ Jefferson/99-01-02-2187. (This is an Early Access document from *The Papers of Thomas Jefferson*. It is not an authoritative final version.)

36. Jensen, Kaminski, and Saladino, *DHRC*, 10:1373.

37. Jensen, Kaminski, and Saladino, *DHRC*, 10:1098.

38. Jensen, Kaminski, and Saladino, *DHRC*, 10:1371.

39. Jensen, Kaminski, and Saladino, *DHRC*, 10:1371; Jensen, Kaminski, and Saladino, *DHRC*, 10:1375–76.

40. Jensen, Kaminski, and Saladino, *DHRC*, 10:1098 (Randolph); Jensen, Kaminski, and Saladino, *DHRC*, 10:1412 (Madison).

41. Jensen, Kaminski, and Saladino, *DHRC*, 10:968.
42. "Reminiscences of Patrick Henry's Thunderstorm Speech."
43. "From James Madison to James Madison Sr., 20 June 1788," Founders Online, National Archives, https://founders.archives.gov/documents/Madison/01-11-02-0100 (original source: Robert A. Rutland and Charles F. Hobson, eds., *The Papers of James Madison*, vol. 11, 7 March 1788–1 March 1789 [Charlottesville: University Press of Virginia, 1977], 157–58).
44. Maier, *Ratification*, 313.
45. "Obituary for Constitutional Liberty," in Jensen, Kaminski, and Saladino, *DHRC*, 10:1716.

Chapter 3: Electoral College Origins Myths

1. Tara Ross, *Why We Need the Electoral College* (Washington, DC: Regnery Gateway, 2017); "Do You Understand the Electoral College?," PragerU, May 17, 2015 (video), https://www.prageru.com/video/do-you-understand-the-electoral-college.
2. Alexandria Ocasio-Cortez (@AOC), "It is well past time we eliminate the Electoral College, a shadow of slavery's power on America today that undermines our nation as a democratic republic," Twitter, 4:14 p.m., October 6, 2018, https://twitter.com/aoc/status/1048667886527627265?lang=en.
3. Ross, for example, states, "America's method of electing its president remains largely as it was first conceived by the Founders in the summer of 1787" (Ross, *Why We Need the Electoral College*, 30).
4. John Jay, *Federalist* 64, in *The Federalist*, by Alexander Hamilton, James Madison, and John Jay, ed. Jacob E. Cooke (Hanover, NH: Wesleyan University Press, 1961), 432–38.
5. James Madison, *Notes of Debates in the Federal Convention of 1787* (New York: Norton, 1966), 576–77 (originally published in Henry Gilpin, ed., *The Papers of James Madison*, vols. 2–3 [Washington, DC: Langtree & O'Sullivan, 1840]).
6. Ross, *Why We Need the Electoral College*, 7; Donna Carol Voss, "The Electoral College Still Makes Sense because We're Not a Democracy," *The Federalist*, September 16, 2016, https://thefederalist.com/2016/09/16/the-electoral-college-still-makes-sense-because-were-not-a-democracy/.
7. James Madison, *Federalist* 10, in Cooke, *The Federalist*, 65.
8. Akhil Reed Amar, *The Constitution Today: Timeless Lessons for the Issues of Our Era* (New York: Basic, 2018).
9. See Richard Beeman, *Plain, Honest Men: The Making of the American Constitution* (New York: Random House, 2009), especially chapter 17, "The Paradox at the Nation's Core," 308–36.
10. Madison, *Notes*, 327.
11. Importantly, two slaveholding states, North Carolina and South Carolina, voted against the final Electoral College plan. See Madison, *Notes*, 590.
12. Judith Best, *The Case against Direct Election of the President: A Defense of the Electoral College* (Ithaca, NY: Cornell University Press, 1975).
13. "About Save Our States," Save Our States, accessed February 29, 2024, https://saveourstates.com/about/our-story; Trent England, "The Electoral College Preserves Needed

Checks and Balances," National Conference of State Legislatures, March 24, 2020, https://www.ncsl.org/state-legislatures-news/details/debating-the-electoral-college.

14. See Madison, *Notes*, 94.

15. Merrill Jensen, John P. Kaminski, and Gaspare Saladino, eds., *Documentary History of the Ratification of the Constitution* (Madison: Wisconsin Historical Society Press, 1976), 10:1371, 10:1375–76. Subsequent references to this work will be cited as *DHRC*.

16. James Madison, *Federalist* 39, in Cooke, *The Federalist*, 250–57; James Madison, *Federalist* 45, in Cooke, *The Federalist*, 308–14; Jensen, Kaminski, and Saladino, *DHRC*, 10:1412.

17. Madison, *Notes*, 366.

18. Madison, *Notes*, 327.

19. Madison, *Notes*, 576–77.

CHAPTER 4: THE ELECTORAL COLLEGE AND THE ELECTION OF 1800

1. Alexander Hamilton, *Federalist* 68, in *The Federalist*, by Alexander Hamilton, James Madison, and John Jay, ed. Jacob E. Cooke (Hanover, NH: Wesleyan University Press, 1961), 457–62.

2. "From Alexander Hamilton to James Wilson, [25 January 1789]," Founders Online, National Archives, https://founders.archives.gov/documents/Hamilton/01-05-02-0075 (original source: Harold C. Syrett, ed., *The Papers of Alexander Hamilton*, vol. 5, June 1788–November 1789 [New York: Columbia University Press, 1962], 247–49).

3. Though officially the party name was "Democrat-Republicans," they often shortened it simply to "Republican." Throughout the remainder of this book, I refer to Jefferson and Madison's party as Republican. Notably, scholars agree that they were the forerunners of the Democratic Party that emerged in the 1830s.

4. The description of this meeting of electors in the following pages is based on Oliver Wolcott Sr.'s account in a letter to his son, Oliver Wolcott Sr. to Oliver Wolcott Jr., December 12, 1796, in *Memoirs of the Administrations of Washington and John Adams, Edited from the Papers of Oliver Wolcott, Secretary of the Treasury*, ed. George Gibbs (New York, 1846), 1:407–9.

5. R. J. Purcell, *Connecticut in Transition, 1775–1818* (Middletown, CT: Wesleyan University Press, 1963; originally published by the American Historical Association, 1918).

6. These quotations are taken from letters to and from Oliver Wolcott Jr. in the months leading up to the election, in particular Oliver Wolcott Sr. to Oliver Wolcott Jr., October 3, 1796, in Gibbs, *Memoirs*, 385–86; Oliver Wolcott Sr. to Oliver Wolcott Jr., November 28, 1796, in Gibbs, *Memoirs*, 403; Oliver Wolcott Jr. to Oliver Wolcott Sr., November 19, 1796, in Gibbs, *Memoirs*, 397; Chauncey Goodrich to Oliver Wolcott Sr., November 15, 1796, in Gibbs, *Memoirs*, 394.

7. Chauncey Goodrich to Oliver Wolcott Sr., November 15, 1796, in Gibbs, *Memoirs*, 394; Oliver Wolcott Jr. to Oliver Wolcott Sr., November 27, 1796, in Gibbs, *Memoirs*, 402; Oliver Wolcott Sr. to Oliver Wolcott Jr., November 21, 1796, in Gibbs, *Memoirs*, 397; Oliver Wolcott Jr. to Oliver Wolcott Sr., October 17, 1796, in Gibbs, *Memoirs*, 387.

8. Oliver Wolcott Sr. to Oliver Wolcott Jr., December 12, 1796, in Gibbs, *Memoirs*, 407–9; Chauncey Goodrich to Oliver Wolcott Sr., November 19, 1796, in Gibbs, *Memoirs*, 397.

9. Oliver Wolcott Sr. to Oliver Wolcott Jr., December 12, 1796.

10. Chauncey Goodrich to Oliver Wolcott Jr., December 17, 1796, in Gibbs, *Memoirs*, 411–12; *New York Diary*, February 1797.

11. This account draws heavily from Richard Beeman, *The Old Dominion and the New Nation, 1788–1801* (Lexington: University Press of Kentucky, 1972), 212–22, as well as Noble E. Cunningham Jr., *The Jeffersonian Republicans, 1789–1801* (Chapel Hill: University of North Carolina Press, 1957), 144–54.

12. Beeman, *Old Dominion*, 216. "To James Madison from Charles Pinckney, 30 September 1799," Founders Online, National Archives, https://founders.archives.gov /documents/Madison/01-17-02-0175 (original source: David B. Mattern, J. C. A. Stagg, Jeanne K. Cross, and Susan Holbrook Perdue, eds., *The Papers of James Madison*, vol. 17, 31 March 1797–3 March 1801 and Supplement 22 January 1778–9 August 1795 [Charlottesville: University Press of Virginia, 1991], 272–74).

13. Brockenborough to Joseph C. Cabell, 5 December 1799 [ViU: *Joseph Carrington Cabell Papers*], cited in Editorial Note to "The Report of 1800, [7 January] 1800," Founders Online, National Archives, https://founders.archives.gov/documents/Madison/01 -17-02-0202 (original source: Mattern, Stagg, Cross, and Perdue, *The Papers of James Madison*, 17:303–51).

14. Beeman, *Old Dominion*, 216.

15. Beeman, *Old Dominion*, 216.

16. Beeman, *Old Dominion*, 216.

17. Beeman, *Old Dominion*, 221.

18. Beeman, *Old Dominion*, 221–22.

19. "A Vindication of the General-Ticket Law, Passed by the Legislature of Virginia, on the 18th Day of January 1800" (Richmond, March 1800), *Early American Imprints*, series 1, no. 38942.

20. John Marshall to John H. Pleasants, March 29, 1828, reprinted in *Niles Weekly Register*, April 12, 1828.

21. "From Thomas Jefferson to James Monroe, 12 January 1800," Founders Online, National Archives, https://founders.archives.gov/documents/Jefferson/01-31-02-0256 (original source: Barbara B. Oberg, ed., *The Papers of Thomas Jefferson*, vol. 31, 1 February 1799–31 May 1800 [Princeton, NJ: Princeton University Press, 2004], 300–301).

22. This account draws on Edward J. Larson, *A Magnificent Catastrophe: The Tumultuous Election of 1800, America's First Presidential Campaign* (New York: Free Press, 2007), 101–9, as well as Cunningham, *Jeffersonian Republicans*, 176–84, and John Ferling, *Adams vs. Jefferson: The Tumultuous Election of 1800* (New York: Oxford University Press, 2004), 126–31.

23. "From Alexander Hamilton to John Jay, 7 May 1800," Founders Online, National Archives, https://founders.archives.gov/documents/Hamilton/01-24-02-0378 (original source: Harold C. Syrett, *The Papers of Alexander Hamilton*, vol. 24, November 1799–June 1800 [New York: Columbia University Press, 1976], 464–67).

24. "From Alexander Hamilton to John Jay, 7 May 1800," editorial footnote 4.

25. "From Thomas Jefferson to Thomas Mann Randolph, 12 December 1800," Founders Online, National Archives, https://founders.archives.gov/documents/Jefferson/01-32 -02-0202 (original source: Barbara B. Oberg, *The Papers of Thomas Jefferson*, vol. 32, 1 June 1800–16 February 1801 [Princeton, NJ: Princeton University Press, 2005], 300).

26. "From Thomas Jefferson to Aaron Burr, 15 December 1800," Founders Online, National Archives, https://founders.archives.gov/documents/Jefferson/01-32-02-0208 (original source: Oberg, *The Papers of Thomas Jefferson*, 32:306–7).

27. "From Thomas Jefferson to Hugh Henry Brackenridge, 18 December 1800," Founders Online, National Archives, https://founders.archives.gov/documents/Jefferson /01-32-02-0218 (original source: Oberg, *The Papers of Thomas Jefferson*, 32:318–19).

28. "John Adams to Thomas Boylston Adams, 17 December 1800," Founders Online, National Archives, https://founders.archives.gov/documents/Adams/04-14-02-0221 (original source: Hobson Woodward, Sara Martin, Christopher F. Minty, Amanda M. Norton, Neal E. Millikan, Gwen Fries, and Sara Georgini, eds., *The Adams Papers*, Adams Family Correspondence, vol. 14, October 1799–February 1801 [Cambridge, MA: Harvard University Press, 2019], 488–89).

29. "From Alexander Hamilton to Oliver Wolcott, Junior, 16 December 1800," Founders Online, National Archives, https://founders.archives.gov/documents/Hamilton/01 -25-02-0131 (original source: Harold C. Syrett, ed., *The Papers of Alexander Hamilton*, vol. 25, July 1800–April 1802 [New York: Columbia University Press, 1977], 257–59); "From Alexander Hamilton to Oliver Wolcott, Junior, [December 1800]," Founders Online, National Archives, https://founders.archives.gov/documents/Hamilton/01-25-02-0151 (original source: Syrett, *The Papers of Alexander Hamilton*, 25:286–88); "From Alexander Hamilton to Theodore Sedgwick, 22 December 1800," Founders Online, National Archives, https://founders.archives.gov/documents/Hamilton/01-25-02-0139 (original source: Syrett, *The Papers of Alexander Hamilton*, 25:269–71); "From Alexander Hamilton to Harrison Gray Otis, [23 December 1800]," Founders Online, National Archives, https: //founders.archives.gov/documents/Hamilton/01-25-02-0140 (original source: Syrett, *The Papers of Alexander Hamilton*, 25:271);"From Alexander Hamilton to Gouverneur Morris, 24 December 1800," Founders Online, National Archives, https://founders .archives.gov/documents/Hamilton/01-25-02-0141 (original source: Syrett, *The Papers of Alexander Hamilton*, 25:271–73); "From Alexander Hamilton to James McHenry, 4 January 1801," Founders Online, National Archives, https://founders.archives.gov/ documents/Hamilton/01-25-02-0155 (original source: Syrett, *The Papers of Alexander Hamilton*, 25:292–93).

30. Thomas N. Baker, "'An Attack Well Directed': Aaron Burr Intrigues for the Presidency," *Journal of the Early Republic* 31, no. 4 (2011): 553–98, http://www.jstor.org/stable /41261652.

31. Baker, "'An Attack Well Directed.'"

32. Larson, *Magnificent Catastrophe*, 262–63.

33. "From Thomas Jefferson to James Monroe, 15 February 1801," Founders Online, National Archives, https://founders.archives.gov/documents/Jefferson/01-32-02-0430 (original source: Oberg, *The Papers of Thomas Jefferson*, 32:594).

34. "From Thomas Jefferson to James Monroe, 15 February 1801."

35. Larson, *Magnificent Catastrophe*, 267.

36. "From Alexander Hamilton to James Bayard, April 6, 1802," Founders Online, National Archives, https://founders.archives.gov/documents/Hamilton/01-25-02-0315 (original source: Syrett, *The Papers of Alexander Hamilton*, 25:587–89).

37. *Mercury and New England Palladium*, January 20, 1801; Gary Wills, *Negro President: Jefferson and the Slave Power* (Boston and New York: Houghton Mifflin, 2003), 2.

38. "From Alexander Hamilton to James Bayard, April 6, 1802."

39. 11 Annals of Cong. 191 (1802).

40. 11 Annals of Cong. 191 (1802); "From Alexander Hamilton to James Bayard, April 6, 1802."

41. 11 Annals of Cong. 190 (1802); 10 Annals of Cong. 627 (1800); 12 Annals of Cong. 449 (1803); 13 Annals of Cong. 380–81 (1803). "Albert Gallatin to Thomas Jefferson, 14 September 1801," Founders Online, National Archives, https://founders.archives .gov/documents/Jefferson/01-35-02-0222 (original source: Barbara B. Oberg, *The Papers of Thomas Jefferson*, vol. 35, 1 August–30 November 1801 [Princeton, NJ: Princeton University Press, 2008], 284–89).

42. This description follows Ron Chernow, *Alexander Hamilton* (New York: Penguin, 2004), 703–4.

Chapter 5: "Hideous the Deformity of the Practice": The Tortured Path to Winner-Take-All

1. Anthony Pitch, *The Burning of Washington* (Annapolis, MD: Naval Institute Press, 1998), describes the destruction of Washington's government buildings in detail; specifics here are based on Pitch's account.

2. J. Herman Schauinger, *William Gaston: Carolinian* (Milwaukee, WI: Bruce, 1949), 77 (Gaston's viewing of Washington after the British invasion); Schauinger, *William Gaston*, 70 (Hannah's death).

3. Schauinger, *William Gaston*, 50–52.

4. 26 Annals of Cong. 836 (1814). Lucius Wilmerding Jr., *The Electoral College* (New Brunswick, NJ: Rutgers University Press, 1958), 63–64, relates the North Carolina incident, as does Schauinger, *William Gaston*, 59. Sarah McCulloh Lemmon, *Frustrated Patriots: North Carolina and the War of 1812* (Chapel Hill: University of North Carolina Press, 1973), offers good description of the war's impact in North Carolina.

5. Senator Mahlon Dickerson recounted the New Jersey ordeal before the Senate in 1818. 31 Annals of Cong. 182–83 (1818).

6. Schauinger, *William Gaston*, 71–72.

7. This figure is based on the calculations of Herman Ames, *The Proposed Amendments to the Constitution of the United States* (New York: Lennox Hill, 1970), 80–87.

8. Alexander Keyssar, *Why Do We Still Have the Electoral College?* (Cambridge: Harvard University Press, 2020), 66–67. See especially the helpful chart on 62.

9. 26 Annals of Cong. 842 (1814).

10. 29 Annals of Cong. 223–24 (1816).

11. 1430 Annals of Cong. 138 (1817); 30 Annals of Cong. 303 (1816).

12. 30 Annals of Cong. 339–40 (1816); 26 Annals of Cong. 831 (1814); 26 Annals of Cong. 838 (1814).

13. 36 Annals of Cong. 1905 (1820); 31 Annals of Cong. 181 (1818).

14. 26 Annals of Cong. 839 (1814); 31 Annals of Cong. 183 (1818).

15. 26 Annals of Cong. 840 (1814).

16. 29 Annals of Cong. 220–21 (1816).

17. 29 Annals of Cong. 213–19 (1816).

18. "From James Madison to George Hay, 23 August 1823," Founders Online, National Archives, https://founders.archives.gov/documents/Madison/04-03-02-0109 (original source: David B. Mattern, J. C. A. Stagg, Mary Parke Johnson, and Katherine E. Harbury, eds., *The Papers of James Madison, Retirement Series*, vol. 3, 1 March 1823–24 February 1826 [Charlottesville: University of Virginia Press, 2016], 108–11; "From James Madison to Thomas Jefferson, 14 January 1824," Founders Online, National Archives, https://founders.archives.gov/documents/Madison/04-03-02-0217 (original source: Mattern, Stagg, Johnson, and Harbury, *The Papers of James Madison*, 3:201–2).

19. "From Thomas Jefferson to Robert Selden Garnett, 14 February 1824," Founders Online, National Archives, https://founders.archives.gov/documents/Jefferson/98-01-02-4052. (This is an Early Access document from *The Papers of Thomas Jefferson, Retirement Series*. It is not an authoritative final version.)

20. 41 Annals of Cong. 74 (1823).

21. The portrait of Van Buren and New York politics in these pages is drawn from Robert V. Remini, *Martin Van Buren and the Making of the Democratic Party* (New York: Columbia University Press, 1959); Jabez Hammond, *The History of Political Parties in the State of New York* (Syracuse, NY: Hall, Mill, 1852); Martin Van Buren, *The Autobiography of Martin Van Buren*, ed. John Clement Fitzpatrick (New York: Kelly, 1969); and Lisa Thomason, "Jacksonian Democracy and the Electoral College: Politics and Reform in the Method of Selecting Presidential Electors, 1824–1833" (PhD diss., University of North Texas, May 2001).

22. The portrait of Clay developed here, including the details of his Ashland estate, relies on James Klotter, *Henry Clay: The Man Who Would Be President* (New York: Oxford University Press, 2018); and Robert Remini, *Henry Clay: Statesman for the Union* (New York: Norton, 1991). See also David P. Callahan, *The Politics of Corruption: The Election of 1824 and the Making of Presidents in Jacksonian America* (Charlottesville: University of Virginia Press, 2022).

23. On Clay's calculations regarding the race and the prospect that a contingent election would boost his chances, see Remini, *Henry Clay*, 234–41.

24. Chase C. Mooney, *William H. Crawford, 1772–1834* (Lexington: University Press of Kentucky, 1974).

25. Robert Remini, *Andrew Jackson and the Course of American Freedom*, vol. 2 (New York: Harper & Row, 1981).

26. Recent scholarship suggests that New York would likely have chosen pro-Adams electors, had the electors been chosen by popular vote. See Donald Ratcliffe, "Popular Preferences in the Presidential Election of 1824," *Journal of the Early Republic* 34, no. 1 (2014): 45–77, http://www.jstor.org/stable/24486931.

27. These pages draw heavily on Remini, *Henry Clay*, 251–63.

28. Remini, *Henry Clay*, 252–53.

29. Remini, *Henry Clay*, 254.

30. Remini, *Henry Clay*, 254.

31. Remini, *Henry Clay*, 253.

32. Remini, *Henry Clay*, 259.

33. *Columbia Observer*, January 28, 1925.

34. Margaret Bayard Smith, *The First Forty Years of Washington Society, in the Family Letters of Margaret Bayard Smith*, ed. Gaillard Hunt (New York: Ungar, 1965), 186.

35. 1 Reg. Deb. 526–27 (1825).

36. Smith, *Forty Years*, 183.

37. Thomason, "Jacksonian Democracy," 89–90.

38. George McDuffie, *Speech of Mr. McDuffie on the Proposition to Amend the Constitution of the United States, Delivered in the House of Representatives Respecting the Election of the President and Vice President, February 17, 1826* (Washington: Gales and Seaton, 1826), 7, 11, 10.

39. McDuffie, *Speech of Mr. McDuffie*, 12, 9.

40. William Rawle, *A View of the United States Constitution of the United States of America*, 2nd ed. (Philadelphia: Nicklin, 1829), 22.

41. Joseph Story, *Commentaries on the Constitution* (Boston: Hilliard, Gray, 1833; Cambridge: Brown, Shattuck, 1833), 3:1457, 3:1458.

42. Story, *Commentaries on the Constitution*, 3:1458.

43. Thomason, "Jacksonian Democracy," 121–22.

44. Until after the Civil War, the South Carolina legislature chose the state's electors.

45. 2 (Part 1) Reg. Deb. 694–95 (1826).

46. Thomason, "Jacksonian Democracy," 139–41.

Chapter 6: "The Everlasting Principle of Equal and Exact Justice": Reconstruction's Radical Vision, the Electoral College, and the Election of 1876

1. This description has been drawn from reports in the *New York Times*, November 29, 1876.

2. Two years earlier, Republicans had won almost 1,700 votes in the parish, but after this terror campaign the number plummeted to 793. Totals recorded in Paul Leland Haworth, *The Hayes-Tilden Disputed Presidential Election of 1876* (New York: Russell and Russell, 1906), 118.

3. Haworth, *Hayes-Tilden Disputed Presidential Election*, 118.

4. *New York Times*, February 1, 1865.

5. Rebecca E. Zietlow, *The Forgotten Emancipator: James Mitchell Ashley and the Ideological Origins of Reconstruction* (Cambridge: Cambridge University Press, 2017), 127.

6. For Ashley's life work against slavery, see Zietlow, *Forgotten Emancipator*. For his specific efforts to pass the Thirteenth Amendment, see Zietlow, *Forgotten Emancipator*, 108–29.

7. Ashley introduced amendments to abolish the Electoral College several times. Cong. Globe, 40th Cong., 2nd Sess. 2722 (1868).

8. Alexander Keyssar, *Why Do We Still Have the Electoral College?* (Cambridge, MA: Harvard University Press, 2020), 173–79.

9. Many Radical Republicans who favored women's voting rights did not champion them in Congress because they believed doing so would sabotage their efforts on behalf of the freedmen. Cong. Globe, 40th Cong., 2nd Sess. 2722 (1868).

10. Cong. Globe, 40th Cong., 2nd Sess. 2714 (1868).

11. Cong. Globe, 40th Cong., 2nd Sess. 2718 (1868).

12. Other Reconstruction-era Republican congressmen who introduced amendments on direct election of the president include Senator Charles Sumner, as well as representatives John Lynch, Nathaniel Banks, and Charles Porter. See Keyssar, *Electoral College*, 181–82.

13. See Eric Foner, *The Second Founding: How the Civil War and Reconstruction Remade the Constitution* (New York: Norton, 2019).

14. See Jeremi Suri, *Civil War by Other Means: America's Long and Unfinished Fight for Democracy* (New York: PublicAffairs, 2022), 181–84.

15. This account relies on William Darrow, "The Killing of Congressman James Hinds," *Arkansas Historical Quarterly* 74, no. 1 (Spring 2015): 18–55.

16. Darrow, "The Killing of Congressman James Hinds," 25.

17. *St. Cloud Journal*, November 19, 1868, in Darrow, "The Killing of Congressman James Hinds," 43.

18. Suri, *Civil War by Other Means*, develops this theme and describes many of the instances of violence identified in the following paragraphs.

19. Glenn Feldman, *The Irony of the Solid South* (Tuscaloosa: University of Alabama Press, 2013), 1–20, describes this violence in Alabama. Quotes: Feldman, *The Irony of the Solid South*, 5. The Texan's quote is found in "Reconstruction in America: Racial Violence after the Civil War, 1865–1876," Equal Justice Initiative, 2020, https://eji.org/report/reconstruction-in-america/documenting-reconstruction-violence.

20. The Colfax massacre is well documented and described in many sources. This account draws on Suri, *Civil War by Other Means*, 185–87.

21. A. James Fuller, *Oliver Morton and the Politics of the Civil War and Reconstruction* (Kent, OH: Kent State University Press, 2017). On Morton's paralysis, see 193–95.

22. Cong. Globe, 40th Cong., 2nd Sess. 725, 727 (1868).

23. Cong. Globe, 40th Cong., 2nd Sess. 725 (1868)

24. Cong. Globe, 40th Cong., 2nd Sess. 727 (1868).

25. Cong. Record, 43rd Cong., vol. 3, pt. 1, 627 (1875).

26. Cong. Record, 43rd Cong., vol. 3, pt. 1, 628 (1875).

27. Cong. Record, 43rd Cong., vol. 3, pt. 1, 626 (1875).

28. Cong. Record, 43rd Cong., vol. 3, pt. 1, 629 (1875).

29. Cong. Record, 43rd Cong., vol. 3, pt. 1, 629–31 (1875).

30. Edward Foley, *Ballot Battles: The History of Disputed Elections in the United States* (New York: Oxford University Press, 2016), 48–74, offers good analyses of the

ballot-counting disputes that Kent and Story witnessed, as well as their comments on these controversies.

31. Cong. Record, 43rd Cong., vol. 3, pt. 1, 627 (1875).

32. I have drawn from four accounts to describe this disputed election: Haworth, *Hayes-Tilden Disputed Presidential Election of 1876*; Michael Holt, *By One Vote: The Disputed Presidential Election of 1876* (Lawrence: University Press of Kansas, 2008); Foley, *Ballot Battles*; and Roy Morris, *Fraud of the Century: Rutherford B. Hayes, Samuel Tilden and the Stolen Election of 1876* (New York: Simon & Schuster, 2004).

33. *New York Herald*, November 20, 1876; Lew Wallace, *Autobiography* (New York: Harper Brothers, 1906), 2:901–2.

34. The classic treatment of this effort of journalists and operatives is C. Vann Woodward, *Reunion and Reaction: The Compromise of 1877 and the End of Reconstruction* (New York: Oxford University Press, 1991).

35. Foley, *Ballot Battles*, 139–45.

36. Quoted in Woodward, *Reunion and Reaction*, 221.

37. See, for example, Oliver P. Morton, "Our Electoral Machinery," *North American Review* 117, no. 241 (October 1873): 383–401; Oliver P. Morton, "The American Constitution," *North American Review* 124, no. 256 (1877): 341–46, http://www.jstor.org/stable/25110045; and Oliver P. Morton, "The American Constitution. II," *North American Review* 125, no. 257 (1877): 68–78, http://www.jstor.org/stable/25110077.

Chapter 7: "Samson with His Locks yet Unshorn": The White South, the Electoral College, and the Civil Rights Movement

1. This account drawn from the *Birmingham News*, July 18, 1948, and Joseph Crespino, *Strom Thurmond's America* (New York: Hill & Wang, 2012).

2. *New York Times*, July 16, 1948.

3. Charles Wallace Collins, *Whither Solid South? A Study in Politics and Race Relations* (New Orleans, LA: Pelican, 1947), 258.

4. The "five-fifths" clause comes from Alexander Keyssar, *Why Do We Still Have the Electoral College?* (Cambridge, MA: Harvard University Press, 2020), 190.

5. James Madison, *Notes of Debates in the Federal Convention of 1787* (New York: Norton, 1966), 327 (originally published in Henry Gilpin, ed., *The Papers of James Madison*, vols. 2–3 [Washington, DC: Langtree & O'Sullivan, 1840]); Walter Clark, "The Electoral College and Presidential Suffrage," *University of Pennsylvania Law Review* 65, no. 8 (June 1917): 74.

6. "Twelfth Census of the United States, Taken in the Year 1900," United States Census Bureau, accessed February 27, 2024, https://www2.census.gov/library/publications/decennial/1900/volume-1/volume-1-p3.pdf.

7. Notably, before passage of the Nineteenth Amendment in 1920, southern states did not allow women to vote. These disenfranchised women also boosted the political power that southern white men enjoyed in congressional representation and the Electoral College.

8. Joseph Warren Keifer, "Power of Congress to Reduce Representation in Congress and in the Electoral College: A Reply," *North American Review* 182, no. 591 (1906): 228–38, http://www.jstor.org/stable/25105525; *New York Times*, December 5, 1916.

9. Figures on Electoral College reform proposals taken from Gary Bugh, *Electoral College Reform: Changes and Possibilities* (Burlington, VT: Ashgate, 2010), 239–53. No proposals to alter or abolish the Electoral College were introduced in the 69th Congress (1925–1927).

10. *St. Louis Post-Dispatch*, November 23, 1916.

11. *St. Louis Post-Dispatch*, November 23, 1916.

12. *New York Herald*, November 11, 1916; *Philadelphia Inquirer*, November 13, 1916; *Washington Herald*, quoted in *St. Louis Post-Dispatch*, November 19, 1916.

13. Keyssar, *Electoral College*, 192–95.

14. The foregoing account is based on Kari Frederickson, *The Dixiecrat Revolt and the End of the Solid South, 1932–1968* (Chapel Hill: University of North Carolina Press, 2001), 54–56.

15. Frederickson, *Dixiecrat Revolt*, 56–57.

16. Frederickson, *Dixiecrat Revolt*, 65.

17. Frederickson, *Dixiecrat Revolt*, 130.

18. Charles Wallace Collins to Mr. Graves (John Templeton Graves), October 31, 1948, Series III, Box 2, folder 8, *Charles Wallace Collins Papers*, Special Collections and University Archives, University of Maryland Libraries, College Park, MD.

19. Collins, *Whither Solid South?*, vii, 54.

20. Collins, *Whither Solid South?*, x, 79, 66–67.

21. Collins, *Whither Solid South?*, ix, 262, 265–66.

22. Collins, *Whither Solid South?*, 255–57.

23. Collins, *Whither Solid South?*, 148–66.

24. Merritt H. Gibson to Honorable Charles Wallace Collins, August 28, 1948, Series III, Box 2, folder 8, *Charles Wallace Collins Papers*; Charles Wallace Collins to Norman Farrell, Esq., October 28, 1948, Series III, Box 2, folder 8, *Charles Wallace Collins Papers*.

25. Neal Peirce and Lawrence D. Longley, *The People's President: The Electoral College in American History and the Direct Vote Alternative* (New Haven, CT: Yale University Press, 1981), 284.

26. "1948 Presidential General Election Results: Mississippi," Dave Leip's Atlas of US Elections, accessed February 27, 2024, https://uselectionatlas.org/RESULTS/state.php?year=1948&fips=28&f=1&off=0&elect=0.

27. Crespino, *Strom Thurmond's America*, 82.

28. Frank Newport, "Americans Support Proposal to Eliminate Electoral College System," Gallup News, January 5, 2001, https://news.gallup.com/poll/2140/americans-support-proposal-eliminate-electoral-college-system.aspx.

29. Cong. Record, 81st Cong., vol. 96, pt. 1, 1260 (1950); John Templeton Graves, "This Morning," *Dothan Eagle* (Dothan, AL), October 3, 1948.

30. Account of Thurmond's filibuster based on Crespino, *Strom Thurmond's America*, 114–16; *New York Times*, August 29, 1957; *New York Times*, August 30, 1957; and *Columbia Record* (Columbia, SC), August 30, 1957.

31. See, for example, the uncertainty around unpledged electors in Georgia, described ably in Patrick Novotny, "John F. Kennedy, the 1960 Election, and Georgia's Unpledged Electors in the Electoral College," *Georgia Historical Quarterly* 88, no. 3 (2004): 375–97, http://www.jstor.org/stable/40584789.

32. John R. Williams, "Aspects of the American Presidential Election of 1960," *Australian Quarterly* 33, no. 1 (March 1961): 25–36.

33. Some calculate that Kennedy actually lost the popular vote. Popular-vote tabulators were unsure how to count Alabama's unpledged electors, especially since voters there selected both unpledged and Kennedy electors.

34. *New York Times*, March 2, 1964.

35. John Dittmer, *Local People: The Struggle for Civil Rights in Mississippi* (Urbana: University of Illinois Press, 1994), 212.

36. "Gray v. Sanders," Oyez, accessed September 25, 2023, https://www.oyez.org/cases /1962/112.

37. Keyssar, *Electoral College*, 212–17.

38. *Journal-Herald* (Dayton, OH), January 10, 1966.

39. "Electing the President," *American Bar Association Journal* 53, no. 3 (March 1967): 219–24.

40. Bugh, *Electoral College Reform*, 245.

41. Account based on the *Post-Crescent* (Appleton, WI), October 20, 1968.

42. *Post-Crescent*, October 20, 1968.

43. *Wisconsin State Journal* (Madison, WI), September 18, 1968.

44. *Wisconsin State Journal*, September 6, 1968; *Post-Crescent*, October 20, 1968.

45. *New York Times*, October 25, 1968; *Wisconsin State Journal*, September 6, 1968.

46. *Standard-Star* (New Rochelle, NY), September 19, 1969.

47. Cong. Record, 91st Cong., vol. 115, pt. 18, 24963 (1969).

48. Cong. Record, 91st Cong., vol. 115, pt. 19, 26007–8 (1969).

49. *New York Times*, March 4, 1970.

50. *Union Springs Herald* (Union Springs, AL), May 21, 1970.

51. Cong. Record, 91st Cong., vol. 116, pt. 23, 30999–31002 (1970).

52. Bugh, *Electoral College Reform*, 97. For the 1979 effort, see Keyssar, *Electoral College*, 263–307.

CHAPTER 8: DECEPTIONS, DISTORTIONS, DANGERS, AND DYSFUNCTION: THE ELECTORAL COLLEGE TODAY

1. "Proposals to Revise the Virginia Constitution: I. Thomas Jefferson to 'Henry Tompkinson' (Samuel Kercheval), 12 July 1816," Founders Online, National Archives, https://founders.archives.gov/documents/Jefferson/03-10-02-0128-0002 (original source: J. Jefferson Looney, ed., *The Papers of Thomas Jefferson, Retirement Series*, vol. 10, May 1816 to 18 January 1817 [Princeton, NJ: Princeton University Press, 2013], 222–28).

2. Two states, Maine and Nebraska, essentially use the old district system. Both states allot two electors to the winner of the state's overall popular vote, but voters choose the remainder of the electors in districts.

3. Samples of early presidential ballots are reproduced in Neal Peirce and Lawrence Longley, *The People's President: The Electoral College in American History and the Direct Vote Alternative* (New Haven, CT: Yale University Press, 1981), 278–79.

4. George C. Edwards III, *Why the Electoral College Is Bad for America*, 3rd ed. (New Haven, CT: Yale University Press, 2019), 19–20. North Dakota, South Dakota, Arizona, Indiana, Oklahoma, and Louisiana retain the names of electors on their ballots.

5. For a list of states that bind electors, see "State Control of Electors," Fair Vote, accessed February 28, 2024, https://archive.fairvote.org/?page=967.

6. Data from "Understanding Electoral Representation in the U.S.," USAFacts, accessed February 28, 2024, https://usafacts.org/visualizations/electoral-college-states -representation/.

7. "Understanding Electoral Representation in the U.S."

8. "Understanding Electoral Representation in the U.S."

9. These traditional election maps can be found in many places; this one has been repro- duced from Wikipedia, s.v. "2020 United States Presidential Election," accessed February 28, 2024, https://en.wikipedia.org/wiki/2020_United_States_presidential_election. For a county-based election map, see "2020 US Presidential Election Map by County and Vote Share," Brilliant Maps, accessed February 28, 2024, https://brilliantmaps.com/2020 -county-election-map/.

10. For the color spectrum map, see "Four Maps That Show How America Voted in the 2020 Election with Results by County, Number of Voters," *USA Today*, accessed February 28, 2024, https://www.usatoday.com/in-depth/graphics/2020/11/10/election-maps-2020 -america-county-results-more-voters/6226197002/.

11. "Four Maps That Show How America Voted."

12. Results taken from "General Election," Board of Elections (Augusta, GA), accessed February 28, 2024, http://appweb2.augustaga.gov/election/results/electab_gen_ 2020/ElectionResults.html#Races?Race=For%20Presi- dent%20of%20the%20United%20States; and "St. Louis County, Missouri: 'General Election' and 'St. Louis County,'" St. Louis County Board of Elections, accessed February 28, 2024, https://stlouiscountymo.gov/st-louis-county-government/board-of-elections /election-results-archive/2020-election-results/november-3-2020-general-election/ official-election-results/.

13. Megan Brenan, "61 Percent of Americans Support Abolishing Electoral College," Gallup News, September 24, 2020, https://news.gallup.com/poll/320744/americans -support-abolishing-electoral-college.aspx.

14. Edwards, *Why the Electoral College Is Bad for America*, 4–7; George E. Condon Jr., "It's Down to Just Eight States for Obama and Romney," *The Atlantic*, October 18, 2012, https://www.theatlantic.com/politics/archive/2012/10/its-down-to-just-8-states -for-obama-and-romney/443223/.

15. John R. Koza, Barry Fadem, Mark Grueskin, Michael S. Mandell, Robert Richies, and Joseph F. Zimmerman, *Every Vote Equal: A State-Based Plan for Electing the President by National Popular Vote* (n.p.: National Popular Vote Press, 2013), 439, https://www.every -vote-equal.com/sites/default/files/eve-4th-ed-ch9-web-v1.pdf.

16. "Reaction Poll on Elián González," Gallup News, April 22, 2000, https://news.gallup.com/poll/2971/reaction-poll-elian-gonzalez.aspx.

17. William Schneider, "Elián González Defeated Al Gore," *The Atlantic*, May 1, 2001, https://www.theatlantic.com/politics/archive/2001/05/elian-gonzalez-defeated-al-gore/377714/. The article estimates that the González affair cut support for Democrats in Florida's Cuban American community by 15 percent.

18. Kyle Kondik, "Electoral College Ratings: Expect Another Highly Competitive Election," Sabato's Crystal Ball, University of Virginia Center for Politics, June 29, 2023, https://centerforpolitics.org/crystalball/articles/electoral-college-ratings-expect-another-highly-competitive-election/.

19. Judith Best, *The Choice of the People? Debating the Electoral College* (Lanham, MD: Rowman & Littlefield, 1996), 20. Best testified before Congress on the Electoral College four times, in 1977, 1979, 1992, and 1997. For more information on Best, see her obituary, "Judith A. Best," *Ithaca Journal*, accessed February 28, 2024, https://www.ithacajournal.com/obituaries/bps126590.

20. Katherine Shaw, "'A Mystifying and Distorting Factor': The Electoral College and American Democracy," *Michigan Law Review* 120, no. 6 (2022): 1294.

21. Edwards, *Why the Electoral College Is Bad for America*, 3; Jeffrey M. Jones, "Last Trump Job Approval 34 Percent; Average Is Record-Low 41 Percent," Gallup News, January 18, 2021, https://news.gallup.com/poll/328637/last-trump-job-approval-average-record-low.aspx#:~:text=Trump%20is%20the%20only%20president,presidential%20job%20approval%20in%201938.

22. Jeffrey M. Jones, "U.S. Party Preferences Evenly Split in 2022 after Shift to GOP," Gallup News, January 21, 2023, https://news.gallup.com/poll/467897/party-preferences-evenly-split-2022-shift-gop.aspx; Philip Bump, "1.7 Million People in 33 States and DC Cast a Ballot without Voting in the Presidential Race," *Washington Post*, December 14, 2016, https://www.washingtonpost.com/news/the-fix/wp/2016/12/14/1-7-million-people-in-33-states-and-dc-cast-a-ballot-without-voting-in-the-presidential-race/.

23. Ezra Klein, *Why We're Polarized* (New York: Simon & Schuster, 2020), offers an accessible analysis of the factors driving this polarization.

24. Jonathan Haidt, "Why the Past 10 Years of American Life Have Been Uniquely Stupid," *The Atlantic*, April 11, 2022, https://www.theatlantic.com/magazine/archive/2022/05/social-media-democracy-trust-babel/629369/.

CHAPTER 9: AN INDEFENSIBLE SYSTEM

1. Dan Mclaughlin, "What the Electoral College Saves Us From," *National Review*, April 5, 2019, https://www.nationalreview.com/2019/04/what-the-electoral-college-saves-us-from/.

2. Save Our States often produces these kinds of arguments. As one example, see their handout "National Popular Vote and Rural America," Save Our States, accessed February 28, 2024, https://cdn2.assets-servd.host/saveour-states/production/NPV-and-Rural-America.pdf?v=1600200769&dm=1611941292. See also examples from the organization's X (formerly Twitter) feed: Save Our States (@saveourstates), X, 10:59 a.m., September 22, 2023; 3:55 p.m., September 20, 2023.

3. Data on the 1980 presidential election found at "Statistics: 1980," American Presidency Project, accessed February 28, 2024, https://www.presidency.ucsb.edu/statistics/elections/1980.

4. Data on the 2008 presidential election found at "Statistics: 1980," American Presidency Project, accessed February 28, 2024, https://www.presidency.ucsb.edu/statistics/elections/2008.

5. The possibilities for these kinds of minority wins vary, of course, from cycle to cycle depending on population and the distribution of electoral votes among the states. See George C. Edwards III, *Why the Electoral College Is Bad for America*, 3rd ed. (New Haven, CT: Yale University Press, 2019), 162–63.

6. Biden won slightly fewer votes from these ten states, with 2,443,995 popular votes, while Trump won slightly more, with 2,463,370. Underscoring Electoral College distortions, Biden nonetheless got seventeen electoral votes from the smallest states, while Trump garnered just sixteen.

7. Save Our States (@saveourstates), X, 2:54 p.m., August 22, 2023.

8. John Hendrickson, "The Electoral College: Last Defense of Federalism," Center Square, September 15, 2021, https://www.thecentersquare.com/national/op-ed-the-electoral-college-last-defense-of-federalism/article_d665135a-1666-11ec-9ae7-dfe75c022391.html.

9. James Madison, *Notes of Debates in the Federal Convention of 1787* (New York: Norton, 1987), 221 (Wilson) (originally published in Henry Gilpin, ed., *The Papers of James Madison*, vols. 2–3 [Washington, DC: Langtree & O'Sullivan, 1840]); Madison, *Notes*, 215 (Hamilton).

10. Madison, *Notes*, 215.

11. "Fact Check: Yes, Trump Lost Election, Despite What He Says," Associated Press, May 6, 2021, https://apnews.com/article/donald-trump-michael-pence-electoral-college-elections-health-2d9bd47a8bd3561682ac46c6b3873a10. For the statement from the Election Infrastructure Government Coordinating Council Executive Committee, see "Joint Statement from Elections Infrastructure Government Coordinating Council and the Election Infrastructure Sector Coordinating Executive Committee," Cybersecurity & Infrastructure Security Agency, accessed February 28, 2024, https://www.cisa.gov/news-events/news/joint-statement-elections-infrastructure-government-coordinating-council-election. The vote in New Mexico was the only one of the seven where the margin of victory was greater than 3 percent. North Carolina finished with a margin of 1.3 percent, but no allegations find a fake elector scheme in that state.

12. Gallup polling on the Electoral College back to 2000 is described in Megan Brenan, "61 Percent of Americans Support Abolishing the Electoral College," Gallup News, September 24, 2020, https://news.gallup.com/poll/320744/americans-support-abolishing-electoral-college.aspx. Trends before 2000 are described in Frank Newport, "Americans Support Proposal to Eliminate Electoral College System," Gallup News, January 5, 2001, https://news.gallup.com/poll/2140/americans-support-proposal-eliminate-electoral-college-system.aspx.

13. Brenan, "61 Percent of Americans Support Abolishing the Electoral College."

14. "Proposals to Revise the Virginia Constitution: I. Thomas Jefferson to 'Henry Tompkinson' (Samuel Kercheval), 12 July 1816," Founders Online, National Archives, https://founders.archives.gov/documents/Jefferson/03-10-02-0128-0002 (original source: J. Jefferson Looney, ed., *The Papers of Thomas Jefferson, Retirement Series*, vol. 10, May 1816 to 18 January 1817 [Princeton, NJ: Princeton University Press, 2013], 222–28).

15. "Proposals to Revise the Virginia Constitution: I. Thomas Jefferson to 'Henry Tompkinson' (Samuel Kercheval), 12 July 1816."

16. "Proposals to Revise the Virginia Constitution: I. Thomas Jefferson to 'Henry Tompkinson' (Samuel Kercheval), 12 July 1816." Virginia's constitution had none of these features at the time. See the overview of the provisions of the state's 1776 constitution at "1776 Constitution," Library of Virginia, accessed February 28, 2024, https://www.lva.virginia.gov/constitutions/discover/#constitution-1776.

17. The website of the Library of Virginia offers a good summary of the changes in Virginia's successive constitutions: https://www.lva.virginia.gov/constitutions/discover/#constitution.

18. Cong. Globe, 40th Cong., 2nd Sess. 725 (1868).

CONCLUSION: "THE EARTH BELONGS ALWAYS TO THE LIVING GENERATION"

1. Save Our States (@saveourstates), X, 11:19 a.m., August 7, 2023.

2. This idea paraphrases Robert A. Dahl, "I do not mean to suggest that the Connecticut Compromise should be undone; but I do mean to say that it is rather muddleheaded to romanticize a necessary bargain into a grand principle of democratic politics." Robert A. Dahl, *A Preface to Democratic Theory: An Expanded Edition* (Chicago: University of Chicago Press, 2013), 118.

3. "Presidential Election Margin of Victory," American Presidency Project, University of California, Santa Barbara, https://www.presidency.ucsb.edu/statistics/data/presidential-election-mandates.

4. James Madison, *Notes of Debates in the Federal Convention of 1787* (New York: Norton, 1987), 653 (originally published in Henry Gilpin, ed., *The Papers of James Madison*, vols. 2–3 [Washington, DC: Langtree & O'Sullivan, 1840]). "From George Washington to Benjamin Harrison, 24 September 1787," Founders Online, National Archives, https://founders.archives.gov/documents/Washington/04-05-02-0316 (original source: W. W. Abbot, ed., *The Papers of George Washington*, Confederation Series, vol. 5, 1 February 1787–31 December 1787 [Charlottesville: University Press of Virginia, 1997], 339–40. "From James Madison to Thomas Jefferson, 24 October 1787," Founders Online, National Archives, https://founders.archives.gov/documents/Madison/01-10-02-0151 (original source: Robert A. Rutland, Charles F. Hobson, William M. E. Rachal, and Frederika J. Teute, eds., *The Papers of James Madison*, vol. 10, 27 May 1787–3 March 1788 [Chicago: University of Chicago Press, 1977], 205–20).

5. "An Address to the Freemen of North Carolina," *State Gazette of North Carolina*, March 20, 1788," in *Documentary History of the Ratification of the Constitution*, ed. Merrill Jensen, John P. Kaminski, and Gaspare Saladino (Madison: Wisconsin Historical Society Press, 1976), 16:48; Jensen, Kaminski, and Saladino, *Documentary History*, 10:1412.

6. Steven Levitsky and Daniel Ziblatt, "How American Democracy Fell So Far Behind," *The Atlantic*, September 5, 2023, https://www.theatlantic.com/ideas/archive /2023/09/american-constitution-norway/675199/; Richard Priest Dietzman, "The Four Constitutions of Kentucky," *Kentucky Law Journal* 15, no. 2 (1927): 117–21.

7. "II. Thomas Jefferson to James Madison, 6 September 1789," Founders Online, National Archives, https://founders.archives.gov/documents/Jefferson/01-15-02-0375 -0003 (original source: Julian P. Boyd, ed., *The Papers of Thomas Jefferson*, vol. 15, 27 March 1789–30 November 1789 [Princeton, NJ: Princeton University Press, 1958], 392–98).

8. "Proposals to Revise the Virginia Constitution: I. Thomas Jefferson to 'Henry Tompkinson' (Samuel Kercheval), 12 July 1816," Founders Online, National Archives, https:// founders.archives.gov/documents/Jefferson/03-10-02-0128-0002 (original source: J. Jefferson Looney, ed., *The Papers of Thomas Jefferson, Retirement Series*, vol. 10, May 1816 to 18 January 1817 [Princeton, NJ: Princeton University Press, 2013], 222–28).